# THE SPARK

Kristine Barnett lives in Indiana with her husband, Michael, and their children. In 1996 she founded Acorn Hill Academy, a daycare serving local families. She and Michael currently run a charitable community centre for autistic and special-needs children and their families, called Jacob's Place.

# The Spark

*A Mother's Story of Nurturing,
Genius and Autism*

## KRISTINE BARNETT

PENGUIN BOOKS

PENGUIN BOOKS

Published by the Penguin Group
Penguin Books Ltd, 80 Strand, London wc2r orl, England
Penguin Group (USA) Inc., 375 Hudson Street, New York, New York 10014, USA
Penguin Group (Canada), 90 Eglinton Avenue East, Suite 700, Toronto, Ontario, Canada m4p 2y3
(a division of Pearson Penguin Canada Inc.)
Penguin Ireland, 25 St Stephen's Green, Dublin 2, Ireland (a division of Penguin Books Ltd)
Penguin Group (Australia), 707 Collins Street, Melbourne, Victoria 3008, Australia
(a division of Pearson Australia Group Pty Ltd)
Penguin Books India Pvt Ltd, 11 Community Centre, Panchsheel Park, New Delhi – 110 017, India
Penguin Group (NZ), 67 Apollo Drive, Rosedale, Auckland 0632, New Zealand
(a division of Pearson New Zealand Ltd)
Penguin Books (South Africa) (Pty) Ltd, Block D, Rosebank Office Park,
181 Jan Smuts Avenue, Parktown North, Gauteng 2193, South Africa

Penguin Books Ltd, Registered Offices: 80 Strand, London wc2r orl, England

www.penguin.com

First published in the United States of America by Random House, an imprint of
The Random House Publishing Group, a division of Random House, Inc., New York 2013
First published in Great Britain by Fig Tree 2013
Published in Penguin Books 2014
001

*The names of many of the children and parents appearing in this book have been changed and some
biographical details have been altered. A small number of individuals described are composites*

Set in 11/13pt Bembo Book MT Std
Typeset by Jouve (UK), Milton Keynes
Printed in Great Britain by Clays Ltd, St Ives plc

isbn: 978-0-241-96181-0

www.greenpenguin.co.uk

MIX
Paper from
responsible sources
FSC
www.fsc.org   FSC™ C018179

Penguin Books is committed to a sustainable
future for our business, our readers and our planet.
This book is made from Forest Stewardship
Council™ certified paper.

*For Michael, who makes the impossible possible every day*
*And for everyone who's ever been told they can't*

# Introduction

I am sitting at the back of a university physics class while the students cluster in small groups around the whiteboards lining the lecture hall, ready to tackle the day's equation.

Work proceeds in fits and starts. There's a great deal of erasing. As the teams of students begin to bicker, I catch a glimpse of my nine-year-old son at the front of the room, chatting easily with the professor. The frustration level in the room mounts. Finally, my son pulls a chair over to a whiteboard and steps up on it. Even so, he must stand on his tiptoes, straining his arm as high as it can go.

This is his first encounter with the equation, just as it is for all the other students in the class, but he doesn't pause to deliberate. Instead, the numbers flow fast and fluently from his pen. Before long, everyone in the room is watching. The students from the other teams stop their work to stare at this little kid in the backward baseball cap. My son doesn't notice the gaping onlookers because he's happily engrossed by the numbers and symbols flying onto the board. They mount up at impossible speed: five lines, then ten, then fifteen, spilling over into the whiteboard space of the group next to his.

Soon he's talking to the others on his team, pointing and explaining and asking leading questions, the way a teacher would. A serious woman with a French braid breaks away from her own group, drawing closer to listen. She's joined by a stoop-shouldered young man, who nods his head vigorously as comprehension dawns.

In a matter of minutes, all of the students at the front of the auditorium have gathered around my little boy. When he points out a trick he's found in the equation, he bounces on the balls of his feet in delight. A bearded student calls out a question. I glance over at the professor, who is leaning against the wall with a smile on his face.

Now that they get the problem, the college students rejoin their own groups, and their markers begin to move as well, but the tension in their body language is unmistakable: No one in the room loves the equation like my son.

Class is dismissed, and the auditorium empties. My son packs up his markers, talking animatedly to a fellow classmate about a new NBA videogame they both want. As they come up the stairs toward me, the professor approaches and extends his hand.

'Mrs Barnett, I've been wanting to tell you how much I enjoy having Jake in my class. He's bringing out the best in the other students, to be sure; they're not used to being lapped like this. To be honest, I'm not completely confident I'll be able to keep up with him myself!'

I laugh along with him.

'Oh, gosh,' I say. 'You've just pretty much described the story of my life.'


My name is Kristine Barnett, and my son Jake is considered to be a prodigy in math and science. He began taking college-level courses in math, astronomy, and physics at age eight and was accepted to university at nine. Not long after, he began work on an original theory in the field of relativity. The equations were so long they spilled over from his gigantic whiteboard onto the windows of our home. Uncertain how to help, I asked Jake if there was someone he might show his work to, and a renowned physicist I contacted on Jake's behalf generously agreed to review an early iteration. He confirmed that Jake was indeed working on an original theory and also said that if the theory held, it would put him in line for a Nobel Prize.

That summer, at age twelve, Jake was hired as a paid researcher in physics at the university. It was his first summer job. By the third week, he had solved an open problem in lattice theory, work that was later published in a top-tier journal.

A few months earlier, in the spring of that year, a tiny article had appeared in a small local newspaper about a small charity my husband, Michael, and I had founded. Unexpectedly, that piece led to a story about Jake in a larger newspaper. The next thing we knew, camera crews were camped out on our lawn. Our phone rang off the hook with film people, talk shows, national news outlets, talent agencies, publishers, elite universities – the reporters and producers all desperate to interview Jake.

I was confused. I can honestly say that at the time, Michael and I had no idea why so many people were interested in our son. Sure, we knew Jake was smart. We understood that his abilities in math and science were advanced and that it wasn't 'normal' for him to be in college. But Michael and I were squarely focused on celebrating different victories: the fact that Jake had a decent batting average, a close group of friends his own age who liked to play Halo: Reach and watch movies together in our basement, and (although he'll kill me for mentioning it) his first girlfriend.

These typical things in Jake's life are, to us, the most extraordinary. So when the media descended, we were utterly baffled. It wasn't until we had talked with some of those reporters and read or heard the stories they wrote that we began to understand our disconnect. The truth is, it took a glaring spotlight to show Michael and me that the story line of our lives with our son had changed.

You see, what those reporters didn't understand was that

Jake's improbable mind is all the more remarkable for the fact that it was almost lost. When the media showed up on our lawn, we were still living inside the diagnosis of autism Jake had received when he was two. We had helplessly looked on as our vibrant, precocious baby boy gradually stopped talking, disappearing before our eyes into a world of his own. His prognosis quickly went from gloomy to downright grim. When he was three, the goal the experts set for him was the hope that he'd be able to tie his own shoes at sixteen.

This book is the story of how we got from there to here, the story of a mother's journey with her remarkable son. But for me, more than anything, it is about the power of hope and the dazzling possibilities that can occur when we keep our minds open and learn how to tap the true potential that lies within every child.

# The Spark

# An Inch, or Ten Thousand Miles

*November 2001*
*Jake, age three*

'Mrs Barnett, I'd like to talk to you about the alphabet cards you've been sending to school with Jacob.'

Jake and I were sitting with his special ed teacher in our living room during her monthly, state-mandated visit to our home. He loved those brightly colored flash cards more than anything in the world, as attached to them as other children were to love-worn teddy bears or threadbare security blankets. The cards were sold at the front of the SuperTarget where I did my shopping. Other children snuck boxes of cereal or candy bars into their mothers' shopping carts, while the only items that ever mysteriously appeared in mine were yet more packs of Jake's favorite alphabet cards.

'Oh, I don't send the cards; Jake grabs them on his way out the door. I have to pry them out of his hands to get his shirt on. He even takes them to bed with him!'

Jake's teacher shifted uncomfortably on the couch. 'I wonder if you might need to adjust your expectations for Jacob, Mrs Barnett. Ours is a life skills program. We're focusing on things like helping him learn to get dressed by himself someday.' Her voice was gentle, but she was determined to be clear.

'Oh, of course, I know that. We're working on those skills at home, too. But he just loves his cards . . .'

'I'm sorry, Mrs Barnett. What I'm saying is that we don't think you're going to need to worry about the alphabet with Jacob.'

Finally – finally – I understood what my son's teacher had been trying to tell me. She wanted to protect me, to make sure I was clear on the objectives of a life skills program. She wasn't saying that alphabet flash cards were premature. She was saying we wouldn't ever have to worry about the alphabet with Jake, because *they didn't think he'd ever read*.

It was a devastating moment, in a year that had been full of them. Jake had recently been diagnosed with autism, and I had finally come to understand that all bets were off as to when (or whether) Jake would reach any of the normal childhood developmental milestones. I had spent nearly a year stepping forward to meet the gaping, gray uncertainty of autism. I had stood by helplessly watching as many of Jake's abilities, such as reading and talking, had disappeared. But I was not going to let anyone slam the door shut on the potential of this child at the tender age of three, whether he was autistic or not.

Ironically, I wasn't hopeful that Jake would ever read, but neither was I prepared to let anyone set a ceiling for what we could expect from him, especially one so low. That morning, it felt as if Jake's teacher had slammed a door on his future.

For a parent, it's terrifying to fly against the advice of the professionals, but I knew in my heart that if Jake stayed in special ed, he would slip away. So I decided to trust my instincts and embrace hope instead of abandoning it. I wouldn't spend any time or energy fighting to convince the teachers and therapists at his school to change their expectations or their methods. I didn't want to struggle against the system or impose what I felt was right for Jake on others. Rather than hiring lawyers and experts and advocates to get Jake the services he needed, I would invest directly in Jake and do whatever I felt was necessary to help him reach his full potential – whatever that might be.

As a result, I made the scariest decision of my life. It meant going against the experts and even my husband, Michael. That day, I resolved to stoke Jake's passion. Maybe he *was* trying to learn to read with those beloved alphabet cards, maybe he wasn't. Either way, instead of taking them away, I would make sure he had as many as he wanted.

Three years before, I'd been ecstatic to find out I was pregnant with Jake. At twenty-four, I'd been practicing for the role of mother as far back as I could remember.

Even as a little girl, it was clear to me (and to everyone around me) that children were likely to hold a special place in my future. My family had always called me the Pied Piper, because wherever I went, there was sure to be a trail of little ones on my heels, waiting for an adventure to begin. My brother, Benjamin, was born when I was eleven, and right from the start he was never far from my hip. By the time I was thirteen, I was the go-to babysitter for the whole neighborhood, and by fourteen I was in charge of the Sunday school at our church. So nobody was the least bit surprised when I went to work as a live-in nanny to help pay my way through college. Then, after I got married, I opened my own daycare, a lifelong dream. I'd been around children my whole life, and now I couldn't wait to have my own.

Unfortunately, the road leading to Jake's birth was not easy. Although I was still young, the pregnancy was touch and go from the beginning. I developed a dangerous high-blood-pressure condition called preeclampsia, which is common in pregnancy and can harm both mother and child. My mother helped out with my daycare, as I was desperate to hold on to the baby. But the pregnancy became more and more fraught, as I went into preterm labor again and again. Eventually, my doctors became so concerned that they put me on medication and strict bed rest to help prevent premature labor. Even so, I was hospitalized nine times.

Three weeks before my due date, I was rushed to the hospital once again, this time in labor that couldn't be reversed. A cascade of events made the outcome increasingly uncertain. For me, the scene was a kaleidoscope of people rushing in and out, alarms sounding constantly, as the faces of the nurses and doctors crowding the room grew increasingly tense. Michael says this was the day he saw exactly how tough and stubborn I could be. I didn't know it at the time, but my doctor had pulled him aside to tell him that labor wasn't going well and he needed to be prepared: It was likely he would be going home with either a wife or a baby, but not both.

All I knew was that in the middle of the hazy blur of noise, pain, medication, and fear, suddenly Michael was by my side, holding my hand and looking into my eyes. He was a tractor beam, pulling my attention – my whole being – into focus. That moment is the only clear memory I have of that frantic time. I felt as if a camera had zoomed in on us and all the commotion surrounding us had ceased. For me, there was only Michael, fiercely strong and absolutely determined that I hear him.

'There aren't just two but three lives at stake here, Kris. We're going to get through this together. We have to.'

I don't know whether it was the actual words he said or the look in his eyes, but his urgent message broke through the fog of my terror and pain. He willed me to understand the unending depth of his love for me and to draw strength from it. He seemed so certain that it was in my power to choose life that he made it true. And in a way that felt sacred, he promised in return to be a never-ending source of strength and happiness for me and for our child for the rest of his days. He was like the captain of a ship in a terrible storm, commanding me to focus and to survive. And I did.

Real or imagined, I also heard him promise me fresh flowers in our home every day for the rest of my life. Michael knew that I had always been wild for flowers, but a bouquet from a florist was a luxury we could afford on only the most special occasions. Nevertheless, the next day, while I held our beautiful baby boy in my arms, Michael presented me with the most wonderful roses I have ever seen in my life. Thirteen years have passed since that day, and fresh flowers have arrived for me every week, no matter what.

We were the lucky ones – the happy miracle. We couldn't know it then, but this would not be the last time our family would be tested or that we would beat incredible odds. Outside of romance novels perhaps, people don't talk seriously about the kind of love that makes anything possible. But Michael and I have that kind of love. Even when we don't agree, that love is our mooring in rough waters. I know in my heart it was the power of Michael's love that pulled Jake and me through the day Jake was born, and it has made everything that has happened since then possible.

When we left the hospital, Michael and I had everything we'd ever wanted. I'm sure every new family feels that way, but we truly felt that we were the most fortunate people on the planet.

On the way home, with our brand-new bundle in tow, we stopped to sign the final mortgage papers on our first home. With a little help from my larger-than-life grandfather Grandpa John Henry, we were moving into a modest house at the end of a cul-de-sac in a working-class suburb in Indiana, where I also would operate my daycare business.

Glancing over Jake's fuzzy newborn head at a beaming Michael, I was suddenly reminded that it was pure serendipity that Michael and I had found each other – especially when our first meeting seemed so ill-fated.

Michael and I met while we were in college. Our seeming 'chance encounter' was actually the ploy of my meddling sister,

Stephanie. Completely unbeknownst to me, she had felt compelled to play matchmaker – a ludicrous notion, since I was emphatically *not* in the market for a beau. On the contrary, I was on the giddy cusp of becoming officially engaged – I hoped – to a wonderful young man named Rick, my very own Prince Charming. We were blissful together, and I was looking forward to our happily ever after.

Stephanie, however, had a 'feeling' about me and a boy from her public-speaking class – a boy who was not just brilliant but electrifying, a boy she was convinced was my true soul mate. So she hatched a scheme.

On the afternoon she sprung her trap, I was busy in her powder room, readying myself for a date with Rick, with at least twenty different shades of lipstick and eight pairs of shoes out for consideration. When I finally emerged, I found that the person standing before me was not my boyfriend, but a boy I'd never laid eyes on before. There, in her tiny studio apartment, under false pretenses, Stephanie introduced me to Michael Barnett.

Confused by this unexpected visitor, I looked to my sister for an explanation. She pulled me aside to confide in a hushed whisper things that made no sense at all. She said that she'd invited this boy over so that we'd be forced to meet. She'd even called my boyfriend with an excuse to cancel our date that evening.

At first I was too dumbstruck to react. As it slowly dawned on me that Stephanie was trying to play Cupid, I truly thought she'd lost her mind. Who fixes up someone who's hoping her boyfriend is about to propose?

I was furious. She and I hadn't been raised to play the field. In fact, I hadn't gone on my first date until I was in college. We certainly hadn't been taught to be dishonest or disloyal either. What could she have been thinking? But as much as I felt like screaming at her – or storming out of the apartment altogether – we'd been raised with good manners, and Stephanie was counting on that.

I extended my hand to the boy, who was as much a pawn in Stephanie's charade as I, and took a seat with him and my sister in the living room. Stilted chatter ensued, although I wasn't really paying attention. When I finally looked at the boy, really registering him for the first time, I noticed his backward baseball cap, his bright eyes, and his ridiculous goatee. With his laid-back, scruffy appearance, I assumed that he lacked substance. The contrast with my crisply formal, preppy boyfriend could not have been more pronounced.

Why had Stephanie wanted us to meet? I was a country girl, from a family that for generations had lived a modest, simple life. Rick had shown me a very different world – one that included penthouses, car services, ski vacations, nice restaurants, and art gallery openings. Not that any of that mattered. Stephanie could have brought Brad Pitt into the living room, and I still would have been angry at her for disrespecting my relationship. But the contrast between this disheveled college student and the shiny penny I was seeing made me wonder all the more what my sister had been thinking.

Before long, Stephanie yanked me from my silent perch and, trying to find a bit of privacy within her tiny studio apartment, chided me sternly. 'Where are your manners?' she demanded. 'Yell at me later if you like, but give this boy the courtesy of a proper conversation.' She was, I saw immediately and with embarrassment, right. Being rude to a stranger – a guest! – was unacceptable. Courtesy and graciousness were qualities that had been instilled in us since birth by our parents, our grandparents, and the tight-knit community in which we'd been raised, and so far I had been as cold as ice.

Shamefaced, I went back to sit down and made my apologies

to Michael. I told him that I was in a relationship and didn't know what Stephanie could possibly have been thinking when she'd arranged this meeting. Of course, I explained, I wasn't angry with him – only at my sister for putting the two of us in this ridiculous situation. With that out in the open, we laughed at the utter preposterousness of it and marveled at Stephanie's audacity. The tension in the room eased considerably, and the three of us fell into easy conversation. Michael told me about his classes and about an idea he had for a screenplay.

That's when I saw what Stephanie wanted me to see. The passion and drive that animated Michael when he spoke about his screenplay were unlike anything I'd seen in anyone I'd ever met. He sounded like me! I felt my stomach lurch and experienced a kind of vertigo. Instantly, I knew that my future, so certain only moments before, would not go according to plan. I would not be marrying my boyfriend. Although he was a wonderful man, that relationship was over. I had no choice in the matter. I'd known Michael Barnett for less than an hour, and yet with a certainty impossible to explain or defend, I already knew that I would be spending the rest of my life with him.

Michael and I drove to a coffee shop and talked the whole night through. As corny as it sounds, each of us felt as though we were reconnecting with someone we'd lost. Being with Michael felt like coming home. We were engaged three weeks later and married three months after that. And still, after sixteen years of marriage, it feels as necessary and right for me to be with Michael as it did on that first improbable night when we met.

The rest of my family did not embrace Michael immediately – or our whirlwind courtship and sudden engagement. What on earth had gotten into their sensible daughter? Even Stephanie, responsible for our meeting, was now as worried and confused as the others. True, she'd felt compelled to introduce us, but she didn't understand how we could be so sure about a lifelong commitment in such a short time. Our differences were obvious to everyone, including the two of us: I was a sheltered country girl with deep spiritual roots, raised with the constancy of a loving family, while Michael was a city boy, raised on the wrong side of Chicago, with a tough family life.

Whereas I wouldn't leave the house, even for a quick trip to the grocery store, without making sure every hair was in place, Michael, a leather-jacketed nonconformist, was unconcerned with outward trappings. Pride of home also was important to me. When I was growing up, you would have been more likely to come across a live chicken in our kitchen than to find a roll of paper towels or a stack of paper napkins – only slightly less true in my own home today. My world seemed utterly alien to Mike, who had grown up eating meals that were mostly catch-as-catch-can and seldom served at a table, and it provided endless fodder for his jokes.

Michael's sharp wit and keen, satiric humor surely served to compound my family's discomfort. Yet his ability to make me laugh – especially when things got tough (or when we began taking ourselves a little too seriously) – was one of the things that made me fall instantly in love with him.

My family's deep and vocal concern was unanimous, with one exception. Grandpa John Henry saw something in Michael and took an instant shine to him. It was his opinion that carried the most weight with me, and so it meant the world to me when he said that he trusted my inner compass and that I should, too.

Life with Michael was my destiny and a certainty I didn't question, but there was a wrenching consequence to our love: breaking with the church in which I had been raised – the church of my parents, and their parents, and many generations of my family before them.

I was raised Amish – not horse-and-buggy Amish, but city Amish. Like many Amish of their time, my grandparents wanted to embrace the modern world while still holding fast to their old-world traditions and beliefs. So they became part of a new order of Amish – sometimes referred to as the New Amish – who maintained their faith and community while making some concessions to modern life. We wore regular clothes, enjoyed modern conveniences, and went to public school. Even so, church for us was not just a Sunday event. It was the very fiber of our everyday lives.

In the Amish faith, if you don't marry someone from the church to which you belong, you cannot remain a member of that church. My beloved grandpa John had himself been cast out of his when he'd wed for love. (Although my grandmother was Amish, she was not from the same community.) My father was not Amish, but when he proposed to my mother, he joined her church, allowing her to remain in the fold.

As difficult as it was to imagine breaking with a tradition so important to me, I had always known that the Amish custom of arranged marriages was simply not for me. Although there had been many offers for my hand, my dad (to my mother's chagrin) had turned them all down. He also didn't believe in arranged marriages, and certainly not for his own girls. As much as I loved my church and our way of life, if I couldn't marry Michael and stay in the church, I really had no choice but to leave.

# A Baby Boy

From day one, Jake was as affectionate and curious as a baby can be. He talked early and quickly learned the power of 'Hi!' My sister, Stephanie, used to laugh at the way he could charm an entire restaurant by greeting everyone who passed by with a sunny wave. He loved stuffed animals and would hide himself in a heap of them, squealing with delight every time he was discovered.

I had, of course, already seen the softer side of Michael, but even I was tickled by the way he threw himself into the role of devoted dad. He was working long hours at Target in those days, but even if he'd worked a double or an overnight shift, he would always find the energy to wrestle with Jake, WWF-style, on a big pile of couch cushions on the living room floor. One of baby Jake's favorite games with Michael was to 'share' a piece of cake – which mostly meant smearing frosting all over Michael's face and laughing hysterically while his dad pretended to gobble up his hands.

I went back to work at my daycare less than a week after Jake was born. I was eager to return to work because I loved it, and having been on bed rest for so long, I was concerned about taking even more time off. I didn't want to lose the trust of the families who had given me their children to take care of. Some days, I was in the daycare from six in the morning until seven at night, and Jake was right there with me. The kids treated him like a life-sized Cabbage Patch Kid. They dressed him up and sang songs to him and taught him to play patty-cake. I laughed to see how territorial some of the little girls in particular could be. 'I should put her on the payroll,' I told one mom one evening when her daughter was finding it difficult to leave 'her' baby, Jake, with me.

There were some early signs that Jake was quite clever. He learned the alphabet before he could walk, and he liked to recite it backward and forward. By the time he was one, he was sounding out short words such as 'cat' and 'dog' by himself. At ten months, he'd pull himself up using the arm of the couch so that he could insert his favorite CD-ROM into the computer. It contained a program that 'read' Dr Seuss's *The Cat in the Hat* – and it sure looked to us as though he was following the little yellow ball bouncing on top of the words and reading along with it.

One night I found Michael standing outside Jake's room after he'd put him down for the night. He put his finger over his lips and motioned for me to join him. I snuck up next to him to listen to our son, who was lying in his crib, sleepily babbling to himself – in what sounded like Japanese. We knew that he knew all of his DVDs by heart, and we'd seen him switch the language selection on the remote, but it came as a real shock to realize that he'd memorized not only the English versions but apparently much of the Spanish and Japanese versions, too.

We were also struck by Jake's precision and dexterity, especially at an age when most boys are barreling their way through the world like miniature Godzillas. Not Jake, who would often sit quietly, meticulously lining up his Matchbox cars in a perfectly straight line all along the coffee table, using his finger to make sure the spacing between them was even as well. He would arrange thousands of Q-tips end to end on the carpet, creating elaborate, mazelike designs that covered the entire floor of a room. But if we felt the occasional swell of pride when it seemed as if Jake might be a little advanced compared to his peers, we were also aware that all new parents think that they have the most remarkable child on earth.

When Jake was about fourteen months old, however, we started to notice little changes in him. At first they were all minor enough that we could easily explain them away. He didn't seem to be talking or smiling as much, but maybe he was cranky, or tired, or teething. He was prone that year to terrible and painful ear infections, one after another, which helped explain why he didn't seem to laugh as hard when I tickled him, or why he would sometimes wander away when I covered my eyes to play peekaboo. He was no longer as eager to wrestle with his dad, a game he'd previously dropped anything to play, but maybe he just wasn't in the mood. And yet, with each passing week, we noticed that he wasn't as engaged, curious, or happy as he'd been. He no longer seemed like himself.

Jake seemed to be getting lost in some of his early interests. He had always been captivated by light and shadows and by geometric shapes. But now, his fascination with those things started to feel different to me.

We had discovered when he was very little, for instance, that he loved plaid. Our duvet cover at the time had a plaid pattern, and it was the only thing that would soothe him when his ears hurt. Just as other mothers won't leave the house without a pacifier for their babies, I was never without a scrap of plaid material. But after that first year, he began to roll over onto his side and stare intently at the cover, his face just inches from the lines, and he'd stay there as long as we'd let him. Sometimes we'd find him fixated on a sunbeam on the wall, his body rigid with concentration, or lying on his back, moving his hand back and forth through the sunlight, just staring at the shadows he was making. I had been proud of and intrigued by the early signs of his independence, but these behaviors no longer felt like independence to me. They felt like he was being swallowed up by something I couldn't see.

Jake had always been the coddled younger 'sibling' in the

daycare group, and he had loved every minute of it. He'd spent his whole first year finger-painting alongside the daycare kids and bouncing right along with them when they did Freeze Dance. He took his nap when they took their naps, and he ate his snack when they ate theirs. But now I found that he'd rather look at shadows than crawl after his favorite kids, and their most outrageous bids for his attention often went ignored.

Michael was sure I was worrying unnecessarily, rightly pointing out that children go through phases. 'He's fine, Kris. Whatever it is, he'll grow out of it,' he'd reassure me, snuggling us tightly into a family bear hug, and eliciting a squeal of delight by nuzzling Jake's ticklish tummy.

In fact, my mother was the first person in the family to suspect that whatever Jake was going through wasn't just some funny toddler phase. We didn't know it yet, but our perfect world was already starting to fray around the edges.

# Something's Wrong

I grew up in central Indiana, close to farm country. We even had some farm animals of our own out back, usually a goat or a rooster. Every spring, my mother would borrow a brand-new baby bird from a farm for the day. It was a tradition I loved as a child, one I looked forward to every year, so of course I couldn't wait to share it with Jake.

Jake's second spring, the adorable baby was a duckling. Fourteen-month-old Jake was sitting at the kitchen table in my grandmother's house, filling page after construction paper page with hundreds of hand-drawn circles. They were strangely beautiful, but they were odd, too, more like the type of doodle you'd expect to find in the margins of an architect's notepad than in the drawings of a child not yet two.

As my mother tenderly cupped the duckling to scoop it out of its wicker basket, I could barely keep the lid on my own giddy anticipation. Laughing at me, she put her finger to her lips as she snuck up behind Jake, placing the adorable little fuzz ball right on top of the paper where he was drawing.

But the reaction we expected never came. Jake didn't light up with delight at the fluffy baby duck waddling inches in front of his nose. Instead, my son reached out one finger and gently pushed the duckling off his paper. He never stopped drawing his circles.

My mom's eyes met mine again, and this time they registered fear. 'I think you've got to get him checked out, Kris,' she said.

Our pediatrician immediately arranged for a hearing test,

but there was nothing wrong with Jake's hearing, even though by that time he was no longer reliably responding to his name when we called him. We all agreed it was time to have Jake evaluated by a developmental specialist. The doctor suggested that we contact First Steps, a state-funded early intervention program that provides assessments and therapy for children under the age of three who appear to have developmental delays.

After an initial assessment showed significant delays, First Steps sent a speech therapist to our house each week to do therapy with Jake. Despite these sessions, he spoke less and less as the weeks passed, retreating further and further into a private, silent world. His speech therapist ramped up the number of sessions to three a week, the maximum allowed by First Steps, and before long a developmental therapist was added to the team. We set up a therapy area in our kitchen, and I bought a big wall calendar to keep track of all the appointments. By this point, Jake was barely talking.

Michael didn't mind the stream of specialists coming in and out of our home every day, but privately he admitted that he thought it was overkill – a sign of the times, an overreaction. 'Kids develop at their own rate, Kris. You've said so yourself. Not long ago, nobody would have been making such a fuss about this. Whatever he's going through, he'll grow out of it.' Still, if the state was willing to provide all these services to speed the process, that was okay, too. Michael was confident that Jake would be fine either way.

I was also feeling more optimistic, encouraged by the fact that we had our very own personal brigade of therapists. One of the children I'd taken care of when I was a live-in nanny had experienced some early speech problems, and I'd seen his speech therapist work wonders in an extremely short time. Surely, with all these experts helping us and a little elbow grease and patience, we'd get our boy back.

There were other reasons to rejoice as well. My daycare, Acorn Hill Academy, was thriving. Acorn Hill didn't look like a typical daycare; it looked more like the backstage at a theater preparing for a production. Money was always far too tight for me to purchase the supplies I needed to fuel the children's creative impulses from a proper crafts store, so I was constantly on the lookout for resourceful ways to get these materials. The number of possibilities that might spring from, say, a refrigerator box is staggering, and I discovered that as long as I was willing to haul such things away, people were happy to let me have them.

Before long, several stores in the neighborhood began saving boxes of throwaway items for me – boxes filled with treasures. One carpet store kept us well stocked with sample squares, and a paint store gave us old wallpaper books, along with specially mixed paint that people had ordered but not picked up, and damaged brushes. We always had one special project or adventure in the works: an enormous mural, for example, or a room-sized chess game (another donation!) with figures and pieces so large, the children had to form teams to move them.

Parents didn't seem to mind if their children were covered head to toe in paint once they saw the gigantic, elaborately constructed castle we'd spent the day building out of refrigerator boxes. They looked right past the messy clothes when their children, beaming with pride, took them on a tour of the brightly colored castle, which consisted of several separate rooms.

Even more exciting, I was pregnant again, and Michael was thrilled. Our vision of a house filled to the brim with kids was coming true.

Although I didn't realize it at the time, this bubble of restored domestic bliss was just the eye of the storm. The gravity of what was happening to Jake – this thing we couldn't name or understand – hit me some weeks later, while the three of us were attending another child's birthday party.

Very few things thrill young children like interacting with a character they know and love from books or TV, and our neighbor's Clifford the Big Red Dog birthday party was no exception. When the big red dog came in, the toddlers in the room erupted into gleeful hysteria. Michael joked that it was like happening upon Michael Jackson at the mall.

Not one kid in that room could take his or her eyes off the giant red dog, except my son, who remained glued to the alphabet book he'd brought with him. We tried to engage him – 'Look, Jakey, it's Clifford!' – but Jake wouldn't even look up. In a room filled with squealing children, festooned from floor to ceiling with balloons and streamers, with gigantic bowls of candy everywhere – not to mention the six-foot man in the furry red dog suit – Jake was lost in the letter $K$.

My anxiety level was rising. 'Put him up on your shoulders so he can see,' I urged Michael, who did, bouncing and singing along with Clifford's birthday song. But Jake simply opened his alphabet book again and rested it on top of Michael's head. In a last-ditch attempt to get Jake involved, Michael gently opened Jake's fingers to give him a balloon. Jake looked down at the red ribbon in his hand, then up at the shiny, helium-filled foil balloon, and then back down at his book. Slowly, he opened his fingers, releasing the ribbon. I stood there, watching my silent, serious boy, lost in his alphabet, while the balloon drifted to the ceiling, and I knew in that instant my mother was right: Something was wrong with my son.

First Steps continued to send therapists to work with Jake in our home. I was still going through the motions, of course, but after that day at the birthday party, my sense of optimism had deflated like the balloon we'd brought home with us. I no longer felt confident that therapy would be enough to reverse whatever was happening to Jake. He seemed to be withdrawing even more, and nothing could stop his downward spiral.

An hour with his therapist might elicit a word or a sound; sometimes he'd randomly echo song lyrics or parrot a phrase one of us had said. But real communication with Jake – anything remotely resembling a conversation, even something as simple as 'Hi' or a request for a cookie – was gone.

Looking back, I realize that Jake was exhibiting the textbook signs of autism: the gradual change in speech, the inability to make eye contact or to engage with us or his therapists. But this was 1999, before the PBS specials, before anyone knew we were dealing with an epidemic. In 1999, autism meant one thing to most laypeople, and that was *Rain Man*, and I saw no similarities between our baby boy and the character Dustin Hoffman played in that movie.

Although I still did not know what to name it, I had begun to accept in my heart the seriousness of what was unfolding. But it was essential to me to maintain the traditions that made our family life uniquely ours.

One of those traditions, and perhaps the most important one to me, was Sunday dinner at my grandparents' house. My mother's job as a corporate accountant meant long hours and frequent trips to New York, so growing up, we spent a great deal of time with my grandparents, who lived directly across the street. An irrepressible, wonderfully eccentric inventor, my grandfather loved more than anything to play with us. He turned life for everyone around him into an endless, elaborate series of adventures.

Grandpa John Henry was an incredible man, not only a machinist, an engineer, and an inventor but also an expert craftsman and carpenter. After his stint in the U. S. Navy during World War II, he had come back to his hometown of Mansfield, Ohio, to work as a machinist on the floor of Westinghouse's tool and die plant, as his father had before him. In addition to his day job, Grandpa John earned a contractor's license and began building commercial and residential buildings. He was written up in the local newspapers as the epitome of America's can-do spirit, living proof of the rags-to-riches optimism and enterprise that had made our country great. And that was before he had performed his best trick.

When Grandpa began his job at Westinghouse, he couldn't help noticing inefficiencies in the process known as annealing. To drill a hole in steel, workers had to heat the metal to soften it to the point where a tool could pierce it. Often as not, once the steel had cooled, the precisely drilled hole would lose its shape, and the whole process would have to be repeated. This was true for every steel manufacturer in the world, and knowing Grandpa John, it must have driven him nuts.

We never saw him without a little notebook in his pocket, each one filled with drawings and ideas and projects he was working on. I don't know how long it took him or how many notebooks he worked his way through, but Grandpa John and a partner eventually solved the puzzle by inventing a new set of tools and a new process that allowed workers to drill hard steel, which revolutionized steel manufacturing.

The Ford Motor Company took notice of Grandpa John's invention and was the first to purchase nonexclusive rights to it from the team. They subsequently sold it to other major companies as well, and there isn't a car on the road today or a toaster in your kitchen that didn't benefit from my grandfather's innovation.

Ford changed my grandfather's life. Grandpa John moved directly from the machine shop in Mansfield to Ford's famous Glass House in Dearborn, Michigan. Even when he became an executive, the machine shop remained Grandpa's favorite place to be. Eventually, Ford asked if he'd be willing to move to Indianapolis to head up the tool and die division of its largest manufacturing plant, and that's how he (and later we) came to live in Indianapolis.

Grandpa's invention and his position at Ford, which he held

until he was in his seventies, made him a wealthy man. But he never bought a fancy house or traveled the world. Grandpa lived in the same single-story brick house on the east side of Indianapolis to which he and my grandmother moved from Dearborn for the rest of his life, and my grandmother lives there to this day.

The money he earned did afford my grandfather the freedom to take a five-year leave of absence to help my parents take care of Stephanie and me when the need arose, and every day Grandpa John delivered us into a world of pure enchantment. He was the only adult we knew whose inventiveness and energy matched our own. With him at our side, we spun all the wonders of our imagination into playthings as concrete as the ground beneath our feet.

Grandpa John could truly build *anything*. At the same time that he was helping to raise us, he was also working on another project close to his heart. The one extravagance he'd allowed himself was to purchase a nearby plot of land in order to build a sanctuary for the New Amish community in Indiana. The church was very much a hands-on project for him. Grandpa John had been raised in a culture of barn raisings and carpentry, and he'd earned his contractor's license, so it was completely in character when he insisted on building every pew in the new church himself. When the crew responsible for sanding and varnishing the timber beams to support the roof didn't perform up to his standards, he redid them himself with the help of his family – even enlisting Stephanie and me, the very youngest members. He was at the construction site practically every day, more often than not with us in tow. We'd make little statues out of dampened sawdust and discarded screws while he answered a question or consulted on the plans, and then we'd head out with him onto the lake on the church's property, fishing for croppies and bluegills in a boat my grandfather had built with his own hands.

When we weren't at the church site, we were by his side in the superb mess of his garage workshop. Other children may have fantasized about Santa's workshop, but I grew up in the real thing. Piles of fragrant wood rested on strong brackets in the garage, waiting for my grandfather to call them into service to make a cradle for a new baby in the family, or for one of our dolls. Hammers and clamps and other small tools, handles burnished from years of good use, hung haphazardly from nails on the wall. Handmade oak drawers with shiny brass pulls opened to reveal thousands of screws and washers and bolts of every size and description, while handmade cabinets held lacquer and paint, brushes and honing stones, chisels and anything else he might need to turn imagination into reality.

In the evenings, tired after our long, busy days with Grandpa, Stephanie and I slid into the soothing routines of my grandmother Edie's immaculate kitchen. A little stern where Grandpa John was free-spirited, Grandma enlisted our help in late summer to can corn and berries and to make pickles. Later, we'd put up great vats of spiced applesauce from the Yellow Transparent and Lodi apples we picked in the fall. On winter nights, we made peanut brittle, caramel corn, and, when the temperature fell below freezing, clothesline taffy.

After dinner, we spent the final hour of the day in my grandparents' front room, where we might feast on cheddar cheese and apples or one of the amazing German baked goods in Grandma Edie's repertoire. Stephanie and I particularly loved the giant puff pastry cookies sprinkled with sugar and cinnamon that we called knee patches. In the summer, Grandma's homemade vanilla ice cream was loaded with just-picked strawberries, and in the winter she'd spoon the peaches she'd canned over our bowls.

In this room, my grandmother taught Stephanie and me how to quilt, and how to embroider, too, patiently untangling the jewel-colored threads when they snarled. When the whole family sat down for dinner on Sunday nights, we did so at a table that my grandfather had built himself, then sanded and polished to a mirror finish. The table was set with linen place mats and napkins that the women in our family had embroidered ourselves. There was always care and quality at that table, and there was love.

Given how central the relationship with my grandparents was to me, it was only natural that I would want Jake to grow up close to them, too. So every week, our new little family joined them for Sunday dinner, just as I always had when I was growing up.

Michael loved going for Sunday dinner as much as I did. Before he met me, he'd never known how wonderful it felt to come out of the winter cold into a toasty house filled with the intoxicating smells of roasting meats and baking pies. He'd never given thanks at a table set with homemade beeswax candles or joked with relatives as everyone worked together to get the food on the table while it was still hot. I came to see that welcoming Mike into this domestic embrace was one of the greatest gifts I could give him.

Mike wasn't the only one who enjoyed our Sunday outings. As picky as Jake was about what he ate, he'd wolf down a giant piece of my grandmother's homemade apple pie – and another if we let him. He loved to play with the beautiful wooden toys that Grandpa John had made for his grandchildren when we were small. The marble run was Jake's favorite, as it had been mine. And I was certain that when he got bigger, I'd see Grandpa John and him at the workbench in the garage, both bent over one of my grandfather's notebooks.

One Sunday evening when Michael had been called in to work, Jake and I went alone to Sunday supper. Usually, my grandfather welcomed us at the door, but that night he didn't.

I assumed he was either finishing a project or cleaning up. My grandmother wouldn't allow him anywhere near her table until he'd washed the machine grease and wood dust off his hands with gritty black soap and changed into one of the soft flannel shirts she always kept pressed and stacked neatly for him. But when he finally appeared at the head of the table to carve the roast, I was stunned to see that he was in a wheelchair.

Over the course of the previous year, he had suffered a series of small strokes and we'd seen him gradually lose ground. Even so, I was shocked that he was now too weak to stand. My heart caught in my throat, but the way he proudly showed off the engineering behind his wheelchair to my brother, Ben, helped me also to see that he was still very much himself.

There was a funny convergence that night. My grandfather's occupational therapist had given him some soft putty to squeeze so that he could regain the strength in his affected hand. When he brought it out, Jake's eyes widened, and he began, somewhat shockingly, to hum a little tune under his breath. 'What's that song he's singing?' my grandmother asked me, bewildered. It was the only sound we'd heard out of Jake all night. I smiled and sang along with him: 'Make a snake, make a snake' – the song that Mike and I always sang to encourage Jake to roll out the very same putty in the way *his* occupational therapist had instructed.

The levity, however, didn't last. Later that night, as I was helping Jake into his car seat, my mother handed me a newspaper article describing what autism looks like in a very young child. As I read the article, my stomach dropped: Many of the behaviors on the checklist were all too familiar to me. On the drive home, I had to pull over because I was crying too hard to see the road.

# Scattered Skills

Every parent has had a moment of inattention while shopping. You think, 'Hmm, this dress is cute. I wonder if they have it in my size?' and by the time you turn back around, your child is nowhere in sight, having vanished into thin air. That feeling of mounting terror that claws at your throat as you wildly start calling his or her name – that moment is what it feels like to watch your child disappear into the dark well of autism. But instead of a few terrible seconds before that little face pops out from behind a rack of sweatpants, the moment of powerlessness and desperation can last for years, or a lifetime.

Michael was having none of it. He was still pushing back the encroaching darkness, fighting fiercely to hold on to our picture-perfect life. After all, this was his little buddy, his Jake, his *boy*. So when a therapist used the word 'autism' in relation to Jake – the first health professional to do so – Michael fired her on the spot. We're not proud of that now, but it's a common reaction.

Over the next few weeks, however, it became clear to both of us that we were losing Jake. In October 2000, First Steps came to the house to conduct a formal evaluation.

The night before, I was such a wreck that Michael called my brother, Ben, to come and lend moral support. Ben is always hatching some wacky new plan, whether it's turning the guest bedroom into a yoga studio or draping sheets of meat over every surface in his house to make homemade beef jerky. But even high-spirited, practical-joke-playing Ben was solemn on the day of Jake's evaluation, and nobody on earth could have brought a smile to my face.

As we shook hands with the evaluating therapist, Stephanie Westcott, I was keenly aware that everything in our world was riding on the next few hours. This woman's verdict would either leave us rejoicing or cast us out even further into the desert – and we'd seen enough to know exactly how bleak that landscape could be. My hands shook so badly that Michael had to press them hard between his own hands to get them to stop.

By midmorning, I felt physically ill. We didn't need special training to see how badly the evaluation was going. Most of the time, Jake didn't even respond when Stephanie spoke to him. He wouldn't make eye contact with her. He wouldn't point at the circle, put the star in the shape stacker, or put the rings on the tower. He wouldn't sort objects by shape or by color, even though he spent a lot of time doing those types of activities on his own. He wouldn't sing along with her for Itsy Bitsy Spider or show her with his fingers how the spider crawls up the spout.

When he recited the alphabet, my heart lifted. But Stephanie didn't look as impressed as I'd hoped, not even when he recited it backward. At one point, when she tried to guide Jake to a new activity after playing with crayons on the floor, he cried and refused, his whole body stiffening. By the time she had convinced him to move along to the next exercise, my blouse was soaked in sweat.

Then Stephanie asked Jake to do a wooden puzzle with her. I let out a breath I didn't know I'd been holding, and Michael and I allowed ourselves to exchange a glance of relief. We both felt certain that he would do well on this one. Jake had loved to do puzzles since his pudgy baby hands were big enough to hold the pieces, and he was a whiz at them. The puzzle she was asking him to do was similar to some of the ones he had – easier, even – so we were confident that here, at least and at last, Jake would score well.

But just then, as Jake's moment to shine finally arrived, he decided that he wanted to play with his alphabet magnets.

Jake was obsessed with the colorful plastic alphabet magnets we kept on the fridge. He had dozens of them and carried them everywhere he went. Hoping to avoid a possible distraction during the evaluation, we'd put his magnets away in a box on a bookshelf, thinking that out of sight would be out of mind. The tactic, unfortunately, backfired, and Jake's single-minded focus was now squarely on getting those magnets off the shelf.

Jake would get up and make a beeline for the box, and Stephanie would gently but firmly lead him back to the table. The battle raged on as the minutes ticked by. I couldn't bear to watch, staring instead at Michael's hand clutched over my own, his knuckles a startling white. Finally, and after quite a bit of time, Jake agreed to stay seated, but his whole body was craning over the back of his chair toward the box of magnets. After even more coaxing, he finally did the puzzle – without looking at the puzzle itself or at Stephanie sitting across from him, instead still leaning over the back of his chair, his eyes trained on the box.

I felt as if the whole world had come crashing down. After all, this was something he *could* do, something he was good at. We'd been banking on this puzzle to be a bright spot in what had been a dismal performance so far. I realized how desperately hopeful I was that a success here could somehow make a significant difference in the overall results, and Michael must have been feeling the same way.

'Listen,' Michael said. 'Sorry to interrupt, but he's really distracted. He's doing it by feel, and he's using his left hand – he's a *righty*! Give him another chance to show you how fast he can do it?'

Stephanie looked at Michael in open disbelief and said, 'Mr Barnett, usually it takes children of Jake's age approximately two minutes to do a puzzle of this complexity.' She told us it had taken Jake – even with his nondominant hand and while looking behind him toward the box of magnets the whole time – just fourteen seconds.

'Attaboy!' Mike said, punching his fist into his open hand, and I felt a weight lift, too. He'd aced one! Now we were on the right track. I was sure that once Stephanie could see what Jake was capable of, those strengths would offset all the other tasks he either couldn't or wouldn't do. For the first time in weeks, I allowed a little hope to creep in. We'd do more therapy. We'd do whatever they wanted us to do. All I wanted was to hear her tell me that my baby angel was eventually going to be okay.

After the hours of testing were finally over, Stephanie sat down with us and said, her face grave, 'Jacob has Asperger's syndrome.' A wave of relief washed over me; I had been prepared for worse.

'Oh, that's great news,' I told her. 'We were afraid he had autism.'

Stephanie went on to explain that Asperger's is a form of autism. Ultimately, however, the distinction wouldn't matter. Jake's diagnosis would soon change from Asperger's to full-blown autism.

That day was our introduction to the concept of scattered skills. Stephanie explained that it's quite common for autistic children to be relatively high functioning in some areas, even if they're coping with significant delays. At two, for instance, Jake could easily do a complicated maze more quickly than I could, but he couldn't make eye contact, which is a developmental hurdle that a baby ordinarily clears between one and three months – and something that Jake had also been able to do until he was about sixteen months of age, when he began to regress. The term for these peaks and troughs in standard developmental milestones, Stephanie told us, is 'scattered skills.' Children are diagnosed on the autism spectrum when their skills, instead of lining up neatly, are scattered all over the developmental map.

That was when I lost it. I suddenly understood that the bright spots Michael and I had pinned our hopes on during the evaluation wouldn't lift his score or change the outcome of the assessment. Suddenly, it was all too clear: All the little things we'd been so quietly proud of – Jake's early reading, his speedy ease with puzzles, his ability to concentrate and focus for long periods – didn't contradict the autism diagnosis but instead confirmed it.

Jake's gifts were inextricably tied up with all these terrifying shortfalls, and for the first time I allowed myself to face the ugly reality of what those shortfalls would mean for Jake and for the life we had dreamed of for him. I felt like a fool. What did it matter now if he could do a puzzle faster than some other kid if it meant that he'd never be able to ask a girl out on a date or shake hands with someone interviewing him for a job?

Stephanie Westcott's report from that day reads in part: 'Interested in shadows, bright lights. Twirls himself. Limited response to minor pain.'

We went to bed absolutely shattered. Michael held me tight, but I didn't close my eyes once all night. When I wasn't consumed with worry about Jake's future, I was racked with anxiety about whether the same fate was in store for our new baby – another son, we'd recently learned – who was on the way.

# Inside the Diagnosis

Autism is a thief. It takes your child away. It takes your hope away, and it robs you of your dreams.

Whatever you did with your child, I did with mine. I took him to the petting zoo and the aquarium. I bought that cute little outfit with the matching hat. And I worried about which was better, Huggies or Luvs. We were an ordinary family, and Jake was an ordinary baby, having an ordinary babyhood. Then he began to withdraw from us, and with that initial diagnosis of Asperger's, any hope of normalcy disappeared.

By age two and a half, Jake was a shadow of the little boy he'd been. Most of the time, it didn't even feel as though he was in the room. He had stopped speaking entirely. He no longer made eye contact with anyone, nor did he respond when he was spoken to. If you hugged him, he'd push you away. The best you could hope for was that he'd let you hold him for a few seconds while he ignored you, staring at the shadows on the wall. He wouldn't ever ask for food or drink, and would eat only plain foods prepared and served in particular ways. I had to keep close track of his liquid intake so that he wouldn't get dehydrated.

He'd spin in circles until he got dizzy. He'd spin objects in his hands or on a flat surface, sometimes staring so intensely at the spinning object that his whole body would shake. These spinning behaviors are hallmarks of autism, referred to as 'self-stimulation,' or 'stimming,' in the autism world. He loved flash cards of any type, especially ones with the letters of the alphabet on them, and he carried them everywhere. He was obsessed with cylinders and would spend hours putting smaller objects into an empty flower vase. His preoccupation with shadows and mirrors and light was all-consuming. He could spend a whole morning walking back and forth past the chairs arranged around the kitchen table, head down, studying the shadows cast by the spindles onto the floor and the way they changed as he moved.

Many of these new behaviors were truly mystifying. Even as a baby, Jake had shown a curious penchant for upturning any cereal box in reach. Now no cereal box was safe: No matter how cunningly I hid them, he'd find, open, and upend them, emptying the contents on the floor. Every time I looked around, one of the daycare kids would be gleefully running through a big pile of cereal that Jake had dumped out. No amount of sweeping could contain the mess. Michael and I grew used to finding rogue Cheerios in the most unlikely places – our winter boots, the glove compartment, the bathtub.

A great deal of the time, though, Jake simply disappeared into his own quiet world. When he carried his soft baby blanket around – a yellow Afghan with an open weave – it wasn't for security, as it would have been for most children. Instead, he'd fixate for long stretches of time on it, staring, I now think, at the geometric shapes created by the weave. His obsession with plaid and any other pattern involving straight lines was so extreme as to be frightening. I'd had a lot of experience with toddlers, usually so active and squirmy it was hard to keep them still long enough to get a pair of shoes on them. But Jake could spend hours staring silently at a shadow pattern on the wall or floor, never moving a muscle.

Like many autistic kids, Jake liked to be in small, contained spaces. The bottom of his closet was a favorite place to line up his Matchbox cars. The tighter the quarters, the better. Often he'd cram himself into the bottom shelf of the armoire we had in our living room, or into one of the small plastic storage tubs we used to hold toys.

One panicked afternoon, I spent forty-five minutes searching desperately for him. I was about to call the police when I found him scrunched cozily atop some freshly folded towels in a small laundry basket. Deep down, I had been reassuring myself that there was nothing to fear, not in our carefully child-proofed house, where Jake usually had at least two sets of eyes trained on him at all times. But in those horrifying minutes, the boy who seemed to be disappearing a little more each day was suddenly – if only momentarily – *gone*. It was almost too much for me to bear.

Later that year, after another formal assessment administered by another therapist, Jake's diagnosis was revised. She explained to us that Jake had likely been diagnosed with Asperger's (a mild form of autism characterized by relatively high functioning) instead of full-blown autism because his IQ was so high – a shocking, off-the-charts 189 on the Wechsler Intelligence Scale for Children. Michael and I had seen that number when we'd pored over the reports together after the first battery of tests, but we had completely ignored it, in part because we were distracted by everything else in the report, but also because neither of us thought the IQ scale even went that high. We simply thought it was a typo.

It hadn't been a mistake. But what did it matter? An astronomical IQ wasn't preventing Jake from sinking ever more deeply into his own isolated world. By the time of the second evaluation, right before his third birthday, the diagnosis was full-blown, moderate to severe autism. Despite his remarkably high IQ, his functional scores put him in the so-called 'retarded' range.

When my brother, Ben, heard the revised diagnosis, he said, 'Get ready, Kris. This is going to be the fight of your life.' Even though I'd always been the easygoing peacemaker in our family, he knew – more, maybe, even than I did – that I would fight for Jake. But none of us yet understood the magnitude of what was to come.

Once you've gotten a diagnosis of autism, a horrible stranglehold takes hold of everyone in the family. You eat, breathe, and sleep autism. You fight autism every moment you're awake, and you fall asleep knowing that you could have – that you *should* have – done more. Because there's quite a lot of evidence that improvement depends on how much intervention a child gets before the age of five, life with an autistic child is a constant race against the clock to do more, more, *more*.

The year before he turned three, Jake had state-funded speech therapy for an hour every day, five days a week. He also had an occupational therapist, a physical therapist, and a developmental therapist coming to the house once a week, each for an hour or more. Independent of his work with First Steps, we started doing another therapy protocol called applied behavior analysis (ABA), which required forty hours or more a week – an ordinary person's workweek! – on top of all the other therapy. On the recommendation of Marilyn Neff, a wonderful therapist who worked with Jake, we later settled on a different type of therapy called Floortime, which is more child directed and more closely modeled on natural styles of play. Floortime required less drilling, but it was still inordinately time-consuming.

It was almost impossible to squeeze those additional Floortime hours in on top of all the other appointments and therapies and interventions. The calendar on the kitchen wall was so jam-packed that nobody but I could read the microscopic handwriting I used to cram it all in. A friend who worked as the secretary to a busy executive took one look at it and commented that my little boy's lightest day made her boss's worst one look like a walk in the park.

On top of all the hours with the therapists, the whole family (even Ruby, the young woman who worked with me at the daycare) was learning American Sign Language, in the hope that Jake would eventually be able to communicate with us that way. Every wall in our house was papered with sign language materials. My belly growing bigger every day, I was still also operating the daycare, and Michael was working full-time. We were exhausted.

It seemed there was no respite, ever, for any of us. Right after breakfast, it would start: The doorbell would ring, announcing the first therapist of the day. Then, for hours, Jake would sit at the little table we had set up in the kitchen. The therapists would encourage him to make eye contact or to label what he was doing or what he saw: 'in,' or 'fish,' or 'one.' Often they would use a technique called 'hand over hand,' using their own hands to demonstrate how to perform simple tasks such as opening a box.

You could see how frustrating all of it was for him. I learned that many autistic children get upset during therapy; they throw toys, scream, or have tantrums. Jake didn't do any of that. He was simply unresponsive, preoccupied as always with the shadows on the wall. Occasionally, he'd get upset, usually when the therapist did something differently than he was used to. One of the only times I remember him losing it was when his developmental therapist, Melanie Laws, asked him to do one of his favorite puzzles upside down.

Most of the time, he simply looked peeved – and today I think, *No wonder!* The emphasis all day and every day was on what Jake *couldn't* do. He couldn't hold a pencil with a proper grip. He couldn't go up the stairs one leg after the other. He couldn't imitate clapping. He couldn't mimic the facial expressions or the noises the therapists made. Those compassionate and dedicated therapists would sit there at that little table in our kitchen with Jake, laboring hour after hour. But despite their patience and determination, he'd look right through them as if they weren't there at all.

It never ended. After Jake went to sleep, Michael and I would spend hours reading books or combing the Internet for new research, new therapies, or other parents' groups. The news out there was even bleaker than we'd thought. Michael memorably nicknamed one newsgroup ParentsWithoutHope.com.

I think of that year as living inside the diagnosis. Obviously, the toll on families with an autistic child is extreme, and the fallout is well documented. It is common knowledge that divorce rates skyrocket after a child is diagnosed. Thankfully, Michael and I weren't among those casualties. If anything, Jake's diagnosis seemed to bring us closer together. We didn't always agree, but we remained each other's port in the storm. I was completely focused on Jake, doing anything and everything I could for him, and Michael channeled whatever anxiety he had into taking care of me. Sometimes he'd bring home dinner, and after Jake was in bed, we'd spread out a blanket on the living room floor and have a date-night picnic. And without fail, a bouquet of fresh flowers arrived every week.

There was more heartbreak on the way for us, though. Now in his early eighties, my indefatigable grandfather was gradually losing his battle against the strokes that had battered his body over the previous year. He moved into hospice care. I spent a great deal of time with him there, often getting into the car to go visit him as the last daycare child was leaving. Sometimes I sat with him while he slept.

When he talked, he sounded the same as he always had. Certainly, his sense of humor was still very much intact, and he delighted in teasing me about my ever-expanding belly. (Along with the rest of me. I am naturally quite petite, but I gained ninety pounds with that pregnancy!)

It was hard for me to believe that he was dying, that this pillar of strength and good sense – the bulwark of my childhood – could now be so weak and frail. One afternoon I drove up to the church he'd built to drop off some baked goods for my mother, who was cooking the church lunch that week. As I got out of the car, I heard the sound of the tractor used to mow the grounds.

My grandfather had never hired anyone to landscape the grounds. He took pride in keeping the property beautiful for the people who used it. As meticulous as he was, he never failed to make the chore fun, inscribing figure eights and zigzags in the grass to keep the grandchild on his knee screaming with delight.

Before my brain could catch up, my heart lifted, and I turned, fully expecting to see him careening toward me on the tractor he'd fixed a thousand times. But someone else was driving the tractor, soberly edging the church lawn, and my heart broke at the sight.

It was from his example that I'd learned the value of lifelong curiosity, the pleasure to be found in hard work, and the importance of family. I'd seen the sense of purpose he felt in dedicating his life to ideals larger than himself, and the satisfaction he derived from doing so. As sad as I was about his decline, I felt incredibly grateful that I'd had the opportunity to tell him how much he had meant to me.

Late one afternoon, while I was changing the water in a vase of flowers in his room, he asked, 'What is this autism?' I was startled by the question. Not wanting to worry him, I hadn't told him about Jake's official diagnosis. Apparently, someone else in the family had, and now I searched for the simplest way to talk about it.

'Jake can't talk to us right now, and they don't think he ever will,' I explained.

He nodded and was silent for a while. And then he put his gnarled hand on top of mine, looked right into my eyes, and said, 'It's going to be all right, Kristine. Jake is going to be all right.'

I truly believe that those words were his last gift to me. From anyone else, the comment would have felt like a shallow platitude, the kind of meaningless comment that people make when they don't know what else to say. But when my grandfather told me that Jake was going to be all right, he said it with complete conviction, and I believed him. For a minute, in that hospital room, I was a little girl again, and he was the pillar of strength, the person who could fix anything in the world at his tall workbench in his garage. I gave myself over to the comfort of the idea that my strong, brilliant grandpa knew something about my son that I couldn't see.

# An Ending, and a Beginning

My grandfather's funeral was beautiful. He had been deeply beloved in the community, and his had been a life worth celebrating.

I was, however, sick with grief. Although I'd been able to say everything I wanted to say to him, his passing had left a gaping hole in my life. I missed him so much, and the fact that he would never know the baby I was carrying devastated me.

After the funeral, my sister, Stephanie, was supposed to drive me back to my grandparents' house for food and remembrance. We pulled into the procession at the graveyard, but as she was about to turn right, I put my hand on her arm and said, 'Go left.' She turned to me, confused.

'We need to get to the hospital,' I said. 'The baby is coming.'

It was a month early, but no matter. I had felt the first telltale pangs as my grandfather's coffin was being lowered into the ground.

John Wesley was in fact born the next day. Michael and I decided to name him John after my grandfather.

The feeling of those early days with baby Wes are marked indelibly in my mind. Although I was still actively mourning my grandfather, even that terrible sadness was blunted by the sheer delight of having this wonderful brand-new child at home. Michael and I couldn't get enough of Wesley's delicious milky smell. We marveled over his impossibly tiny feet and wondered at all the funny, adult-seeming expressions that flitted over his face. Grandpa John, with his strong faith, would have appreciated the symmetry: As one life had ended, another had begun.

As I'd done after Jake was born, I reopened Acorn Hill a few days after Wes arrived. Once again, the daycare kids had a new baby to play with. From the very beginning, it was clear that Wesley was a boy's boy. Planes, trains, automobiles: If it had wheels, he loved it. Michael would hold him in the back of one of Jake's oversized toy trucks while I'd gently roll it around the room. This induced gales of contagious baby laughter, and the faster we went, the louder Wes laughed. He would kick and shriek with excitement every time our beagle puppy (so loving and utterly useless as a guard dog that Michael ironically insisted on calling him Cujo) entered the room. We couldn't stop ourselves from laughing, too.

Jake seemed unperturbed by Wesley's arrival, which was, of course, disturbing in itself. It was the first time (though not the last) that I'd wistfully hope for a little sibling rivalry between the two of them. But after so many months of tension and anxiety, Mike and I were grateful simply to relish the tiny, ordinary moments with the new baby.

Then we noticed that Wesley seemed to gag and cough more than was usual when we were feeding him. I became hypervigilant, carrying him with me everywhere, snuggled inside a baby sling. One day while I was giving him a bottle when he was about two and a half months old, he not only stopped moving but also began turning blue. He looked like he was dead.

Leaving my terrified assistant, Ruby, in charge of the daycare, I rushed over icy roads to the emergency room at St. Vincent Carmel Hospital. Michael met me there. We'd been through a lot, and we didn't scare easily, but this was terrifying. Our pediatrician happened to be away, so we waited and watched as a team of covering doctors did test after test. Nobody could tell us what was wrong. Eventually, someone told us that our doctor was flying home from his vacation to speak to us in person.

Our doctor, who had already been through so much with us, looked heartbroken to share more bad news. He explained that Wesley had been diagnosed with a disease called reflex sympathetic dystrophy (RSD), a neurologic disorder that can affect every system in the body. Although no one knows for sure what causes the condition, the doctor explained that it is widely suspected to be the result of a malfunction in the nervous system.

Locking eyes with me, he went on to say that RSD is almost never seen in infants. When it is, it can be catastrophic, because it can interfere with the autonomic nervous system – all those essential actions our bodies do that we don't think about or control, such as maintaining a normal body temperature, a steady heart rate, and regular breathing.

Our doctor knew that Michael and I were fighters, but he gently explained that he'd seen only two other cases of RSD in infants over the course of his long career, and both those babies had died before the age of one. How we made it out of his office and back home, I don't know. We allowed ourselves briefly to fall to pieces and then soldiered on, determined to help our baby fight to beat the odds.

Wesley began to have seizures, sometimes eight or nine a day. His beautiful new body seemed rigid all the time, and to us it appeared that he was in more or less constant pain. He now had his own battery of therapists who came to administer neurodevelopmental therapy, stretching exercises designed to improve his range of motion and train his muscles.

I knew the treatment was necessary, but there is absolutely nothing worse for a mother than hearing her baby cry, which meant that this stretching therapy was torture for both of us. Poor little Wes would scream and scream and scream, and I would pace the kitchen, my clammy fists clenched and my heart rate skyrocketing. It took every bit of faith I had to believe that we were helping our son, not making things worse.

Michael surprised me one day by coming home from work right in the middle of one of Wesley's sessions, just to check in. During the session I was, as usual, beside myself in the kitchen – white, shaking, and in tears. I'd told him how awful the sessions were, of course, but nothing could have prepared him for experiencing it firsthand.

He took one look at me and said, 'Stretching therapy? More like screaming therapy.' Then he picked up the phone to call his boss. That afternoon, Mike rearranged his work schedule so that he could be home during Wesley's therapy sessions. It meant he would have to work Saturdays, but Wes would get the care he needed – and I could be in the daycare, safely out of earshot.

It was a harrowing time. We were in the emergency room a couple of times a week for months. Wes couldn't swallow liquids, so he survived on formula thickened with rice cereal. Sleep was impossible for me. I was convinced that without constant vigilance, Wesley would stop breathing, so I spent every night by his crib. I couldn't entrust his care to anyone else; I knew I would never be able to forgive them or myself if anything happened to him. All this was happening amid everything that was going on with Jake. And while I was doing daycare, Wesley was once again with me in a baby sling, every second of the day.

# Rainbows

Wesley's urgent health issues and therapy didn't change Jake's needs, of course, so it was important for us also to maintain his schedule and ordinary routines. We were still spending hours upon hours at that little table in the kitchen, but we weren't seeing much improvement – and certainly nothing commensurate with the tremendous amount of work being done. Life was doubly difficult at this time because of the daycare, where I was surrounded by typical kids. I remember watching a child much younger than Jake zoom by his therapy area, effortlessly reaching over to drop a ball in a cup – a skill that Jake's therapists had spent six months working on, to no avail. I tried to accept that a little girl I'd known for only a week would give me a huge hug goodbye at the end of the day when my own child no longer acknowledged that I was in the room. But it was hard.

Still, I couldn't help noticing that when Jake's therapists had left and he was playing by himself, he seemed deeply engaged. To others, it might have looked as though he was simply zoned out, but I didn't see his focus as blankness. When he was spinning a ball in his hand, or drawing geometric shapes over and over, or dumping those boxes of cereal onto the floor, he seemed to me to be completely transfixed. His attention didn't seem random or thoughtless. He looked like someone who was lost in very important, serious work. Unfortunately, he couldn't tell us what it was.

Occasional glimmers of light did come through, though, and when they did, they were extraordinary.

Because of the daycare, I always had hundreds of crayons stored in big tins, and Jake loved to dump all of them onto the floor and then line them up side by side, just as he liked to arrange his toy cars. Late one evening, while I was tidying up the living room, I stopped for a moment to take a breath and to appreciate the precise and harmonious pattern Jake had left on the rug, a beautiful array that transformed hundreds of ordinary crayons into a rainbow.

As I knelt to pick them up, tin in one hand, a murky memory from high school science bubbled up out of the deep recesses of my brain: the mnemonic ROYGBIV, for the colors red, orange, yellow, green, blue, indigo, violet. A chill went up my spine. The pattern that Jake had made didn't just *look* like a rainbow – it *was* a rainbow. Brick red was placed neatly next to burnt umber, cadet blue next to purple mountain majesty. The crayons weren't only lined up meticulously, which would have been unusual enough for a child of two and a half, but they were also in the precise order of the color spectrum.

Jake was at the breakfast table the next morning when I told Michael about the crayon rainbow. Frankly, I was a little freaked out. 'How can he possibly know the order of the color spectrum?' I asked. 'I could barely remember ROYGBIV!' As if in response, Jake reached out to the table and turned the faceted water glass in front of Michael so it caught the morning sunshine pouring in from the sliding door, splashing a gorgeous, full-spectrum rainbow across the kitchen floor. All three of us turned to look at the vivid rainbow.

'I guess that's how he knows,' Michael said.

Another day around the same time, I was hurrying to find the right gift at a toy store before Wesley started to fuss. Jake was occupying himself at a shelf full of music boxes, opening and closing the lids and listening to the songs. As I was paying for the gift, Jake went over to an electronic roll-out piano mat the store had set up for demonstration purposes by the cash register. While the woman behind the counter wrapped my present, Jake cocked his head to one side and, without missing a single note, began playing the tunes he'd just heard. The saleswoman's jaw hit the floor. He was able to play each song after hearing it only once. That was shocking enough, but the saleswoman didn't know that this was the first time Jake had ever seen a piano keyboard.

Sometimes I felt as if I was the only person who could see any of Jake's special abilities. The therapy reports grew more and more alarming, and Jake's distance from Michael and me felt nearly complete. Our once affectionate boy didn't talk to us, didn't hug us, didn't tell us he loved us. He wouldn't even look at us unless we happened to get in the way of one of the shadows he was staring at.

Every day, it seemed as though there were fewer activities Jake would – or could – participate in. But I wouldn't relinquish all of them. Because Michael worked in retail, his hours could be crazy. During the holidays, for instance, he might work from three in the afternoon until three in the morning. Whenever Michael's work schedule had robbed him of coveted family time, Jake and I would wake him up for a quick good-morning hug and kiss before starting our own day. I can't describe how happy it used to make me to open the door to our bedroom and see Jake's face light up at the sight of Michael. 'Daddy!' he would cry, and at the sound of his son's voice Michael's eyes would open – and his arms, too.

All that, of course, had gone away, but still I persisted, hoping that Jake would once again reach out for his father. One morning, with my hand on the doorknob to our bedroom, I thought about the look on Michael's tired face the day before, wondering if it was fair to wake him up for nothing. Ultimately, though, I turned the knob. Maintaining routines that had once been filled with laughter and love was our way of keeping the candle burning in the window, lighting the way for Jake to come back to us.

It wasn't easy. Every night, I'd get into the shower after I'd cleaned up the daycare space and put the boys down, and I'd just cry and cry – from the exhaustion, from the fear and the sense of hopelessness, from knowing another day had passed and I hadn't done enough, and from knowing that we'd have to get up the next day and do the whole thing all over again. That year was so hard, some nights I'd stay in the shower crying until the hot water ran out.

Some days, it was especially hard to keep the faith. Joey, a little boy almost exactly the same age as Jake, had been coming to the daycare since he was a newborn and had been diagnosed with autism at roughly the same time as Jake. We began working with Joey and Jake together, and when we started hearing good reports about a casein-free, gluten-free diet, we started both of them on it.

Jake didn't respond to the diet at all. But it worked for Joey, and so quickly that it felt like a miracle. After two weeks, Joey was speaking again. Every parent of an autistic child dreams of hearing his or her child's voice again, and when Joey spoke for the first time, I wept with gratitude. Later that night, I wept again, because my own son still couldn't talk, and I was starting to believe all the therapists and experts around me who didn't think he ever would.

# Breakthrough

The state-funded First Steps program ends on a child's third birthday, and all services stop. It's possible to apply for a waiver to keep some of the therapy going, but there's a long waiting list. I've heard of cases where the child was twelve or thirteen before he or she qualified for additional help.

Jake's birthday is in May. His autism diagnosis meant that he would be eligible to get therapy through a developmental preschool – special ed – in the fall. But with First Steps over, we had an empty summer before school started, and I had no intention of wasting it.

All the research indicates that the best window for reaching autistic children is before they turn five. So every day for us was a race against the clock. We've all heard the urban legend about the mother who found the strength to lift a car to save her child. That was exactly the kind of drive I felt. I was going to do everything within my power to make sure Jake didn't slip further away.

Michael and I knew enough, as most parents would, to keep the basic protocol going. But we wanted to do more. Some of Jake's therapists, such as Melanie Laws, had become friends and were kind enough to answer when we pestered them with question after question. There was still a great deal to learn. Michael and I stayed up late every night, reading every book we could get our hands on. Our bedroom looked like a dorm room during exam time, open textbooks and notebooks strewn everywhere.

That summer, as we began working with Jake on our own, I was determined to find a way to communicate with him again.

Unfortunately, even though the whole family had learned it, our attempts with sign language had been fruitless. Watching Jake in his therapy sessions, I could see these were empty gestures for him, and finally, in a state of complete frustration, I ripped every one of the sign language posters down.

On an Internet newsgroup I read about a set of flash cards that had been developed for stroke patients. Called the Picture Exchange Communication System (PECS), the cards hadn't been widely used with autistic children, and they were extremely expensive. But I kept thinking about the alphabet flash cards Jake loved so much and the way he gravitated toward pictures, and I thought that PECS might work for him.

It did. Within a few weeks, he could point to the right card when we said the word that corresponded to the picture. It felt like a tremendous breakthrough. After a year of practically no communication whatsoever, Jake was responding.

I rushed in to fill the void. I remember walking into the kitchen to find Michael, a puzzled look on his face, flipping through a set of photos he'd picked up from the drugstore. In the envelope, along with pictures of Wesley and Jake at the zoo and an apple-picking farm, as well as a few shots of Jake lining up Matchbox cars on the coffee table, he'd found some still lifes I'd asked to have printed on the extra-long paper used for panoramic shots. These included a basketful of crayons, a gallon of milk next to a sippy cup, a bowl of mac and cheese, and a CD player with some CDs next to it. In Michael's hand was a giant portrait of our toilet. I laughed and explained: I had been trying to make Jake his own customized PECS cards, so he could use them to point to what he wanted to do.

Melanie was very excited by how quickly the cards had worked and advised me to keep going. 'Let's try to get him back to the high end of the spectrum this summer,' she said. 'Let's not let him lose any more ground.'

So the two of us put together a highly sensory program for Jake. Michael and I couldn't do it all ourselves, so we got National Honor Society kids from my old high school to come to our house to help. They needed volunteer hours, and we needed volunteers.

The kids were great, but nobody was having much fun. Jake wasn't speaking, but it didn't take a trained professional to interpret the way he felt about the activities we made him do. He was bored. Sometimes Melanie and I would laugh because he looked so much like a jaded teenager, his toddler body lolling away from the table, chin dropped wearily onto his chest. Sometimes when she'd take out an exercise, he'd roll his head back in exasperation, as if to say, 'This again?' If he did the exercise, it was clear he was indulging us. 'C'mon, Jake, work with me here, buddy,' Melanie would say, teasing and cajoling him along. Sometimes he'd yawn right in her face. Yet I continued to notice that when he was playing by himself, his focus was ferocious.

You can't make too many generalizations about autistic kids, but I feel comfortable making this one: They *love* string. Jake would get into my knitting basket and play for hours with the yarn. One morning when I walked into the kitchen to refill my coffee cup, the scene before me took my breath away.

Jake had run different-colored yarn all around the kitchen – crisscrossing through the refrigerator handle and around the garbage pail, the table and chair legs, the cabinet pulls, and the knobs of the stove. The result was a series of brilliantly colored, intricate, overlapping webs. Using yards of yarn, he had created not a terrible, tangled mess, but a design of complexity, beauty, and sophistication. I was awestruck.

That phase went on for months. It must have seemed a little crazy to let him take over the house this way. Some days it was even impossible to get into my kitchen. But his intricate designs were spectacular to look at, and when the sun streamed through the windows, the shadows they threw moved and changed as the day progressed, involving the whole room in a complex play of light and dark. These creations were evidence to me that my little boy was in there, busy working on something magnificent. They gave me a way in, a glimpse into his private world and his extraordinary mind.

The contrast with his behavior in therapy was stark. When working with the yarn, Jake was engaged and alert. Obstacles didn't frustrate him, and nothing could distract or divert him. He was unstoppable. I began to find that if Jake had time to spin his webs in the morning, he was more tolerant of whatever therapy he had to do later in the day.

I also prioritized his comfort, even during therapy itself. Like many autistic children, Jake really liked to be squished. I had read all the research showing that compression is comforting for people with autism. I knew about the wonderful autism and animal rights activist Dr Temple Grandin and the 'squeezing' machine she had designed to compress herself when she was a child. So I made Jake a special pouch by folding a hammock, sewing it lengthwise up the back, then hanging it from the ceiling. When he was in the pouch, it enclosed him completely, but because it was woven, he could still see out. That was important to me. It meant that even when he was tucked up comfortably inside, he was still in the room with us. I'd swing him three or four times, which he loved, and then I'd hold up two flash cards, name the object on one of them, and ask him to point to the correct card. Invariably, we found that his ability to focus on the recognition games was much better when he was in his sling.

We snuck therapy in wherever we could. I took the wooden toy train table from the daycare, but instead of filling it with trains, I lined it with a velvety blanket and then dumped in thousands of dried beans I'd gotten from the bulk section of the supermarket. One of Jake's favorite comfort rituals, especially if he'd experienced a stressor such as a change in his schedule, was to climb up and burrow into the beans with an alphabet book. I took advantage of the fact that the other children in the daycare also loved playing in the beans (it was like a sand table, only easier to clean up) and would ask Jake to take a break from his book to hand them a funnel or a sand toy to play with, incorporating some social goals into what would otherwise be solitary play.

The other change we implemented that summer was more subtle, but in my heart of hearts I credit it with Jake's emergence from autism.

One afternoon Jake was working with one of the high school students at his little table in the living room. It was the first truly hot day of the summer, so hot we decided to turn the sprinklers on for the kids in the daycare. After a long winter cooped up together, they burst out into the yard, their bare feet slipping on the wet grass as they laughed and squealed and splashed around. It was a glorious moment – the kind of typical childhood experience, I realized with a start as I looked out the window at them, that Jake hadn't had since his diagnosis.

The sight and sound of those kids breaking free, sliding and shrieking as they laughed under the cold water, brought me up short. For the past year and a half, every moment that Jake had been awake had been about autism: drills and therapy and pattern recognition to work on his lowest skills. In all of this, we had forgotten something vitally essential: *childhood*.

Typical childhood experiences – like watching your cold fingers wrinkle up under a sprinkler on the first superhot day of the year – are important for everyone, not just typical kids. Every family needs to have special traditions that celebrate who they are and what matters to them. I knew from my own days growing up that such traditions don't have to be a big deal to be meaningful. Something as simple as packing a cooler with peanut butter sandwiches and heading to the beach to fly a kite can bring a family together to make a memory. But we weren't doing any of those things with Jake, and suddenly I realized that if I didn't fight for my child to have a childhood, he wasn't going to have one.

I picked up the phone and called Michael at work. 'Sweetheart, I need you to take care of Wesley alone tonight. I've got a date.' Michael was startled. Wesley was so incredibly ill that I hadn't spent more than ten minutes away from him since he'd been born. But that very evening after dinner, I did. As Michael got Wesley into his pajamas, I put Jake in the car, opened the sunroof to the sweet-smelling summer air, and drove out into the Indiana countryside.

In only a few minutes, we'd left our familiar neighborhood behind. The narrow road that stretched out in front of us was only a single lane in each direction, edged by a wall of tall corn on one side and miles of dark green soybeans on the other. After the pavement ended and the gravel began, ours was the only car for miles, and the only lights we could see came from farmhouses in the remote distance. People always say they go to the country for peace, but the truth is that a country night is loud, and the chirping of crickets and the hushed sounds of the wind rustling through the cornstalks filled the car.

I was driving us up to the land surrounding my grandfather's church – miles and miles of open pasture around the lake where Grandpa John had loved to fish. In the summertime, he'd often bring the grandkids along, packing all thirteen of us and a case of grape soda into his van, along with the coffee cans full of night crawlers he'd sent Stephanie and me out into the rain in our ponchos to catch. I spent many long, blissful days with my sister on that lake. All day, we'd chase butterflies and bullfrogs, and when the sun went down, we'd catch fireflies in jam jars to light up our forts. It was a place I so strongly associated with my childhood that it seemed like the right place to begin Jake's.

I turned on the fog lights and cranked up a jazz station as loud as it could go. Leaving my shoes in the car, I got Jake out of his car seat and gathered him in my arms. As I danced with him in the warm night air to Louis Armstrong's *Takes Two to Tango*, it felt as if it had been a long time since we'd just been together, without anything to work on.

When my arms got tired from swinging him around, we lay down on the hood of the car, and I pulled Popsicles out of the big cooler I'd brought. Sticky drips from the ice pops stained our necks as we lay back and looked at the enormous sky. I pointed out the constellations I knew, and when I ran out of the ones I could name, we lay there in silence, looking up. There's very little ambient light pollution from Indianapolis when you're so far out in the country, and that night the stars were so close and so bright, it felt as if we could reach out our hands and grab one.

Jake was utterly transfixed by the stars. I hadn't seen him so relaxed and happy since he'd started therapy. I felt that way, too. As exhausted and scared as I was, for the first time I felt confident that I was doing the right thing.

All that summer, we chased the long, hard, exhausting hours of therapy during the day with a few hours of frivolous kid fun in the evenings. It wasn't easy. After therapy, there weren't very many hours left in the day, and I didn't want to broadcast what we were doing. The received wisdom was unanimous: When children are broken, work supersedes play. The other moms I knew with autistic children would have been appalled if they'd known we were sneaking off, and most of the experts as well. I could hear their shocked reactions in my head: 'But what about your hours? Did you get in your hours?'

I made sure we got in the requisite hours of therapy, of

course, but I knew in my gut that Jake also needed the chance to play and to feel dirt between his toes. I was determined to give him both. There were times when it would have been easy not to prioritize Jake's childhood – to stay an extra hour doing occupational therapy at the gym or spend a little more time at the therapy table. But if it came down to choosing between extra therapy and blowing dandelion fluff at each other in the backyard, we went with the dandelions every time. I truly believe that decision was a contributing factor in enabling Jake to rejoin the world, and it is one that has guided and animated all the decisions, large and small, that Michael and I have made on his behalf in the years since.

Many kids spend their summers playing at the beach. Jake couldn't do that without compromising his therapy because the beach was too far away. But we could still build sand castles together in the backyard sandbox, even if we had to do it by moonlight. We had a little brazier in our backyard. It wasn't a real fire pit, but it was good enough to allow Jake the pleasure of licking melted chocolate and gooey toasted marshmallows off his fingers while the mosquitoes made their own meal of our ankles.

We made frequent trips out to my grandfather's land. Grandpa John's presence was so strong there, it almost felt as though we were visiting him. When I felt frightened and alone, as I often did in those days, I allowed myself to be comforted by his reassurance that Jake would be okay.

Jake loved those trips. It occurs to me now that he may have tolerated dancing under the stars because he was also getting to do what he really loved: looking up at the night sky. But he couldn't tell me that, and I was only trying to cram as much old-fashioned fun as possible into the spare time we had.

That pasture out in the country was where I found my son again. He still wasn't speaking or making eye contact, but by the end of the summer, I could sometimes hear him humming along with the jazz I played, and he'd laugh when I'd swing him around under the bright stars. While we were lying on the hood of the car and looking at the stars, he'd turn around to hunt for the Popsicles, handing me the box to open. It might not seem like much, but it was more of a connection than we'd had in a year. Then, right before he was to start special ed pre-school, we had another breakthrough.

Many parents complain that they have a hard time putting their kids to bed. Not us. Unless Jake and I were out having a nighttime adventure, he would put himself to bed promptly at eight o'clock, every night.

To be honest, this was sometimes a little annoying. In Indiana, summer days are long. Kids run around until nine or ten on weekend nights, sneaking an extra ice cream out of the cooler while the adults talk with their neighbors around the barbecue. Not Jake. If we were at someone's house, he'd put himself to 'bed' on their floor – or, on one memorable Halloween, in the unoccupied bed of our friend Dale's daughter Allison.

We didn't realize exactly how precise his timekeeping was until I tried putting him to bed early one night. We had an out-of-state wedding to drive to the next morning, which meant the whole family would have to be up and out of the house much earlier than usual. Thinking that we'd all benefit from a good night's sleep, I put Jake into his Volkswagen Bug bed and was surprised when I couldn't entice him to lie down. Perplexed, I called Michael into the room. We tried to coax Jake to lie down, but as usual he just ignored us, instead watching the shadow on the wall. There was no clock in Jake's room, but at eight o'clock sharp he lay down and pulled the covers over himself.

'Oh, my,' I said to Michael. 'The shadow on his wall – it's a clock.'

We tested my theory on subsequent nights by throwing towels over the cable box and the kitchen clock and turning our bedroom alarm clock toward the wall. Every night, Jake put himself to bed at exactly eight o'clock – not at 7:57 or 8:03, but at 8:00 on the dot.

Our bedtime routine had become very precise. Like many autistic children, Jake liked the events in his life to be predictable. So I'd always do exactly the same thing when I tucked him in. I'd lean over, kiss his forehead, and say, 'Good night, my baby angel. You're my baby angel, and I love you.'

When he was small, he'd hug me back, but over time he'd become completely unresponsive. People ask what the hardest thing is about having an autistic child, and for me the answer is easy. What mom doesn't want to hear her baby tell her that he loves her or to feel his arms around her? And then one night toward the end of the summer, about six months after we'd started making those trips out into the country, my wish came true. As I was putting Jake to bed, I leaned over to kiss him, and to wish my baby angel good night. Completely without warning he reached up and hugged me back.

I will never forget that moment as long as I live. It was the first sign of affection, or even interest, he had shown toward me in more than a year. I was in a state of complete shock, hiccuping back the sobs, scared to move in case he'd stop. I could have stood there forever, tears streaming silently down my face, his little arms tight around my neck.

And then, his sweet breath hot in my ear, my son spoke for the first time in eighteen months. And what he said was, 'Night-night, baby bagel.'

Through my tears, I started to laugh, and once I'd started, I couldn't stop.

# A Step Backward

All the gains we'd made over the summer were incredibly encouraging. It had even been a little bit fun. But the summer came to an end, and when it did, special ed began. Off Jake went to developmental preschool.

Right from the beginning, these life skills classes felt wrong to me. In regular preschool, the first days include an emphasis on helping the kids separate from their parents for the first time. But there was no such luxury with special ed. Instead, the little yellow school bus showed up outside our door the first day, Jake got on it, and then several hours later the same bus dropped him off at home. What happened in the hours in between remained largely a mystery to me.

To be fair, I suppose the separation anxiety was more my issue than Jake's. With the exception of that one heart-melting bedtime hug, he still barely acknowledged my presence when I was in the room, let alone when I left it. But as a parent, it was terrifying to put him on that bus. At three and a half, he was so *little* – still a baby really. And although he had begun to speak an occasional word here and there, an actual conversation with him was still unthinkable. Jake couldn't tell me about his day at school, about what had happened or how he felt. He couldn't share any of his fears or anxieties or concerns. On any given day, I couldn't even tell if he'd liked his lunch. So I had to put my trust in the system.

Unfortunately, maintaining that trust became increasingly difficult. I had nothing to go on except how Jake acted when he was at home, and what I saw filled me with doubt. He wasn't improving. In fact, it seemed to me that he was losing some of the gains he'd made over the summer. By summer's end, I had for the first time dared to hope that he was rounding a corner. I prayed that the few words we'd been able to coax out of him meant that more would follow, and I was even becoming more optimistic that he might really talk again. But as school started and the weeks passed, my hopes once more seemed out of reach.

The start of special ed prekindergarten also coincided with a host of new behaviors I found alarming. Most notably, one evening when I asked him to come to the dinner table, Jake lay down on the floor and wouldn't budge. When I went over to pick him up, I found that he'd let his body go completely limp, so it was almost impossible to carry him. He wasn't crying or even visibly upset – just floppy. Over time, I noticed him doing this more and more, always when I asked him to do a task he didn't particularly want to do.

His teacher came to our house for a state-mandated conference once a month, and the next time she came, I mentioned this new behavior. She laughed and said, 'Oh, he must be getting that from Austin, another boy in the class. Austin has cerebral palsy, and when he doesn't want to cooperate, he goes limp.' On one level, I could see that it was funny, but on another I felt real concern. How much specialized attention could each child possibly be getting if all of them were lumped together into one classroom, regardless of their special needs? More specifically, I found the floppy behavior itself unsettling. The goal wasn't for him to become *less* responsive.

Michael was sympathetic to my concerns, up to a point, and he'd patiently act as a sounding board whenever my doubts about Jake's progress in special ed surfaced. He became the calm mouthpiece for all the same sentiments I'd repeat over and over to myself whenever he wasn't around: 'They're the experts, Kris. We wouldn't second-guess a cardiologist or an oncologist.

Shouldn't we trust them to know what the best plan is for our son?'

I rode that seesaw for months. My doubts would simmer until they boiled over, and then I'd be steadied by Michael's sensible impulse to stay the course and trust in the experts. But my worries about the school finally came to a head a few months in, when Jake's special ed teacher gently but firmly asked me to stop sending Jake to school with his beloved alphabet cards.

That misunderstanding was a clarifying moment for me. Michael and I were sending Jake to school to learn. But his teachers – the people responsible for his education – were telling me they didn't think he could be taught. As gentle as Jake's teacher had been with me, the underlying message was clear. She had given up on my son.

Later that day, while I was taking a chicken out of the Crock-Pot for dinner, I tried to talk it through with Michael. 'He's not going to read? *Ever?* Why not at least try? This is a kid who's already totally obsessed with the alphabet without any encouragement at all. Why hold him back from what he's naturally doing?'

Michael was slightly exasperated with me. 'Kris! These people have a lot more experience and training than we do. We have to let the experts be the experts.'

'What if carrying around alphabet cards everywhere he goes is Jake's way of saying he wants to read? Maybe it's not, but what if it is? Do we want him with people who won't even try to teach him simply because it's not part of the life skills program? Why would they say no to somebody who wants to learn?'

I realized that all of my questions – indeed, all of the niggling doubts I'd been unable to squelch in the months since Jake had started preschool and even before that – could be boiled down to one big, basic issue: Why is it all about what these kids *can't* do? Why isn't anyone looking more closely at what they *can* do?

Michael's arguments for staying the course had always worked to calm my doubts – until that night. Suddenly, my doubts evaporated. As any mother would instinctively know to snatch her baby back from the edge of a campfire, I knew I had to snatch *my* baby out of special ed.

Michael could sense a tidal shift, and he was alarmed. 'Kris, honey, I understand you're frustrated and upset, but you've got to be reasonable,' he said. He often trusted me to take the lead, but this time he saw me heading into waters he wasn't comfortable sailing, not when the stakes were this high. I understood his position completely. After all, I'd been in complete agreement with him twenty-four hours before. But now it was absolutely clear to me that what he considered to be the more prudent and rational course would only spell disaster for our son.

To look at us, you would have thought that Mike was the rebel. He was the one who drove too fast and played elaborate pranks and wore ripped jeans and a leather jacket. But the fault lines in our relationship were not always turning out to be what we expected. Of the two of us, it was Michael who felt more comfortable proceeding by the book, who needed the safety of a narrowly prescribed set of rules. I was the one, it turned out, who was more likely to embrace the uncharted path when the need arose.

The conversation went on late into the night, even though Michael understood early on that my mind was made up. Over the next few years with Jake, I would come to see over and over again that if one door closes, others can fly open. But as I tossed and turned that night in bed, hearing his teacher's voice in my head, I didn't yet have that knowledge to comfort me, which is why the decision to pull him out of special ed was the scariest thing I'd ever done and required the biggest leap of faith I'd ever made in my life.

I got out of bed without disturbing Michael and walked down the hallway to Jake's little green room, which had an orchard painted on the walls to match the one outside. His quilt had a pattern of black Labrador puppies riding in red pickup trucks through apple trees. Scattered all over it, as always, were hundreds of his alphabet flash cards.

I put my hand on his back to feel him breathe. He was so special, so unique. But he was also autistic, and just because of that, his school had labeled him and then prematurely decided what he could and couldn't do. He needed me to be his advocate, his champion; he needed me to be his voice.

The next day, I did not put Jake on the little yellow school bus. Instead, he stayed home with me.

Michael hit the roof.

'*What do you mean he's not going to school?* Are you crazy, Kris? Have you completely lost your mind?'

'Michael, we're going to lose him if we keep doing what we're doing.'

'This isn't a joke, Kris. School is where Jake gets therapy. We can't afford to have an army of private therapists come to the house. We can't afford a single one of them! How is he going to get the help he needs?'

'I'm going to do it myself.'

'What about the daycare? What about Wes?'

'No one else is going to do it, Michael. The experts have it all backward, and I don't want to waste time trying to change their minds.'

Jaw set, arms crossed, he didn't say anything.

I tried one last time. 'I can do this, Michael. I *have* to.'

Still angry, Michael turned away from me, his shoulders tight. I didn't blame him for being angry. I wasn't formally trained to administer the kind of therapy Jake needed. But like every other parent of an autistic child, I'd been in the trenches with Jake's therapists since day one. Plus, I knew my child better than any expert could. And I saw a spark in Jake. Some days, true, there was only the faintest glimmer. But while I couldn't claim to fully understand Jake's passions and interests, neither could I justify discouraging those interests just because the rest of us didn't understand them, or because they didn't match up with some so-called normal template for childhood development. If we wanted to help Jake, we had to stop focusing on what he *couldn't* do.

After a few moments of tense silence, Michael turned back to face me. I could see that I hadn't so much convinced him as worn him down. He agreed, on the condition that we reevaluate in a few months. I suspected that the outcome might have been very different if we'd been talking about kindergarten and not preschool.

'You'll see, Michael, I promise. By kindergarten, Jake will be ready. And not for special ed, but for regular public school. I'm going to make sure of it.'

# The New Normal

The silence on the other end of the phone was uncharacteristic. Then Jake's developmental therapist, Melanie Laws, said, 'Are you sure?'

Before picking up the phone that day, I sat in my living room and tried to remind myself to keep breathing: in and out, in and out. The enormity of what I had signed myself up for had hit me hard. I'd taken this stand with Michael, and I'd won – but now what? There was no book, no *Ten Easy Steps to Mainstreaming Your Severely Autistic Child* waiting for me on my shelf, and I didn't have the slightest idea where to start.

So I called someone I knew could help: Melanie Laws. But to get her on board, I first had to convince her that I hadn't gone completely bonkers.

Warm and motherly, Melanie had worked with Jake from the beginning, and she and I had clicked right away. She had the effortless authority that comes with experience – in her case, working with hundreds of children over the years, as well as raising seven of her own. I related immediately to her work ethic: Melanie was someone who always went the extra mile. That was something my grandfather had always taught me to do, and he'd taught me to appreciate it when I found it in other people. Melanie also had a great sense of humor, and Jake, even at his most stubborn, cracked her up. 'I've got my work cut out for me with this one,' she'd observed wryly, shaking her head as Jake, never making eye contact, used one finger to push the matching work she was trying to get him to do right off his little table. Most important, Melanie treated the children she worked with as *people*, not problems to be fixed or objects of pity.

Melanie was the perfect person for me to talk to for another reason: She'd been a teacher before she'd been a therapist, which meant she'd know exactly what I'd need to do to prepare Jake to enter regular kindergarten. Still, the silence I heard when I told her I'd pulled Jake from special ed was worrisome. Her reservations were almost identical to Michael's.

'I'm not sure you completely understand what you're getting into,' Melanie said. 'Jake needs a lot of help – a *lot* of help, Kris. And to be frank, that help is best coming from someone who's had years of training and a lot of experience with autistic children. Not to mention you've got your hands full with your sick little one.'

I launched into my argument. Uncertain as I might have been while watching that school bus come and go, my fundamental conviction remained strong. I knew this was the right thing for Jake. But would my conviction be enough? Melanie was a professional, and like Michael, she sounded far from convinced.

We went back and forth for a while, and then Melanie asked for a little time to think about whether she wanted to participate.

The next morning, I heard a honk outside. There in the driveway was Melanie, unloading box after box from the back of her station wagon. She looked at me, then said, 'You just going to stand there? Or are you going to help me carry this stuff in?'

My impassioned arguments hadn't entirely won her over, but she agreed to help me mainstream Jake. And so the two of us spent the day sitting on the floor of the daycare, kids playing all around us, while Melanie showed me every one of the toys and tools and exercises she used in therapy. She pointed out what she thought might be helpful, while I made list after list after list. She had brought books and worksheets and manuals from her own training for me to photocopy.

Then she walked me through every minute of a typical day of kindergarten, from story time to raising your hand; from asking to use the bathroom to Duck, Duck, Goose; from putting your lunch in a cubby to 'The Goodbye Song.' Then I made yet another list – this one of everything a kid would have to know how to do in order to succeed in a mainstream kindergarten.

We were both worn out when she finally got up to leave, but her smile was not unkind when she asked me one more time, 'Are you sure about this, Kris?'

I said that I was.

I set up new routines for Jake. But instead of constantly pushing him in a direction he didn't want to go, drilling him over and over to get his lowest skills up, I let him spend lots of time every day on activities he liked.

For instance, Jake had moved from simple wooden puzzles to complicated jigsaws, blowing through thousand-piece puzzles in an afternoon. (One Saturday afternoon, when we were trying to complete the last, frustrating part of a house project, Michael dumped all the pieces from five or six of those puzzles into the gigantic bowl I use for popcorn on our family movie nights. 'That should keep him busy,' he said. It did – but not for long.)

He also loved the Chinese puzzles called tangrams – seven flat, oddly shaped pieces that you put together to form recognizable figures. I found it incredibly difficult to arrange these irregular shapes so that they resembled an animal or a house, and I always had to shuffle them around, trying many different options before landing on the right arrangement. Jake, however, seemed to have no trouble flipping and rotating the shapes in his mind. Then he'd lay the pieces out easily, as if that was the only way they went. Soon we began combining sets, making large-scale patterns that were much more beautiful and complex than anything the instruction cards suggested.

I spent as much time doing puzzles and tangrams with him as I'd once spent on therapy, and slowly I began to see a change in him. He was more relaxed, more engaged. Over the next month or so, he regained some of the ground I felt he'd lost while he was in school. In particular, Jake's language began to come back. It wasn't conversation – I couldn't ask him a question and get a response, for instance – but he was talking.

Most of the time, he recited strings of numbers. Numbers had always been comforting to Jake. He would carry an old grocery receipt around for a week, smoothing the list of numbers under his fingers. But once the floodgates were open, Jake was actually quite chatty. We couldn't pass a numerical street sign or an address that he didn't read out loud. Running errands with me in the car, he'd call out a constant stream of numbers from the backseat.

This was how we figured out that Jake already knew how to add. At some point, I realized that some of the numbers he was saying were telephone numbers that he was reading off the sides of the commercial trucks and vans we passed on the road. But there was always an extra, larger number at the end – and I practically drove off the road the day I figured out the final number was the sum of the ten digits in the phone number added together.

Driving back from a doctor's appointment with Wesley, I caught fragments of what Jake was saying to himself in the backseat. This time, it wasn't only numbers but the license plates of the cars we were passing. Then it was the names of the businesses: 'Marsh!' 'Marriott!' 'Ritter's!' At age three, just a few months after his teacher had told us we wouldn't ever have to worry about the alphabet with him, Jake could read. I really didn't know how he had learned or when it had happened – maybe it had been that *Cat in the Hat* CD-ROM after all. All I knew was that I had never gone through any of the typical pre-reading steps with him that I'd taken with so many other children in the daycare, teaching them the alphabet and all the different ways letters can sound. I had never so much as sounded out a single word with Jake. And yet now that he was talking a little more, we were learning that I wouldn't have to.

His memory was another surprise. Jake had been obsessed with license plates since he could walk. Everyone in our subdivision had gotten used to seeing him in their driveways, tracing the numbers on their plates with his fingers. But on our nightly stroll, I was still shocked to realize that the numbers and letters I could hear him singing softly under his breath belonged to cars that had already been put away for the night in the garages we were passing. Apparently, Jake had memorized every single license plate in the neighborhood.

That was a cool trick, but there were hints that something much more interesting was happening. Going to the grocery store with Jake during that period took forever. Before I could put an item in the cart, I had to tell Jake how much it cost so that he could say the number back to me. This drove me crazy. Especially with antsy Wes in the sling across my chest, grocery shopping was a chore that already took too long. One day about six months after we'd pulled him out of special ed, I was swiping my credit card at the checkout counter, and Jake started yelling, 'One twenty-seven! One twenty-seven!' I couldn't get him out of the store fast enough, but when I did and had the presence of mind to check the receipt, I saw that he must have been totaling up the prices as I was putting the items in the cart. The checkout person had accidentally rung up a bunch of bananas costing $1.27 twice. After that day, he always gave me the running total as we joined the checkout line.

The 'math people' in our lives found Jake fascinating. One day I was having a cup of coffee with my aunt, a high school geometry teacher, while Jake sat at our feet, playing with a cereal box and a bunch of Styrofoam balls I'd gotten from a craft store so that the daycare kids could make snowmen. He was putting the balls into the box, taking them out, and then doing it again, and it sounded as if he was counting. My aunt wondered aloud what he was doing.

Jake didn't look up. 'Nineteen spheres make a parallelepiped,' he said.

I had no idea what a parallelepiped was; it sounded like a made-up word to me. In fact, it's a three-dimensional figure made up of six parallelograms. Jake had learned the word from a visual dictionary we had in the house. And yes, you can make one out of a cereal box. My aunt was shocked, less by the fancy word than by the sophisticated mathematical concept behind it.

'That's an *equation*, Kristine,' she said. 'He's telling us that it takes nineteen of those balls to fill a cereal box.' I still didn't understand the importance of what he was doing until she explained to me that an equation was a concept that she saw kids in her tenth-grade class struggling with every day.

Jake's capacity to learn certain types of things astonished us. He seemed curious about chess, so we taught him how the pieces move, and soon he was beating the adults in our family, some of them quite competent players.

We bought him a set of plastic alphabet tiles, the kind of toy he'd always loved. As usual, he took them to bed with him. The next day at breakfast, I noticed that he was fooling around with his Cheerios, arranging them in patterns. I didn't get it until I put him down for his nap and noticed that the new tiles featured a series of small raised dots at the bottom of each one. Jake had taught himself Braille.

Maps were another great passion of Jake's at that stage. He could barely contain himself when Dora the Explorer sang the character Map's special song. He loved nothing more than to trace the intertwined roads and train tracks on a gigantic state map with his finger. This particular interest of Jake's was useful. By age four, he'd memorized a driving atlas of the United States, so if you asked him how to get from Indianapolis to Chicago, he would tell you to take I-65 North until you hit I-90 West, including all the little access roads and connections you'd need to make.

In a city, his skills were particularly invaluable. Mike's family is from Chicago, so we went there often. I'm not ashamed to admit that I completely relied on Jake to navigate the maze of downtown. He knew all the buildings and every one of the shortcuts. What four-year-old directs his parents through traffic in downtown Chicago? But Jake loved telling us where to go, earning him the nickname 'JPS,' for 'Jake Positioning System.' Long before GPS became standard in many cars, JPS was standard in ours.

Michael and I marveled at the evidence of his precocity, but in truth the new normal was still hard. In particular, we weren't making much progress on real conversation. He was talking again, and for that we were grateful. But reeling off numbers and store names and answering questions are different from engaging in conversation. Jake still didn't understand language as a way to make a connection with other people. He could tell me how many dark blue cars we'd seen on the trip to Starbucks, but he couldn't say how his day had been, and I was always searching for common ground.

Also, Jake's extraordinary academic abilities wouldn't really help us to mainstream him into public school. Simply put, social skills are more important than academics in kindergarten. Kids in kindergarten have a lot of playtime. They have to interact with their classmates, they have to follow simple directions, and they have to share. If Jake spent the whole day in the corner, even if he was teaching himself the periodic table, they'd send him right back to special ed.

It was imperative that Jake learn to function well in a group. Of course, he was around the kids in daycare every day, but Melanie thought it might be easier for him if there were other autistic kids in the group as well. With her help, I sent an email out to the parents in our community, hoping some of them might want to join.

My call for participation was the first real clue that there was an autism epidemic. I was hoping for five or six responses. Instead, I got hundreds, from parents of children of all ages. I was stunned by the level of desperation in the emails. These were people, just like me, who could see that what they were doing wasn't helping their children. Many of them had run out of options within the system. There wasn't anyplace left that would work with them or their kids. In most cases, I was the port of last resort. 'Please help us,' one mother wrote. 'You're our last hope.'

That was a huge turning point for me. I looked at my flooded in-box and thought, *I'm not going to turn any of you away. You can all come.* Jake was going to learn what he'd need to get into kindergarten, and we were going to take as many kids with us as we possibly could. Nor would we leave the older or lower-functioning kids behind. *We are going to build a community*, I thought. *We are going to believe in our kids, and in each other's kids, and we are going to do this together.*

# Let It Shine

'Kristine, there appears to be a live llama in our living room.'

Michael's tone was resigned. Two years after we'd pulled Jake out of Life Skills, my husband had become accustomed to the scope and scale of my schemes, but nothing had quite prepared him for this. Of course, the llama wasn't supposed to be in the living room. She was *supposed* to be in the finished garage we'd converted to house my daycare, a space that was now also moonlighting twice a week as a highly unorthodox kindergarten boot camp I'd set up for autistic kids. Whatever Michael had been expecting when I'd told him I was determined to mainstream Jake into kindergarten, it wasn't this.

Receiving that flood of emails from those desperate parents had been an eye-opening experience for me. In response, I had decided that in addition to my daycare, I'd start a new program, a series of evening classes for autistic children and their families with the goal of helping the kids to be mainstreamed into public school. Melanie Laws, thankfully, once again agreed to help, and she suggested that I register the program as a charity, because I was determined not to charge anything for it. I couldn't bear the thought that a family might not be able to afford to come, or that they'd have to skip another therapy to do so.

So every morning, I'd open the daycare as usual and work a full nine-hour day there. But twice a week, after the daycare children went home, I'd vacuum the room and set up a mock kindergarten for autistic kids. I called the program Little Light.

From the beginning, I knew that I wanted to approach

autism differently. Typical therapy focused on the lowest skills. Most of the parents who came to Little Light had spent years trying to get their kids to hop up to the next skill on the ladder, usually without much success. I had seen my share of these sessions, hours spent trying to get a kid to put three rings on a post or to feed a cookie to a puppet, all to no avail. I'd watched my own son nod off in a session, still holding a therapy putty ball. So instead of hammering away at all the tasks these kids *couldn't* do, I thought we'd start with what they *wanted* to do.

This approach was far from standard practice. Most therapists would move a beloved toy or puzzle off the table so that a child could concentrate on *their* therapy goals; some would go so far as to hide it. We'd done the same thing with Jake's alphabet magnets during his evaluation. Just as Jake's whole body had strained toward his magnets and away from the task at hand, I saw many a therapy hour pass with a child too distracted by a missing toy to make even a tiny bit of progress that day.

Harnessing the children's passions may not have been the conventional way to work with them, but it was very much the way I'd always worked with my daycare kids. I believe this approach had a lot to do with the way my sister, Stephanie, and I grew up. Stephanie, younger than me by just fourteen months, was an art prodigy as a child. At age three, her art looked like work done by an adult. By the time she was six, she had the skills of a professional.

Stephanie's talent opened up huge creative worlds for both of us. We had store-bought toys, but we rarely played with them. We were far more interested in the toys Stephanie made. The paper dolls and the hundreds of intricately colored outfits she crafted for them while she was still in preschool were better than anything we could buy. I'd invent elaborate scenarios, and Stephanie would paint fully realized, detailed backgrounds to go along with my stories: enchanted castles, book-lined libraries, lush jungles. When I wanted a dollhouse, I didn't tell my mother; I told Stephanie.

Unfortunately, Stephanie's extraordinary art skills didn't help her much in school. She did poorly in all her classes except for art, and she had very few friends. Mostly, she was comfortable when she was alone or with me.

Remarkably, my mother never tried to turn around Stephanie's dismal academic performance. She wasn't in denial about the problem (Stephanie was barely passing, so denial really wasn't an option), but she stayed upbeat. 'If you can't do art, nobody cares. But if you can't do math, everyone's up in arms,' she remarked once to me. 'Why is that?' I found the comment a little surprising, given that she was an accountant and loved numbers herself. But she knew Stephanie.

In third grade, Stephanie took one look at the questions on a reading comprehension test and realized immediately that she was out of her depth. She drew a little frowny face on the front of the paper, right where the teacher would put her grade, turned the test over, and spent the remainder of the hour drawing a beautifully shaded landscape on the back. When my mother found out what Steph had done, she laughed.

I was perplexed by my mother's response. How could she take this so lightly? 'Because your brain works this way,' she said, pointing to the reading comprehension questions, 'and Stephanie's brain works *this* way.' She flipped the test over to show the landscape drawing. 'And you know what? You're both going to be fine.'

Of course, at the time I had no idea there was anything remarkable about my mother's reaction to Stephanie's differences. It was just the way things were. But I believe it was from her example I learned that *everyone* has an intrinsic talent, a contribution to make, even if it comes in an unexpected form. And

I began to believe that each person's potential to achieve great things depends on tapping into that talent as a child.

Maybe my mother would have been more worried if Stephanie's gifts had been less pronounced or less immediately apparent. As it was, the beauty of my sister's work awed adults, more than once bringing a casual observer to tears. In any case, instead of browbeating Stephanie over her failings, my mother focused instead on her gifts, choosing to do what she could to nurture Stephanie's passion. My grandparents were generous, but not ones to splurge, so we didn't have a lot of money to spare. Yet Stephanie didn't have just one paintbrush; she had ten, of every size and thickness and type, as well as an enormous box of expensive European colored pencils.

When Stephanie turned eight, my mother had some kitchen cabinets installed in the laundry room at the back of the house, and that became Stephanie's studio, an area where she could store her art supplies and draw and paint to her heart's content. Most important, these gifts were given freely, without any expectations. Stephanie never felt that she had to churn out masterpieces in her studio; my mother was simply giving her a place to be herself.

Stephanie is an artist today, and she teaches the subject for a living. Her portraits of my children are among my most treasured possessions. My mother's approach to Stephanie's challenges showed me how viewing a situation that seems bleak under a different lens can reveal a gift and a calling.

I had always encouraged the children in my daycare to lean into their passions, and over the years I saw how astonishing the results could be when they had the opportunity and resources to do so. When I noticed Elliott, one of my daycare kids, putting his fingers into the screw holes at the back of Michael's brand-new television, I drove straight over to the nearest electronics repair store (remember those?) and told the guy behind the counter that I'd take all his hopeless cases – all the radios and televisions he couldn't fix. 'As long as it's not radioactive or broken in a truly dangerous way, I'll take it,' I said. What looked like a gigantic pile of junk to most people became hours of fun for Elliott, especially when I presented him with the brand-spanking-new, candy-apple-red, six-head screwdriver he'd need to take everything apart.

My foraging habit turned into a family joke. By the time I'd been running the daycare for a couple of years, everyone knew that I couldn't pass by a garage sale or a thrift store without finding some present for the kids. Michael would roll his eyes and pull over before I'd even ask. At the Salvation Army, I found old alarm clocks for Elliott to take apart and fix and an expensive but never-used watercolor set for artistic Claire.

I'd seen the attention the kids in the daycare gave to the activities they loved and the way they flourished when they were given the time and space to pursue those interests, so it was never a surprise years later to field calls with updates from grateful moms. That was how I learned that so many of the daycare kids had flourished as they'd grown older. Claire, for instance, moved on to art classes and a probable internship at a museum in Indianapolis. Elliott began building computers from scratch at age ten and spent high school 'hackintoshing' in his parents' garage, using PC parts to build hybrid machines that ran the Apple operating system. During an internship at a clinic in our community, he designed a piece of specialized medical equipment that is still used by the doctors there today. He did all this before leaving high school.

Over and over again, I noted how doing what they loved brought all of the children's other skills up as well. Even as a very little girl, Lauren's favorite thing to do was to 'play house' while at daycare. She'd happily help me fold laundry or put the smaller babies down for their naps, but she wasn't very interested in what might be considered more academic pursuits, such as reading or counting. Her mother continued to send her to me for after-school babysitting even as Lauren got older, and I began teaching her to make some of the pastries that Stephanie and I had learned to make in my grandmother's kitchen. We spent hours together measuring and stirring, making more cookies and cakes than we could possibly eat.

Lauren's mother had the idea to drop some of our extra treats off at a food pantry one day, but it was Lauren's idea to begin volunteering there. Her mom was understandably worried that the hours of baking and serving in the soup kitchen would get in the way of Lauren's schoolwork, but I felt confident that her other skills would naturally improve if she was encouraged to do what she loved, and her mother was convinced. By age eleven, Lauren was a fixture at the soup kitchen on weekends and had won a number of community service awards – all while maintaining straight A's in school, as well as starring in school plays and in local theater productions.

Mostly, I think the approach was effective because it helped us to build crucial relationships with the children. Long before Little Light, eight-year-old Jenny joined my daycare for the summer. Her mom warned me over the phone that Jenny had trouble paying attention and doing what she was told to do. My daycare was, as usual, the solution of last resort, after two day camps had sent Jenny home.

That first day, Jenny and her mom arrived quite late. Her mom, visibly harried, started right in. 'This morning, I sent her to her room to get her sneakers. Half an hour later, down she comes talking some nuttiness about elves and an enchanted ring – and she's still not wearing any shoes! That's why we're late. She doesn't ever listen.'

That morning, I let Jenny be, but when my daycare assistant

was putting the smaller kids down for their nap, I asked Jenny to join me in the living room. Her mom had been very dismissive about Jenny's storytelling abilities, and I didn't blame her. It sounded as if it had been a frustrating morning. Still, I knew that this child had an incredibly fertile imagination and once she trusted me with her gift, there'd be no trouble getting her to listen or to be on time.

I showed her an illustration in an old children's book I'd bought for a nickel at a yard sale. In a sun-dappled forest, a beautiful woman with long, flowing hair held an infant, both of them cradled in the roots of a massive, moss-covered tree. It was a beautiful picture, but more important, it cried out for an explanation. Who was this enigmatic woman, and what on earth was she doing with her baby in this ancient and magical place?

When I showed Jenny the picture, her whole face changed, and she instinctively reached out to touch the page. I handed her the book to hold and closed my eyes. 'I wonder if you'd be interested in telling me a story about that lady,' I said.

We sat there for a while in silence, and then Jenny began to talk. I could feel her checking my face, trying to gauge whether I was going to sit up and rein her in. But I kept my eyes closed and a slight smile on my face, and as she built up steam and the story began to twist and turn, she forgot to worry about what I thought.

The story Jenny spun for me was filled with magic and monsters, wild adventures and terrible misfortunes. There were double-crossing villains, misunderstandings with dreadful consequences, and, of course, true love. In ten minutes, Jenny created a world so elaborately fantastic and yet so convincing that it was almost a shock to open my eyes and find myself back in my own living room, with CNN on mute and Michael's cold toast still on the sideboard.

I had been recording Jenny's story on my phone, and that night I typed it into the computer. Before I hit Print, I went into the craft closet and found a few sheets of creamy, luxurious heavyweight bond paper I was saving for a special occasion. I wrote Jenny's name on the cover page in calligraphy, punched three holes along one edge, and bound the 'book' with gold satin ribbon left over from a Christmas present. The next day, when she came in, I said, 'I wanted to thank you for the story you told me yesterday. I couldn't get it out of my head, so I made it into this book.'

I didn't have any trouble getting Jenny to put her shoes on after that. Each day that summer, I brought her a picture I'd found – a page I'd torn out of a magazine, a photo I'd taken of something I thought might pique her interest, or an illustration from a book – and she'd tell me a story. Her talent blossomed, and after her mother learned to see Jenny's storytelling as a gift instead of an impediment, there were no more behavioral issues at home. All it took was a little encouragement and the ability to recognize this precious talent for what it was.

Knowing that the parents felt that my humble daycare had had a profound impact on their children's abilities and accomplishments later in life was really exciting for me. I had believed for years that any child will outperform your expectations if you can find a way to feed his or her passion. Every story like Lauren's, Elliott's, Jenny's, and Claire's fueled my belief that this approach could have the same impact on kids with special needs as it had on all the typical kids I'd worked with over the years. Those powerful examples were in my mind as I set out to help the Little Light kids get into mainstream kindergarten.

Every one of the children at Little Light who had been labeled a 'lost cause' had some subject area (often quite a few!) that engaged him or her passionately. I just needed to find the proper lens to magnify it, just as I had done with the daycare kids. That concept was the inspiration for the charity's name. I was going to find the little light inside each of these children, and we were going to let it shine.

Very often these special gifts were the first things the parents said about their child when they brought him or her to Little Light: 'Oh, Billy knows the earned run average of every pitcher in the major leagues,' or 'I hope you don't mind if Violet keeps her wings on; she loves butterflies!' But while the parents might have recognized their child's talent or passion, they didn't necessarily think of it as a way to connect with him or her or to advance the child's progress.

Meaghan loved anything that engaged her senses. She'd bury her face in the laundry I pulled out of the dryer and loved to pet the supersoft blanket I kept draped over the couch. How could I use touch to draw her out? I thought of where baking had taken Lauren, and so I led Meaghan into the kitchen. Despite having an IQ of only 50, she'd measure the ingredients for homemade play dough along with me and then play with the huge mass we made while it was still warm to the touch. Then we'd go together to choose a cookie cutter from the two hundred I keep in a deep drawer in my kitchen. She'd choose a color, and we'd mix it into the dough, then we'd add a scent.

'Purple peanut butter penguins! You've got to tell me the story behind that,' I'd say. And she would.

Meaghan and I made cinnamon-apple-scented play dough, rosemary-scented play dough, and lavender-scented play dough. I added tiny beads to one batch so that it had an interesting, bumpy texture. We cut out the alphabet together and then made some short words, including both our names and those of the other kids in her Little Light session. We explored how two rectangles can become a square when they're squished together, or how two stacked triangles make a star. We used the cookie cutters to make living things such as dogs and people, then contrasted them with inanimate objects such as boats. We worked hard the whole time, but there are worse ways to spend a rainy evening than at a kitchen counter, elbows-deep in warm, lavender-scented play dough.

Every Sunday night, I went out shopping, using what I bought to completely transform the little garage. On Monday night, the Little Light kids (and their parents!) couldn't wait to see what I'd done in their absence. Michael never knew what he was walking into either. Once it was a full-fledged archaeological dig, complete with different-colored sand to represent different geologic eras, leather-bound journals to record our observations and sketch the artifacts, and buckets of plaster of Paris in the yard so that we could make casts of the dinosaur bones (the bones from a chicken dinner, boiled and bleached) that we'd unearthed. The kids who hadn't started out crazy about dinosaurs certainly were after that – and the ones who had started out loving them were in heaven.

The over-the-top 'muchness' of my schemes was a big part of the way I worked, a holdover, perhaps, from my own childhood. Years before Little Light, I'd had a little boy named Francis in the daycare. Francis loved to play with a set of giant cardboard blocks designed to look like bricks. I soon came to see that he was frustrated by the fact that the set contained only fifteen blocks, which was enough to make a short wall but not any kind of a proper structure.

I instantly understood the problem. In my grandfather's shop, whatever odds and ends were left over from a woodworking project got sanded and polished and turned into blocks for us grandchildren. These weren't boring cubes either. We had triangles, arches, half-moons, cylinders, long planks, and chunky rectangles, along with lots of funky, irregular shapes to keep it interesting. Grandpa John also made us architectural accent pieces such as corbels, gables, bay windows, and mullions. By the time the thirteenth grandchild had arrived, the set was quite substantial – all different sizes, ranging from tiny sugar cubes to bricks the size of cinder blocks – and the number of them meant that we could build a structure big enough to go inside. These weren't blocks to stack into a little tower. They were blocks to build with, and we played with them long after most other children had outgrown theirs.

I may not have inherited the woodworking gene from my grandfather, but I still thought I could help Francis. I took some money out of the grocery jar and bought seven more sets of those gigantic cardboard blocks – so many that I couldn't fit them all in my car. When I finally managed to get them home, I immediately knew that I'd done the right thing. Francis finally had enough blocks to work with. He made bridges and pyramids. He built Jenga-style towers straight to the ceiling and experimented with low, cantilevered Frank Lloyd Wright–style longhouses.

Francis was another daycare kid who went on to follow his dreams. Years later, I saw a program on the Discovery Channel about medieval cathedrals and realized that Francis had been 'discovering' the flying buttress system by using those blocks in my daycare. On a whim, I emailed his mom to share that tidbit. She emailed back to let me know that he'd just spent the summer in a highly competitive, prestigious architecture internship program in England.

Just as it had been in the daycare, 'muchness' became a hall-mark of Little Light. It just made sense to me. How could a petting zoo possibly have the same impact on an animal-loving child as a real live llama, borrowed from a nearby farm, standing right next to the table where she usually had her snack?

The only thing I asked of the Little Light parents was that one of them stay and work with their child during each session. Showing a child that you take his or her passion seriously and want to share in it is the most powerful catalyst in the world. It was crucial for us to work with the family as a whole so that the parents could learn to recognize their child's unique talents.

Many children with autism spectrum disorders are deeply focused on specific subject areas, but because the rest of the world isn't interested in, say, license plate numbers or the geologic history of Indiana's cave system, they don't get a lot of credit. Similarly, I believe that autistic kids hear their parents talking about patty-cake or asking for a hug, but they're just not interested in those things. Have you ever been trapped at a party with someone who's talking about something you don't particularly care about – sports, maybe, or politics or classic cars? I believe that's what much of life is like for an autistic person. Certainly, people with autism are in our world. They're just not thinking about the things we want them to think about.

Imagine that you live in a tree house in a beautiful forest, and the only place you feel safe and calm is up in that tree house. But people keep intruding. 'Hey, come out of the trees!' they yell up at you. 'It's crazy to live in a tree. You need to come down here.'

Then one day somebody comes into the forest, and she doesn't yell or try to make you change, but instead climbs into your tree house and shows you that she loves it as much as you do. Wouldn't you have a completely different relationship with her than you do with anyone else? And when she asks you to come down for a few minutes, because she has something amazing to show *you*, wouldn't you be more inclined to check it out?

That was the analogy I used to explain what we were doing at Little Light. We met the children where they were in order to get them where they needed to be.

Because we all spent so much time together, the parents working with their kids at Little Light began to build a close, caring community. The moms (and it was mostly moms) started to get to know one another, to confide in one another, and to joke around. Before long, they were looking forward to the weekly sessions as much as their children were. For many of us, the time together was a balm for the fear and isolation we'd experienced since our children had been diagnosed.

That first winter of Little Light is a blur in my memory. I'd open the daycare every morning at 6:30 a.m., work a full day, and close it at 5:30 p.m. I'd give myself half an hour to vacuum and transform the room. Then I'd hold an hour-long Little Light class for five kids, including Jake. I'd take a half-hour break for a quick family dinner, after which Mike would be in charge of Wesley's bath, and the next five kids would arrive for the second session of Little Light. After everyone left, I'd read Jake and Wesley a bedtime story, then I'd bathe Jake and put him to bed.

We did that every night. There were some nights when I fell into my own bed, too tired even to brush my teeth. But compared to where we'd been the year before, that was a great problem to have.

After we'd been doing Little Light for about a year, my original daycare began to attract more special-needs children through word of mouth. This mixture of special-needs and typical children during the day and autistic children at night and on the weekends made for a kind of laboratory in my garage where I could quickly determine what worked to reach the kids – and what didn't. Sometimes the tricks that worked were surprising, but they almost always boiled down to building a relationship with the kids.

Jerod was eleven when I met him and nonverbal. He'd been that way since he'd turned three. Over the years, his parents had tried all the traditional therapies, and every doctor they'd seen had told his mother, Rachel, that he would never talk. Rachel's lip quivered when she told me this: 'They say there's nothing to work with.'

The very idea that someone would make a comment like that about a child made me feel sick. I spent ten minutes with Jerod and knew they were wrong. Yes, he was nonverbal, and it was immediately apparent that his autism was severe. Eleven was indeed late not to have any language at all, but there was something more inside him.

Even during that first meeting, while his desperate mom told me all the things he couldn't do, he kept peeking out from behind her. I could see a sense of humor there, a curiosity, and that led me to believe that Jerod was capable of much more than he was letting on. When I'd smile at him, he'd peek back out at me again. The whole time this funny game of peekaboo was going on, his mother kept telling me how she'd been told to give up on her child.

Rachel mentioned that Jerod could make some noises, so I asked her which sounds he could make. (In other words, was there a physical delay or a neurological one?) 'Can he make a hard $k$ sound, like the $c$ in "cat"?' I asked her. At that moment, Jerod started to grunt loudly: 'Uh, uh, uh, uh.' And he started to bang on the rug with his open palm. 'Uh, uh, uh, uh.'

His mom was apologetic. 'I'm so sorry!' she said, as she tried to settle him down. 'Shhh, Jerod, please, we're talking.' Then she reached into her bag, still apologizing. 'Let me give these to him and he'll be okay.' She pulled out a box of chicken nuggets. Jerod took one out and started to eat it in a way that will be instantly familiar to anyone who's spent time with kids with autism – spinning it, nibbling around the edges and taking tiny caterpillar bites, still stealing peeks at me every once in a while. I was smiling because I knew that Jerod had been answering my question. He had been showing me what he could and couldn't do.

The whole thing struck me as hysterically funny, and I started to laugh – and then Jerod started to laugh, too. Poor, astonished Rachel was wiping the tears from her eyes, trying to pull herself together, and there Jerod and I were, cracking up. By the time they left, I was 100 percent sure I'd be able to make strides with Jerod.

The next time Jerod and Rachel arrived, they found hundreds (and I mean hundreds) of customized alphabet cards scattered everywhere, all over the rug and the floor. Alarmed at the mess, Rachel asked helpfully, 'Do you need me to help you pick these up?'

'No, thanks,' I said. Making eye contact with Jerod, I continued, 'Actually, these are for Jerod.'

There were two important details about these cards I knew Jerod would appreciate. The first was the sheer number of them. The floor looked like the bottom of a snow globe. The second was the way they looked. Most alphabet cards are brightly colored or feature cartoon characters, because they're designed for very small children who are learning to read. I had deliberately made these cards small and simple – bold black letters on white card stock. It was intended as a gesture of respect. Even if Jerod couldn't read or speak, he wasn't a baby, and he didn't deserve babyish learning materials. As I had hoped, his eyes lit up when he saw them.

That day – our very first session together – I put the letters *A* and *T* on a blue Velcro bulletin board I'd made for him and asked Jerod to find me the letter that went together with them to spell 'cat.' He looked around, found a *C*, and came right back to me. His mom's mouth dropped open as I put it on the board to form the word. 'Perfect,' I said. Then I ripped the *C* off the board and threw it over my shoulder to show him that we weren't going to go through it a million times. We did the same thing with 'hat' and 'sat.' In short, we made more progress in an hour than he'd made in the previous eight years.

At the very end of the hour, I said, 'Listen, Jerod. I want you to do something very important for me. I don't care how it sounds. I want us to read the words that I spell out together.' I gathered a whole bunch of those little alphabet cards and started picking through them until I found all the letters I needed. Then I used them to spell out 'I love you Mom' on the board.

'Okay, Jerod,' I said. 'We're going to do it together. This is a really important job, okay?' I reached up to touch my own mouth, and then I reached out to touch his. 'I don't care how the sound comes out. We're going to go really slowly.' And then – and I can't think about this without crying, remembering the look of shock on Rachel's face – Jerod and I read the words that I'd spelled out on the board.

By watching and really listening to the children at Little Light, we could get a glimpse of what was inside them – and then all we had to do was get out of their way! I knew that the parents who participated were taking a huge leap of faith. I just hoped I'd be able to reward them for their trust. Because underneath the bravado, I was honestly scared that our kindergarten boot camp wasn't going to work. Special-needs children don't instantly 'get better.' Instead, it's more like two steps forward and one step back. If we were going to achieve our goals – and for Jake, that meant kindergarten readiness by age five – we couldn't afford to lose any of our hard-won gains. We needed to aggressively reinforce any progress the kids made, or it would disappear again.

The llama in the living room was more the rule than the exception. Mike truly never knew what he was going to come home to, especially because I made so many of the things we used at Little Light myself. For instance, I noticed that Jake loved holding and playing with beanbags, so I had the idea of using them to make a sensory-based exercise for Little Light.

I went to the remnant bin at the fabric store and scrounged up as many different types of cloth as I could find: soft velvet, ropy corduroy, slippery rayon, painfully scratchy burlap. I cut the fabric into squares and sewed them on three sides to make pockets. Then I filled them with sunflower seeds, which were inexpensive to buy in bulk (and safe if they happened to find their way into someone's mouth), and left them like that in the kitchen, intending to stitch the last side of each pocket after Jake and Wesley were asleep. I must have made fifty of these beanbags, of all different sizes and fabrics, by the time Michael got home from work. And then from the kitchen I heard, 'Kris, what the heck is going on?'

When I went to investigate, I saw that Jake had dumped all the sunflower seeds, from each and every pocket, into a set of cylindrical glass vases. Of course, his not-quite-four-year-old motor skills meant that there were as many sunflower seeds on the floor as there were in the vases. There were seeds *everywhere*. (We'd had a similar incident a few months earlier with Styrofoam packing peanuts. I'd let the kids at the daycare run wild with them, and we were still finding tiny smashed bits of them all over the place. Lesson learned: At least sunflower seeds are biodegradable.) I threw my hands up in the air, Michael opened the sliding door, and we swept the seeds right out into the yard.

I can't emphasize enough how important it was to have Michael's support, even though he had initially been opposed to the whole idea, and even though my work at Little Light meant that he was frequently coming home to chaos of one kind or another. None of what I was doing would have been possible without him. In fact, the daycare and the charity completely dominated our lives. For instance, sometimes I had to do our household grocery shopping in the middle of the night because there was no other time to do it.

One afternoon, while sitting in the car outside the bank filling out some last-minute forms, Michael noticed a little boy standing by himself at the preschool next door. The boy was off to the side, looking through the fence while his classmates played behind him. Mike noticed him because he was flapping his arms, a telltale sign of autism. Paperwork forgotten, Mike sat and watched for half an hour, then got out of the car and went inside to suggest ways to get the boy more involved with his classmates. When he got home, he held me close. 'The whole time I watched, nobody came to him,' he said. 'There may be glitter on our ceiling, Kristine, but none of the kids who come to Little Light ever feels as alone as that little boy did today. I could not have seen that without you.'

Our shared understanding was essential, especially because I charged nothing for Little Light – not for the sessions themselves or for the materials – which put a serious strain on us financially. In those early years, Mike worked at Target, and I earned money through my daycare. We didn't have an extra $150 lying around to spend on Ring Pops, even if they were great tongue and mouth exercise tools for kids with apraxia. But we always found a way to make it work.

Sometimes families would try to pay me, but I couldn't accept money from them. These people were already living the kind of torment you can't understand unless you've lived through it yourself, and I wasn't going to contribute to that. I felt then – and still do now – that my mission in life is to bring hope to these families and to help realize the full potential of children, both special-needs and typical.

The yard behind our little house was tiny. I often said that we were lucky it wasn't bigger because at that moment in our lives, we didn't have much time to spend on ground maintenance.

Even so, when spring came, I was surprised to see the little patch outside the kitchen completely overrun with weeds.

'What in the world is going on with those weeds?' I asked Mike one morning as I was trying to coax Jake to take one more bite of his breakfast.

Michael headed out to investigate, and I heard him start to laugh. 'These aren't weeds, Kris. They're sunflowers!'

*Ah, right*, I thought. *Sunflower seeds – not just beanbag filler.*

The discarded seeds we'd swept out into the yard in the fall had taken root – and with a vengeance. To my delight, over the course of that summer, those sunflowers grew to over six feet tall. By August, to get into our backyard, we had to wade through a field of those gigantic flowers, all slowly turning their faces toward the light.

# A Window onto the Universe

The news that I was pregnant again was a shock. Michael and I had always said we wanted a houseful of kids, but my previous pregnancies had been so difficult and Wesley so sick when he was born, it seemed impossible to believe that this one could have a happy outcome. My own doctor's response, when he heard the news, was not encouraging. He referred me instantly to a high-risk specialist, saying, 'I don't deal well with casualties.'

But between Wesley and Jake and the daycare and Little Light, we simply didn't have much time to dwell on our fears. Whenever I got scared, Michael would say, 'Whatever happens, we'll deal with it – together, and one day at a time, the way we've dealt with everything else.'

In fact, Michael and I were beginning to feel cautiously optimistic about our sons. Mike had been taking Wesley for aquatic therapy, which was similar to the stretching therapy we'd been doing with him, except that it took place in a pool at the hospital. It seemed to be working. Although Wes still wasn't walking at two and a half, he seemed much more flexible and in much less pain. He was also choking less, and even though he was a long way from being able to eat solid foods, he was beginning to tolerate liquids. At least I wasn't staying up all night anymore just to make sure he was still breathing.

By the time Little Light was in its second year, nobody provided us with more reassurance than Jake. Not long after we pulled him out of special ed, it became clear that Jake's particular passion had to do with astronomy and the stars. By age three, he could name every constellation and asterism in the sky. I believe Jake's interest in the planets had its roots in his obsession with light and shadows, which we'd noticed even when he was a tiny baby.

Right after we started Little Light, Jake became preoccupied with a college-level astronomy textbook someone had left unshelved on the floor at the Barnes & Noble near our house. The book was huge for such a little boy, but he dragged the cover open and then sat absorbed in it for more than an hour.

It was certainly not a book for a three-year-old. Taking a peek over his shoulder, I was put off by the minuscule text and arcane content. Most of the pages were taken up by maps of different parts of the solar system. There was no narrative at all – no retelling of the Greek myths that gave the constellations their names, not even any scientific explanations – just maps. My eyes glazed over as I flipped through it. What did Jake want with this book?

But when it came time to leave, there was simply no separating boy and book. I would put it back where it belonged and take Jake's hand to leave, and he'd break away from me and make a beeline right back to it. After a few go-rounds, I could see we weren't going anywhere unless that book came with us. I heaved the gigantic thing into my arms, took his hand, and got into line. At least it was heavily discounted.

To my complete surprise, that cumbersome book became Jake's constant companion. Its heft meant that his only way of transporting it around the house was to open the cover and drag it with both hands. After a while, it got so beat-up that Michael had to reinforce the spine with duct tape. Every time I looked through it, I couldn't believe that this highly technical manual, clearly intended for advanced astronomy students, could possibly be of interest to my little boy.

But it was, and it turned out to be an in. I always felt a little bit like a detective at Little Light. Whatever the children loved would set us to following the breadcrumb trail, finding out bit by bit who they really were. I knew Jake's fascination with this book, as impenetrable as it might have been, was an important clue. So when I saw in the paper that the Holcomb Observatory, a planetarium near our house on the campus of Butler University, would be doing a special program on Mars, I asked Jake if he'd like to go see Mars through a telescope. You would have thought I'd asked him if he wanted ice cream for breakfast, lunch, and dinner. He pestered me so mercilessly about it that I thought the day would never come.

In our excitement, we arrived a little too early. The grounds were beautifully maintained, and we found an enormous grassy hill to roll down right by the planetarium's parking lot. At the bottom, by a little pond, we found hundreds of horse chestnuts lying in the grass under the trees. While the sun set, we walked slowly around the pond, and Jake picked up as many of those chestnuts as he could carry, packing them into his pockets and filling the fuzzy dog-shaped backpack he took everywhere. The chestnuts were pleasantly round and smooth, and I could see that Jake liked the way they felt in his hands. By the time the doors to the planetarium opened, his pants pockets were as stuffed as a squirrel's cheeks.

The lobby was spectacular, but almost instantly I wished we were back outside. I'd thought we'd be able to zip in to get a quick look through the telescope without disturbing anyone, but I discovered that to look through the telescope, we'd have to take a tour of the planetarium. Worse still, as I learned after we'd already waited in line and bought tickets, the tour included an hour-long, college-level seminar given by a professor at Butler. As the lobby began to fill up with people, the knot in my stomach intensified. A college-level presentation in a silent, crowded auditorium was not at all what I'd had in mind, and it was the last place on earth anyone in her right mind would voluntarily take an autistic three-year-old.

But I'd promised, and Jake was sure jazzed to be there. I told him I'd made a mistake. I explained about the tour and the lecture and asked him if he would rather go get a pizza instead. But he was adamant; he wanted to stay. While we were waiting for the show to start, he took me by the hand and led me up the curving central stairs, along which were hung enormous photographs of deep space. For half an hour, he dragged me up and down those stairs, chattering at me while I scrambled after him, doing my best to contain him – and the occasional chestnut that spilled out of his pockets, bouncing every which way on the majestic marble staircase.

Distracted as I was chasing after those chestnuts, it sounded to me as if Jake was giving a convincing lecture on each photo. He was rattling off terms and language unfamiliar to me, and while I couldn't tell if he was making the stuff up or imitating someone, it sounded pretty impressive.

Eventually, the doors to the lecture hall opened, and the crowd filed in. As soon we got inside, I thought, *Oh, boy, this whole thing is about to go bad*. The room was small and hushed; a PowerPoint presentation was ready to go. The first slide had to do with nineteenth-century telescope resolution. The only seats left were right up front.

I started digging through my bag, desperate to find something – animal crackers? a crayon? some gum? – that might stave off a complete meltdown. By the time the lecturer stepped up to the podium, I was in a near panic, and it only got worse. As the slides started clicking by, Jake began reading, quite loudly, some of the words popping up on the screen: 'Light year!' 'Diurnal!' 'Mariner!'

I shushed him, sure the people around us were going to give

me the stink eye, hissing at me to get my kid out of this place we clearly had no business inhabiting. Sure enough, the people around us *were* starting to notice, and to whisper, but it soon became clear that they weren't so much annoyed as they were amused and a bit incredulous.

'Is that little kid reading?' I heard someone say. 'Did he just say "perihelial"?'

Then the lecturer introduced a history of scientific observations about the possibility of water on Mars, starting with the nineteenth-century Italian astronomer Giovanni Schiaparelli, who believed he saw canals on the planet's surface. Hearing this, Jake started to laugh. In my anxiety, I thought he was going to lose it, but when I looked at him, I could see he was genuinely cracking up, like the idea of canals on Mars was the greatest knee-slapper he'd ever heard. (It was the same delighted giggle I heard every time Dora the Explorer stopped the thieving fox Swiper.) Again, I quieted him down. But I could see the ripple spread through the crowd as people started craning their necks to see what was going on.

Then the lecturer asked a question of the audience: 'Our moon is round. Why do you think the moons around Mars are elliptical, shaped like potatoes?'

Nobody in the crowd answered, probably because no one had the slightest idea. I certainly didn't. Then Jake's hand shot up. 'Excuse me, but could you please tell me the size of these moons?' This was more conversation than I'd seen from Jake in his entire life, but then again, I'd never tried to talk to him about Mars's moons. The lecturer, visibly surprised, answered him. To the astonishment of everyone, including me, Jake responded, 'Then the moons around Mars are small, so they have a small mass. The gravitational effects of the moons are not large enough to pull them into complete spheres.'

He was right.

The room went silent, all eyes on my son. Then everyone went nuts, and for a few minutes the lecture came to a halt.

The professor eventually regained control of the room, but my mind was somewhere else. I was completely freaked out. My three-year-old had answered a question that had been too difficult for anyone else in the room, including the Butler students and all of the adults present. I felt too dizzy to move.

At the end of the lecture, people crowded around us. 'Get his autograph. You'll want that someday!' someone said. Another person actually pushed forward a piece of paper for Jake to sign, which I pushed right back. Usually overwhelmed by crowds, Jake took everything happening around him in his stride, staring contentedly at the last PowerPoint slide, a close-up satellite shot of an enormous mountain on the surface of Mars.

I wanted nothing more than to get out of there. But when it came time for everyone to make their way upstairs to look through the telescope, an astonishing thing happened. The crowd fell back to let Jake go first. The entire auditorium had wordlessly united behind the same goal: Let's get this kid upstairs to see Mars! I know it sounds crazy, but there was a reverence in the air. Jake and I went up the stairs, buoyed by the energy and hopefulness and goodwill of the group. I felt almost as if they were carrying us.

The observatory would soon become a home away from home for Jake and me. Although I've been there many times since that first night, it never loses its magic for me. It feels exactly like what it is, a window onto the universe. The roof of the domed space retracts with the push of a button. Underneath that slice of sky is a tall flight of metal stairs on wheels, with a landing at the top. To look up at the sky, you actually look down through an instrument similar to a microscope, which is connected to an enormous white metal barrel pointing out at the stars.

Jake may have been the first to go up the ladder, but he was too short to see into the eyepiece. Again, the strangers in the crowd graciously extended their hands to help. Someone fetched a stepladder. A couple of people steadied him and held the little ladder as he climbed. One even held his hand as he looked down into the scope. He looked for a long time, but I sensed no impatience or irritation from anyone else in line. I felt numb. It was as if everyone in that room was saying, 'Take your time. This place belongs to you.'

As we drove home that night, Jake couldn't stop chattering about space. I could finally understand what he was saying, but all it did was freak me out even more. How did this child know the comparative densities and relative speeds of the planets?

After I tucked Jake in for the night, I called my friend Alison. Melanie Laws had introduced us because Alison's son Jack was also autistic and the same age as Jake, and we had become dear friends. I told her everything that had happened during our evening at the planetarium. Reliving it raised goose bumps on my arms.

'What am I supposed to do with this child?' I asked her. 'Should I be doing something more, something different? Seriously, should I take him to NASA or something?'

I have thought about that moment again and again in the years since. Like the decision to pull him out of preschool, it was a turning point. We could have gone down a very different road, one I clearly see now would have been wrong for us. I am so grateful to Alison for her good sense. 'You do exactly what you're doing right now,' she told me. 'You play with him, and you let him be a little boy.'

As I fell asleep, I knew that Alison was right. The things that made Jake special weren't going anywhere. He would make his mark eventually – that much was becoming clear – but right now he needed to be comfortable and happy at home with us.

He needed to go to school, to have friends, and to share in family rituals such as going out for pancakes and making s'mores in the backyard. We were going to eat gummy bears and watch VeggieTales. For now, Jake would be a regular kid.

After so much agonizing time searching for him, I could finally catch my breath. I'd found my son.

Even so, that evening at the planetarium, something shifted for me. Michael and I understood that Jake was more than just a smart kid, but he had stunned me, the lecturer, and everyone else in the auditorium with a level of knowledge about the solar system that was frankly bizarre. Suddenly, I was able to see all the cute and remarkable and sometimes odd things Jake could do for what they were: *extraordinary*.

I'd never experienced anything like the awe and veneration I'd felt from the crowd in that lecture hall. In some ways, that had shocked me more than Jake's answer, or anything he'd told me about the radius of Betelgeuse on the way home. Those people in the planetarium had been inspired, transported to a better place, and they'd been delivered there by Jake. That night, I had the distinct feeling – which has never been very far away since – that Jake was going to use his amazing brain to make a significant contribution to the world.

In the meantime, though, I had to get him into kindergarten.

# A Cup of Chicken Soup

For everything Jake knew about the moons around Saturn, the Little Light kindergarten prep classes weren't easy for him. In particular, it was always hard to get him to stay with the group. During any kind of social-relatedness exercise, he'd try to go off by himself. Simply getting him to sit next to another child for ten minutes took a long time – probably a year.

But I had gone too far to go back, so I kept moving forward. Jake and I did kindergarten preparedness every single night, with steady, patient work (and a few tricks). For instance, I bought a bunch of fuzzy toilet seat covers in all different colors and used those as visual markers for the children so that they knew where to sit during circle time. Those social-relatedness exercises became a little easier for Jake, as they did for all the Little Light kids. Activities such as sitting next to another child during circle time became second nature to him because of the repetition. It also felt different than the relentless, monotonous drills of traditional therapy, because he was getting lots of time to pursue everything he loved to do.

One night I looked up to see Michael standing at the door of the garage with Wes in his arms. He said, 'I thought we should stick with the experts, that they knew what was best. But I was wrong, Kris. You've done it.' There was nothing but pride in his voice. I turned back to the room, and for the first time I could see what we'd achieved. Michael voiced what I was thinking: 'It looks just like a kindergarten.'

Jake and I became regulars at the Holcomb Observatory. By the end of the summer, I knew most of the people who worked there by name. The more astronomy Jake was exposed to, the less withdrawn he became. It gave us common ground. Being able to talk to someone else about his love for astronomy helped him to make the connection between talking and actually communicating, and not just with me but with other people, too.

I was delighted and touched to see, for instance, that instead of ignoring my pregnancy as he had when I was pregnant with Wes, Jake actually expressed some curiosity about the baby on the way. I took him to one of my ultrasound appointments. It was a big one – we were going to find out the baby's sex. Jake was, as I had predicted, fascinated by the equipment.

'It's another little boy!' the technician told me. My heart rate shot through the roof. For weeks, everyone had been teasing me about having a third boy. There had been jokes about starting my own baseball team and building a house made up exclusively of padded and washable surfaces. Truthfully, I'd been hoping for a girl, but not because I wanted someone to get a manicure with. Statistically, another boy was much more likely to be autistic.

Ironically, it was Jake who took my mind off the worry. 'Why does she keep calling my sister a boy?' he kept saying, glaring at the technician. Apparently, he'd had his heart set on a girl, too.

Our time at the observatory helped in other, unexpected ways. Sitting on the grass with a picnic waiting for the planetarium to open, I could have all those good 'mom' feelings with Jake that I thought autism had cheated me out of. I could look through an astronomy book with him and stroke the soft down on his cheek while I watched his chubby little hands turn the pages. I could smell his beautiful toddler smell and feel his weight against my leg. I had missed him so much, and now I had him back. It might not have looked like much to an outsider, but in that half hour sitting on the grass, we were both feeding some elemental and important part of ourselves.

Some of the Little Light moms had been so worn down, they weren't even looking at their kids anymore. First they'd lost them to autism, then to the strain of having an autistic child. I could understand that. During that first summer off with Jake, I'd learned this lesson myself. It wasn't only Jake who needed typical childhood experiences; I needed them, too!

Jake began to talk more, and we started to get an idea of what had been going on inside his head all the time he'd been lost to us. He could finally tell us what he'd been doing and thinking about. 'I'm going to need a cup of chicken soup to handle that one,' I'd say (and still do) when he knocked us flat with one of his pearls.

For instance, one of Jake's favorite games had always been to spin people. He would walk around the daycare, choose someone, lead him or her to a very specific spot, and then set the person in motion, spinning him or her like a top. If you were spinning, you couldn't move out of your spot, and you had to maintain your speed. Then he'd lead someone else to a different spot and set that person in motion, too. The kids in the daycare thought this was a blast, so sometimes everyone in the room would be standing and spinning at different speeds.

We had always chalked this up to his autism – a meaningless and repetitive behavior that gave him pleasure – until one afternoon when he was about four and had begun communicating with us a little more. Slightly under the weather, I kept slowing down as I was spinning. Jake returned over and over to correct me, until I finally put my foot down: 'I'll spin, honey, but I have to go slow.'

'You can't spin slow, Mommy,' he said, exasperated. 'The ones closer to the sun go faster.'

We were planets. Only after I searched Google did I fully understand that Jake had been using the children at the daycare to model the planets, which rotate at different speeds depending on where they are in relation to the sun. Jake hadn't picked that up through osmosis, but by intuition. Somehow, while he'd been locked deep inside his autism, he'd figured out Kepler's laws of planetary motion.

The more we learned about Jake, the more I realized how fortunate it was that we hadn't taken away everything he'd been using for self-stimulation in those early days. The cereal he'd dump out onto the kitchen floor? He was figuring out the volume of the boxes. The webs of colored yarn that made it impossible for me to get into the kitchen? Those were equations, using a parallel math system that he'd invented.

After years of what had felt like relentless gray rain, we'd finally gotten a break. There had been glimmers of light all along, glimmers that sometimes only I could see. Now we were learning that in the silence, Jake had been steadily working his way through some of the great breakthrough moments in science. Can you see what I mean about needing to sit down with a little chicken soup to calmly digest it all?

Most amazing to me was the evidence of Jake's creativity. I had heard about savants – human calculating machines, people with photographic memories who could remember every fact they'd ever seen or heard. But Jake wasn't parroting information he'd read somewhere. He actually understood how to analyze the facts he'd been learning; he knew what they meant. Even before he could read, when we thought he'd just been staring at the shadows on the wall, Jake had been making real scientific discoveries. It was incredible to realize that all this potential had been there the whole time. My beloved boy hadn't been missing after all. He'd just been working. And now that we were beginning to understand what he was capable of, it was even more terrifying to think about how much might have been lost.

I'm sure it is no coincidence that some of Jake's work in physics today concerns light waves and how these travel. He believes that his research will lead to a much more efficient electronic transmission of light. That's why I always ask the parents I work with about their children's earliest and most persistent interests. In the case of parents whose children are locked in, I ask what kinds of activities their kids were interested in before the onset of the autism. A good friend of ours is a brilliant engineer. It's no wonder that his mother says he started taking household appliances apart as soon as his fingers were big enough to hold a screwdriver. Our strengths and skill sets are there, right from the beginning, but they need time and encouragement to flourish.

This is an important point. Because of his autism – because we couldn't reach him – Jake had a lot of time and space to do what he was naturally drawn to do. Simply because he was so locked in and unreachable, he was afforded much more time in his day than most kids to focus on the things he cared about: light and shadows, angles and volume, and the way objects move in space. Nobody was telling Jake *how* to learn, because nobody thought he could. In that way, autism had given Jake a bizarre gift.

We think of these children as missing; we think they need to be cured. But I believe that curing autism would be the same as 'curing' science and art. I always told the parents at Little Light that if they could get into their children's worlds, instead of expecting their kids to come out to them, they'd find some beautiful things. It's up to us to build a bridge to our children, so that they can show us what they see and we can begin to draw them back into our world. In Jake's case, astronomy and the stars gave me the connection with him I had so desperately craved. Before the observatory, the planets had always seemed like boring balls to me. But when Jake started giving me glimpses of this world through his eyes, I could see how spectacular it is. Soon after he turned four, he called me over one day to show me some pictures of a nebula on the computer. He had become interested in examining light and colors chemically, and the pictures he showed me knocked my socks off. The nebulae were like fireworks, or spectacular stained glass windows.

Seeing my tiny son point out the chemical signatures of the gases was a revelation for me. I realized that this was art to him, an experience as profoundly moving and emotionally intense as an architecture buff seeing the cathedral at Chartres for the first time, or a lover of Impressionist art left alone in a room lined with Monet's water lilies.

By their second year at Little Light, all the kids were starting to thrive. 'How did you do it?' people would ask me, sure that there was a magic bullet. The gains were tremendous, given how little it sometimes seemed we'd been doing. Sure, we'd done some repetitive therapies with the kids, but not nearly as much as was recommended. Nobody would have believed me if I'd told them what we'd really spent our time on! 'Well, with one of these kids, I spent six hours at the museum looking at a single painting. I bought another one a used drafting table on Craigslist and dropped it off at his mom's house. I taught one of them to read by baking hundreds of cookies with her and then decorating them with the letters of the alphabet in icing. And then there was the llama . . .'

The results we were getting spoke for themselves, and as more and more people heard about what we were doing at Little Light, more and more began to come. They came from all across Indiana, even from Illinois. They brought grandparents and therapists to see their kids do what they'd once thought was impossible.

The fact that people would make this pilgrimage, some driving three hours for an hour-long class on a weeknight, seemed a little crazy to me. I don't know what those parents were expecting at the end of that long drive, but I'm pretty sure it wasn't a daycare in a suburban garage at the end of a cul-de-sac.

They had all been to gleaming, high-tech medical facilities; they'd all paid for cutting-edge therapies; they'd all seen the brightest doctors. Yet here they were, sitting on the floor of my little garage.

As my pregnancy progressed, I was really uncomfortable. As with all of my pregnancies, I had grown very big, and getting up and down off the floor with the kids was increasingly hard. Then one afternoon in July, while I was tidying up some blocks from the daycare, I fell to my knees in excruciating, intolerable pain. Something was seriously wrong.

I was rushed to the emergency room and immediately admitted. I thought the baby was dying. I thought *I* was dying. I was terrified of hurting the baby, so I was on the minimum dose of painkillers. After days of tests and unrelenting pain, my doctor told Michael and me that they'd hit a dead end. To find out what was wrong with me, they'd have to operate. At eight and a half months pregnant, I went in for major exploratory surgery.

I had been in full-on organ failure. The surgeons removed my gallbladder, which had completely failed and turned out to be horrendously infected.

Two and a half weeks later, our third son, Ethan Michael, was born. I do not recommend delivering a baby less than three weeks after abdominal surgery. But on the other side was our beautiful baby boy.

After we'd found out that we were expecting another boy, Michael and I had talked about what it would be like. 'This kid is going to have a hard time, Kris,' Michael mused. 'No matter what he does, we'll have seen it already – twice – with his brothers. He needs to have something cool of his own.' As a joke, he started calling my bump 'Joey Danger,' as in 'My middle name is Danger.'

The closer we got to the birth, however, the less of a joke it became. I was still rolling my eyes, but Mike finally talked me into naming this new baby 'Joseph Danger Barnett.' After all, I thought, it was only a middle name. If he hated it when he got old enough to care, he could drop it.

But when the doctors put Ethan into my arms, both of us knew instantly that Joey Danger wasn't the right name for him. It would absolutely have been the right name for Wes, but we could tell at a glance that there wasn't anything dangerous about this new little boy. So within the first few days, he acquired a much more appropriate nickname, one that stuck for the first couple of years: 'Peaceful.'

Every parent thinks that his or her newborn is perfect, but Ethan actually was. He didn't cry. He didn't fuss. He ate well. He slept through the night. He smiled if you made a funny face, and he smiled if you didn't. He was so quiet and happy that I honestly thought something was wrong with him until our pediatrician convinced me that I was just torturing myself. Unlike both of his brothers, Ethan was 100 percent healthy, right from the get-go.

In truth, we were constantly on the lookout for a problem; we knew the statistics. More than once, I caught Wesley's therapists surreptitiously checking Ethan's muscle tone or his ability to maintain eye contact, in the guise of cuddling or playing peekaboo with him. But they never found anything wrong. Ethan was a perfectly happy, perfectly healthy, sweet, calm baby boy.

And he cuddled! After the first year, Jake had been too autistic for cuddling, and Wesley had been in too much pain and then too active. But 'Peaceful Ethan' would snuggle in for the long haul. The denim sling I carried him in was always covered with finger paint and cookie dough from our activities in the daycare, but I didn't mind. Wherever I went, Ethan went, too.

# Kindergarten Pro

Michael likes to say that I snuck Jake into kindergarten. In a sense, he's right.

By the time the back-to-school sales started in August 2003, the kids in my Little Light groups looked like kindergarten professionals. Even the lowest-functioning children were vastly outstripping whatever forecasts they'd been given when we started. I felt certain we were ready. The bigger question was, were the schools ready for us?

Every year before school starts, the new kindergartners attend a Welcome to School event, where they meet their teachers and see their classrooms for the first time. That was a big night for us. It was my chance to draw parallels for Jake between all the Little Light sensory centers we'd been working with and the classroom he'd be in for the next year. 'That's where you'll be sitting during circle time,' I whispered to Jake, 'and that box is your cubby.'

He nodded to indicate that he knew. But I was glad to meet his teacher, Mrs Hoard. I liked her immediately for her gentle intelligence and warm personality, and I felt grateful for her many years of experience. I could tell that she'd seen a lot of children with different issues and learning styles over the years.

I told Mrs Hoard about Jake's diagnosis and reassured her that I was confident he'd get along fine. We'd been 'doing kindergarten' every single night at Little Light for two years. In response, Mrs Hoard put her arm around my shoulders and said, 'Let's give him a little time and see how it goes.' I was grateful to know that she wasn't going to go looking for an excuse to drop the hammer on him. But I also knew that she'd have twenty-five other kids in her class, each deserving of equal attention, and nobody's patience is limitless. To stay in mainstream school, Jake would need to succeed.

To Mrs Hoard, Jake was a regular kindergartner. But the school administration wasn't so sure. While I was walking in to Welcome to School night, the principal intercepted me and said, 'Mrs Barnett, can I see you in the hallway, please?' She wanted to talk to me about Jake's Individualized Education Program (IEP). After a panel reviews a special-needs child's most recent evaluations, they draw up a document setting down the goals – academic, behavioral, and social – the school has for him or her over the coming year, including details such as how much time the child will spend interacting with nondisabled children and the kinds of supplementary services and aids he or she can expect in the classroom. Jake was still classified as a special-needs student.

Three-year-old Jake had been stimming, nonverbal, and unresponsive. He hadn't seemed like someone who was ever going to speak, read, or make friends. The people evaluating him then didn't think he could learn at all, so the school was expecting him to be the same at age five as he'd been at age three. He wasn't, of course. We'd made tremendous strides since his time in developmental preschool. But the school administrators didn't know that – yet. I didn't want to be confrontational. All I wanted was the chance to show them what Jake was capable of. For that, as Mrs Hoard said, we needed a little time.

So I apologized to the principal and stalled. I told her that I had a brand-new baby and was really busy over the next few weeks. I wouldn't have a spare minute to meet with her until the third week in September. All I wanted was for them to have some time to see that Jake wasn't the same little boy he'd been.

I skimmed through my ultra-packed calendar (daycare, daycare, Wesley's first dentist appointment, more daycare) and set the meeting for three weeks out.

In all fairness, it *was* very hard for me to find someone to take the daycare for the day, and the school didn't mind the delay. The administrators had so many other kids to evaluate that Jake just slid down to the bottom of the list. After all, if it went badly in the mainstream classroom, they knew they could always make updating Jake's IEP a priority.

Jake's first day of kindergarten was a big day for the whole family. That night, Mike made dinner for us, and he thanked me for giving us back our son. Then it was my turn to be grateful. It's one thing to support someone when you agree with him or her, but another thing entirely when you don't. I knew how hard it had been for Mike to take that leap of faith with me. He'd believed with every fiber of his being that I'd been begging for disaster when I'd pulled Jake out of special ed. The counsel of those experts had been more powerful for him than it had been for me, and yet Mike had not only allowed me to take the risk, but he had supported me every step of the way.

Jake didn't give anyone an opportunity to complain. When I called later in September to find out if we needed to meet about his IEP, the principal agreed that we could hold off for a bit. I could hear the bafflement in her voice. 'Is this the same kid?' she asked, only half joking.

Jake was far from the only Little Light success story. That first month, the phone rang off the hook with triumphant Little Light parents all across the state and beyond, calling to share their happiness and relief. Kids who doctors had said would never talk not only talked but also got into mainstream kindergarten. Kids who had come with such serious behavioral issues that their parents were told they'd never be outside a special ed classroom got time in mainstream classrooms. Parents who'd been told that their children would have to be in all-day therapy programs saw those children go to school. Even the lowest-functioning kids needed much less assistance than anyone had dared hope. There were a lot of baffled school administrators across Indiana that year.

I was as proud of the community we'd built as I was of the children. We hadn't waited for the system to come and save our kids. Through resilience and hard work, we'd done it ourselves, and we'd done it together.

Whenever I meet an autistic kid who has made progress, I know that someone fought hard for that kid. No matter what the accomplishment – whether he's toilet trained or in secondary school, whether he's recently started talking again or has gotten his first job, I know that someone behind that child believed in him and that they fought for him.

Every parent has to be a fighter on behalf of his or her kid, not only the parents of kids with autism or developmental disorders. Every parent comes up against difficult choices over the course of the child's life, although those choices might not be as stark as mine were. Whether dealing with physical illness or disability, bullies or mean girls, the politics of a Little League team or competitive college admissions, every parent has to face down challenges on behalf of his or her child. Each of us experiences pain and fear, and each of us needs to muster courage. We *do* fight for our kids; we do it out of love. That willingness is, I believe, what makes us parents.

When confronted by all those experts (and modern parents are dealing with a lot of experts), it's easy to say, 'What do I know? I'm just the person who makes the macaroni and cheese.' But I think my example gave a lot of the parents who came to Little Light, especially the moms, permission to follow what they knew to be true in their hearts.

I came to see my maternal intuition as a compass pointing

true north. Ignoring it could never yield a good result. In those cases where the needle was pointing away from where the experts wanted me to go, I had to trust what I call 'mother gut.' I know that if Jake had stayed in special ed, we would have lost him, and this light that now burns so brightly would have been extinguished forever.

Once he was in kindergarten, it was plain to see that Jake's academic skills were quite advanced compared to the rest of the kids'. Most of his classmates weren't reading, for instance, and certainly not elementary school science textbooks. But we had a deal with Jake that he wouldn't let the cat out of the bag to anyone at school. We'd worked so hard to get him into regular school that we just wanted him to be another kid in the class. That said, his basic reading skills were probably about third- or fourth-grade level by the time he entered kindergarten, and I suspect that if we'd understood exactly what was going on inside his head, we would have seen that he was actually doing high-school-level or college-level math and physics. Our parenting work was far from over, though, because what Michael and I still had to do was teach Jake how to relate to the world.

Mrs Hoard was as good as her word: She did give Jake a chance. But Jake was also a comparatively easy kid, and I think that probably helped quite a lot. Was he distracted? Sure, sometimes. But he was never disruptive, which definitely helped him stay under the radar.

Jake still needed the occasional nudge, though. At Little Light, we'd never done a boys' line separate from the girls' line, which was how they did it at school. So I'm sure Mrs Hoard had to gently remind him which line to stand in, maybe even more than once. But Jake was never a behavioral problem, even at the height of his autism. He was never going to get into a fight with another kid over a tricycle in the schoolyard, for instance, which is the kind of squabble that happens all the time in kindergarten.

He just didn't care. So while little Devin and his buddy Aidan were duking it out over the Big Wheel, Jake would fade to the back of the line. He'd play happily (if silently) next to Corey at the clay table, and if Corey reached out his finger and put a big dimple in Jake's pot, Jake would simply leave Corey with the pot and walk away. Jake didn't throw tantrums or start fights. As long as no one tried to take away his cherished books about rocks and weather systems (and that was a relatively safe bet), he was happy. Mrs Hoard continued on with the occasional quiet reminder, and with a little time and extra help, Jake mastered the routines of his new classroom.

In truth, Jake had difficulty only when something out of the ordinary occurred. The prospect of being called in to discuss his IEP loomed over our heads, so I worked hard to prepare him for any deviation from the regular schedule.

Every morning, I took him out for breakfast, and while he ate his cinnamon roll, I alerted him as best as I could to any anomalies that might be coming up: a field trip or a special movie during lunch, a whole-school assembly in the gym or an early dismissal before a holiday. I thought of those breakfasts together as our pregame meeting. He was the star quarterback, and I was his coach.

'Please don't tell the other children that Santa Claus isn't real,' I'd say a couple of days before a holiday party. 'Even if you can see it's actually Mr Anderson, please don't call him that. Address him as Santa Claus and play along. You might have to sit on his lap and ask for a present while someone takes a picture. Okay?' With preparation, he could tolerate it.

Ironically, nothing alienated Jake more than the goofy activities the school created to appeal to kids his age. He didn't get that wacky, upside-down humor; it confused him. He'd never understood Halloween, for instance, which was one of my favorite holidays, because dressing up didn't make sense to him.

Why would you pretend to be something other than what you were? Why would you ask a neighbor for candy when there was a big plastic pumpkin full of it on your own porch?

I'll never forget the look on his face when I broke the news about another time-honored kindergarten tradition. 'Guess what you're going to be wearing to school tomorrow, Jakey? Your pajamas!' He looked at me, genuinely worried that I'd gone stark raving mad.

'I don't wear pajamas during the daytime, Mommy. I wear them at night.'

I persisted, and he did, too. 'I don't wear my pajamas to *school*,' he kept explaining to me, patient to the end. 'I wear my pajamas to *bed*.'

On one level, it was funny, but I also felt there was an important lesson he needed to learn. I know a lot of parents would have gone to the office to get a note so their autistic kid could be excused from participation. But as my grandfather used to say, you can't get a pass every time life stretches you. Instead, we had to give Jake the tools he needed to overcome his discomfort, so that he could function in a world that sometimes has a Pajama Day.

It's not clear that what we did would work with all autistic children, but I had some insight into Jake and how he'd reacted in the past to the unexpected. A few years before, he'd come with me to the Department of Motor Vehicles so that I could get my license renewed. The storefront was being repaired, so we went around to the back, but Jake just wouldn't – or couldn't – go in through the 'out' door. The DMV was a place with clearly delineated rules. There were arrows painted on the floor showing you where to stand if you needed your picture taken for a learner's permit. There were stanchions marking which line to wait in if you needed a nondriver photo ID. This was a place Jake could relate to, and yet there I was, trying to make him walk in through a door that was clearly marked 'Exit,' and he wasn't having it.

I thought I was going to have to come back after they'd fixed the front door, but I needed my license. I took a deep breath, picked him up, and took the plunge: In through the 'out' door we went. He recovered, eventually, but the incident gave me some insight into his mind. Going through the wrong door was so distressing for him, it almost seemed to be causing him pain.

The real payoff came later that day, when I watched him playing with Wesley on our porch. Jake had a two-level car wash toy that you could drive Matchbox cars into. Both boys loved to play with it, but it was the one toy they couldn't share. As soon as they began playing with it together, there was trouble. After the incident at the DMV, I realized why.

Jake would drive a car through the door marked 'In,' wash the car, and then push the clean car through the ramp marked 'Out' before parking it neatly outside. Wesley was somewhat less interested in operating a well-run car wash. He'd swoop the cars through the air and land them on the roof, drive them in backward at the Matchbox equivalent of seventy miles an hour, or run them off the ramp, staging a ten-car collision at the bottom.

The fact that Wesley didn't take the rules seriously was driving Jake nuts. So I sat him down and explained it to him: 'Jake, you're a very serious boy, and you always do the car wash right, by the rules. But Wesley is a silly boy. When he plays with the car wash, he likes to play it silly, and when it's his turn, that's okay. When it's your turn, you can play it serious. There's more than one way to play with this car wash.'

After that, he got it. The idea that people play differently and that it's okay if someone wants to act silly during his or her turn was surprisingly helpful when trying to explain an event such as Pajama Day. Yes, it was silly, but he needed to learn to tolerate it, as he needed to tolerate the way Wesley played with the car wash.

I always made sure that Jake got his turn. This was hugely important. If I knew that Jake was going to face a challenge that day at school, I'd go out of my way to reassure him at breakfast that he'd be able to do whatever he wanted to later. If he had to sit through a loud movie at lunchtime, for instance, I'd tell him that when he got home, we would count all the coins in his room. If he went to a class with a substitute teacher, when he got home he could do the biggest, baddest five-thousand-piece jigsaw puzzle in the house, or we'd go for a walk and look at license plates for as long as he wanted to.

These promises weren't 'Do this, and I'll give you candy' bribes. That wouldn't have worked. The message was, 'Get through this – and it might not be easy – and later, I promise, you can be your real, authentic self.'

Jake had as much time to do the things that were important to him as he had to do the things that were important to other people, to me, or to the school. I wasn't telling him that he couldn't do his puzzles. He could, and for as long as he wanted, but only after he'd worn his pajamas to school. He did have to get through the day, but he didn't have to change who he was to do it.

# Three Letters

They say that God never gives you more than you can handle, and we never marveled at how easy and sweet baby Ethan was during his first year without thinking about that.

My own health was not great. I never took more than three days off after any of the boys were born because there were so many special-needs children in the daycare. The fact that I didn't rest meant that my healing from the abdominal surgery I'd had at the end of my pregnancy was slow and very painful. In addition, the autumn after Ethan was born and Jake started kindergarten, I started to experience terrible, blinding flashes of pain along the side of my face. These episodes were totally incapacitating. It felt like thousands of hot needles were being inserted into the side of my eye socket and all the way down my face. Most disturbing was that there didn't seem to be a cause. Even a cool gust of wind could trigger an attack.

I was also incredibly exhausted all the time. That, at least, made sense. Everybody is tired during the first six months with a new baby. But no matter how early I went to bed (most nights, minutes after the boys) and no matter how many vitamins I took, I couldn't seem to catch up on my rest.

I woke up on Christmas morning so tired that I could barely drag myself out of bed. Raising our tiny digital camera to take pictures of the boys opening their presents required an effort that felt almost superhuman.

Midmorning, I went into the kitchen to make scrambled eggs for breakfast. I pulled the carton of eggs out of the fridge, put it on the counter, and thought, *I am going to have to sit down to crack these eggs.* I scooted a chair over and sat down on it, and two thoughts occurred to me.

The first was, *Wow. I have to sit down to make eggs?*

An average day for me meant chasing after twelve toddlers for a minimum of thirteen hours, usually while carrying a baby in a sling across my chest and another on my hip. When you run a daycare, you don't need a gym membership; you usually don't get a break until 7:30 at night, after the kids have gone home. So the fact that I couldn't muster the energy to scramble some eggs was odd, to say the least.

The second thought was, *Huh. That's interesting. I can't move my left arm.*

It wasn't scary or painful, simply a fact. I could no longer move my arm – or anything else on the left side of my body.

I sat there for a while until Mike came in, carried me to the car, and drove me to the hospital. At age thirty, I'd had a stroke.

Waiting in the hospital that day, I found myself desperate to get back home. If I wasn't there, who would do what needed to be done? I was coaching Jake through his days at kindergarten, and those play-by-plays of the day to come weren't tasks I could delegate to someone else. I had Wesley, who could actually choke and die if someone gave him liquids that hadn't been thickened, and who still couldn't really move by himself – not to mention having to coordinate the schedules of all his therapists. And I had my brand-new baby, Ethan, who needed his mother.

That night, I felt truly afraid. What would happen to the kids – all of them – if I wasn't there? If an inexperienced caregiver were to give Nancy, one of the children I had in the daycare at the time, the wrong meds (or, worse, miss a dose altogether), she could very well have a fatal seizure. Autistic Ben was a runner, which meant that as soon as you took your eyes off him, he'd make a break for the door. If you didn't watch him every minute, he'd be gone in a flash. (Many autistic children die this way.)

Then I had another, terrifying thought: What if I had another stroke? What if I didn't wake up at all? What would happen to the boys and to Michael?

Instead of sleeping that night, I sat up and composed letters to my sons. They started out as lists of all the wonderful, ordinary moments I wanted them to remember: letting our fingers trail through the water behind the boat we were paddling on the lake, getting sticky from the s'mores we'd made in the backyard, curling up to watch a movie under a fuzzy blanket with a gigantic bowl of popcorn.

But by the time I was done, the letters had morphed into a catalog of everything I loved most about them. I asked them to use their gifts to help one another. I asked careful, thoughtful Jake to check in on his impulsive brother: 'Let Wes have his Maserati. But make sure he has a 401(k), too?' I asked loving Wes to make sure that Jake had fun and to be there for his brother on the inevitable day when Jake's meticulous calculations didn't add up perfectly. To Ethan I simply wrote, 'Don't ever be afraid to be who you are. Find out what you love to do and do it.'

I finally got into bed at about four o'clock that morning, filled with a deep and abiding sense of peace. If I couldn't be around to help my sons hold on to who they were, at least the letters I'd written would be there for them.

Obviously, I did wake up the next morning, and our new life began.

Even after I was finally allowed to go home, my condition required a tremendous adjustment on everyone's part. I was basically paralyzed on my left side. My mouth drooped on that side, I couldn't grasp things with my left hand, and my left leg dragged. Often Michael would have to physically support me so that I could walk.

A common household word such as 'couch' or 'car' would be right on the tip of my tongue, but I was unable to produce it. Sometimes I'd substitute another, completely inappropriate word for the one I meant: 'The groceries are still in the trunk of the elevator.' Or, 'Did you get your lunch from the closet, Jake?' (Jake, being Jake, would dutifully go and check the closet for his sandwich.)

With all the doctors' appointments I had to go to, Mike became my arms and legs. He also had to take time off from work to help with the daycare, but he'd had devastating news there, too. His longtime boss and mentor, Tom, had been diagnosed with advanced lung cancer. (He would live only a couple more months.) Tom had been one of the first people in Mike's professional life to see and to nurture his potential. He was a father figure to Mike and his champion. Losing Tom would be a devastating emotional blow for him.

It was also, unfortunately, one with practical consequences. Tom was replaced by a much younger man, someone less sympathetic to the people Tom had encouraged. So at a time when Mike needed a lot of flexibility and generosity from his workplace, he was instead worried about losing his job. On top of helping with the daycare, taking me to doctors' appointments, and keeping up with work, Mike was still going twice a week to the children's hospital to continue Wesley's aquatic therapy. And he was running the household, doing all the jobs I'd always done, such as shopping for groceries, making lunches, and doing the laundry. I could give instructions from the couch – this yogurt, not that one – but I couldn't drive or shop or do anything that might actually have been helpful to him. He was on his own.

In my eyes, during that time Michael was a superhero. I'd had years to adjust to the daycare, to the addition of special-needs kids to the daycare, to the rigorous demands of therapy schedules.

I'd had a lifetime of experience in running a household. Michael hadn't had any of that. And yet I couldn't believe how strong he was, and how patient. I marveled at his energy. Being physically impaired made me even more grateful – both *to* Michael and *for* him – every day.

But it was too much. Neither of us knew it at the time, but Michael was headed for a personal crisis. Ultimately, however, I don't think it was the grueling schedule, as demanding as it was, that got to him. It was something more.

Mike certainly understood the enormity of Jake's autism and how sick Wesley really was, but he'd always been able to get away from the day-to-day grind by getting in the car and going to work. There was something about actually having to get through the day – *my* day – that brought the reality of the life we'd been living for the past five years home to him with terrible force. He'd never stopped to fully comprehend what we were up against, the overwhelming odds. Every day was a skirmish in a war that didn't seem remotely winnable. What could possibly happen to turn it around?

When I was having Jake, Michael made a solemn vow that he would take care of me. I believe he took that vow even more seriously than the vows we'd made to each other when we were married. At my bedside that day, he told me that he would do everything in his power to keep me happy and comfortable, no matter what. And he had. He had supported me through Jake's autism and therapy, when the doctors told us Wesley might very well die, and through the exhausting uncertainty of Little Light. But now I was crumbling before his eyes, and in his mind that meant he had broken his promise. Somehow, he had let me down, and he felt like a failure.

The tension within him was building, but I didn't realize it until one wintry night, after all the boys were in bed. We were watching television together on the couch; I might even have been napping a little. All of a sudden, Mike said, his voice breaking, 'I can't fix this.' Then he got up, grabbed his truck keys, and left.

I had no idea what was happening. We'd had no argument. In fact, I felt as though we'd never been closer. Plus, I was starting to feel better physically. By that point, I could walk unaided and was beginning once more to participate in daily activities.

I was truly afraid. The streets were icy and wet, and Mike had seemed so shaky and unlike himself when he left, I was worried that he wasn't in any condition to drive. Panicked, I called my brother, Ben, to go looking for him. It wasn't until I hung up the phone that the gravity of the situation hit me: Michael had left, and I had no idea if he was ever coming back.

My mother came over, and together we phoned every one of Michael's friends to see if anyone knew where he was. None of them had seen or heard from him. I knew we had no money for a hotel, so that was out. Ben drove around looking for Mike all night. By 3:00 a.m., when there was still no sign of him, Ben started peering into ditches and ravines for any signs of his car, and my mother took the phone into the other room and called the local hospitals. I sat on the couch and drank pot after pot of the herbal tea my mother brewed for me.

Ben came back as the sun was coming up. He gave me a hug and quietly said, 'I've looked everywhere. He may not be in the area anymore, Kris. I think we have to admit the possibility that he isn't coming back.'

I couldn't accept that, and I convinced Ben to drive out one more time with me while my mom stayed with the boys. Finally, I spotted Mike's Cougar in the parking lot of a hotel right near our house. He'd spent the night out there, in the freezing cold, less than a mile away from home. I was shaking and limping badly as I got out of Ben's truck and approached the Cougar. Ben waited in the truck, his face turned away to give us some privacy.

It had been a long night, and I'd had a lot of time to come up with reasons why Mike might have walked out. First and foremost was my disability. I hadn't been disabled when he'd married me, but now, with my mouth sagging on one side, unable even to return a hug with both arms, maybe I was grotesque to him. As soon as I saw the look of anguish on his face, however, I knew exactly what had caused him to snap. I could almost hear what he'd been thinking, sitting in his truck that whole long, lonely, cold night: *I promised to keep you healthy and happy, and I can't even accomplish that. If I fail at keeping you safe, then I've failed at everything.*

Mike had always been the brave one, the calm one, the one who could make it all better. But that day, it had to be me. I got into the front seat, took him in my arms, and said, 'We're going home.'

And so we did. After that night, our relationship changed. I wouldn't have thought that we could get any closer than we were. I didn't think there was anything about him I didn't know. But maybe I hadn't truly understood the depth of his commitment to our family and to me. We'd been strangers when we got married. All the adversity we'd been through hadn't broken us. Against all the odds, we were still together, still madly in love. But after that night, it felt as if we finally *did* know everything there was to know about each other. At last it had sunk in, for both of us: There was no force on earth that could separate us.

About a month or so later, a doctor finally diagnosed me with lupus, a chronic autoimmune disorder. It sounds ridiculous to say that it was a relief to find out that I had a degenerative and debilitating disease for which there is no cure, but it's true. Now we had an explanation for my poor health: the terrible neuralgia that made my face feel like someone had inserted hot needles into it, why even a garden-variety cold would hit me so hard, and, of course, why I had had a stroke at such a young age. My doctor even explained that lupus eases up in the summertime and gets worse in cold weather, which was why my symptoms had been intensifying as the winter wore on. The lupus diagnosis also explained my difficult pregnancies. My own immune system had been trying to reject the babies. It was a miracle I'd been able to have them at all.

The diagnosis also helped Mike let go a little of his vow to take care of me. He knew that he couldn't cure my lupus.

Today Michael still does all those little things that make my life around the disease a bit easier, like making coffee without me asking him to or bringing me a glass of ice water when I sit down to watch TV. I know that when he goes to the grocery store, he chooses which checkout line to wait in based on whether it has my favorite chocolate treat, Rolo. He can't stop the winter from coming, but he can make sure that I get a pair of fuzzy boots, so at least my feet are warm.

And yes, every week he brings me roses. Our house is filled with dried roses – on top of the kitchen cabinets, at the turn of the stairs, in vases throughout. And with every fresh bouquet, I am even more grateful for what they mean to Michael and me.

# Jelly Beans

Recovery from a stroke is slow going. It takes a long time to rebuild your strength. To this day, when I'm overtired or sick, the grip in my left hand isn't particularly strong, and I often call on the boys to lift heavy packages or books.

In the year after my stroke, our life gradually returned to normal, or whatever normal was for us at that time. Michael left Target for a new job at Circuit City. Peaceful Ethan continued to hit all of his developmental markers. He talked on schedule, walked on schedule, and (maybe most important for me) stayed cuddly. Every time we crossed one of those childhood milestones off the list, I breathed a silent sigh of relief.

But the biggest news had to do with Wesley. The aquatic therapy had continued to pay off, so that his stiff little body was a great deal more flexible. As a result, he could move more easily, and eventually, around his third birthday, he began to walk.

And then he galloped and jumped and sprinted and leaped and crashed. Once mobile, Wes didn't just get out of bed in the morning; he bounded out of it like Tigger in *Winnie-the-Pooh*, usually taking a piece of furniture or one of his brothers out in the process. If I asked him to get me the Scotch tape from the kitchen, he'd turn into a race car to do it, squealing around corners with two wheels off the ground.

Suddenly, our whole house was an extreme-sports obstacle course. Wesley couldn't pass a couch without bouncing on it, a bookshelf without climbing it, a staircase without hurtling down the last six steps. Wesley was never in a room by himself for more than ten seconds before you'd hear a crash. Our middle son was suddenly on the move, and Mike and I couldn't do much more than laugh at his antics. We resigned ourselves to the inevitable cuts and scrapes and bruises (and the occasional emergency room trip). What else could we do? Wes had a lot of lost time to make up for, and nothing in the world was going to slow him down.

Jake was great, too. By the time kindergarten came to an end, it was clear to everyone that he'd been successfully mainstreamed. The school had been checking on him periodically, waiting for the inevitable disruption or tantrum, but it never came. The pride I felt on the last day of school was about more than Jake's individual accomplishment, huge as it was. Maybe, just a little bit, we'd changed people's minds about what it meant to be autistic.

Privately, though, I recognized that we still had some ground to cover. Conversation with Jake was one sticking point. When asked what happened at school that day, most kids say, 'Nothing.' But I knew those kids would *eventually* talk to their parents. For instance, whenever Mike took Wesley along on an errand, such as filling up the car with gas, I'd hear about it for weeks – the kinds of cars they'd seen getting detailed, the crazy hair on the cashier, the lollipop she'd given him.

Not Jake. Every day, when Jake came home from first grade, he'd take my hand, and we'd go out to read license plates until dinner. If I asked him what his day had been like at school, he'd recite the schedule: circle time, then reading, then lunch. If Jake had been my only source of information, I wouldn't have known the name of a single one of his classmates, let alone anything about them. He took 'Just the facts, ma'am' to an absurd degree. He could tell me, for instance, that the class had come in seven minutes late from recess, but not that they'd been late because one of his classmates had gotten a nosebleed.

I felt a little sad that I didn't have more access to his world, particularly when I saw how much shared ground other parents had with their children. One afternoon at the drugstore, I ran into a mom with a kid in Jake's class, and she stopped for a minute to chat. 'Wow, what about that squabble in the playground? I heard Elias's father came in to talk to the principal about the way Jeremy pushes. Isn't it cute the way Oliver and Madison hold hands all the time? It's too bad her family is moving to Chicago next year.'

How on earth did she know this stuff? Had I missed a parent-teacher conference? Was there a newsletter?

'Oh, you know my Caitlin – she's such a Chatty Cathy,' the woman said. She turned to Jake, who was sitting in the back of my cart, reading a book about cloud formations. 'Caitlin tells me you spend a lot of time in the puzzle corner and that you always choose books about weather and rocks on Library Tuesday. Is that right?'

No answer from Jake, of course, and for once I didn't have much more to say than my son. This random woman seemed to have more information about the whos, whats, and whys of Jake's school days than I did. As I loaded Jake and our purchases into the backseat of the car, I felt a little defeated. Thankfully, it's not my nature to stay that way for long. Someday, I knew, Jake would have a conversation with me.

Although school was going well, I was still coaching Jake in the mornings so he'd be able to deal with any anomalies in his day. I couldn't prepare him for everything, so my focus shifted to giving him the tools he'd need to adapt on the spot.

In first grade, right around Halloween, Jake's teacher filled a humongous jar with orange and black jelly beans and told the class that whoever guessed the correct number would get to take the jar home. Jake, of course, had been calculating the volume of cereal boxes since his infancy. The only detail he couldn't be sure about was how much space the teacher had left at the very top of the jar, under the lid. But he was confident that he'd gotten within twenty jelly beans of the correct answer.

It didn't work out. The announced number was lower – much lower – than Jake's formulas had suggested, and the jar of jelly beans went home with a kid who gleefully crowed that he'd pulled a random number out of the air.

When Jake got home, he was beside himself. I couldn't console him, even by promising him every jelly bean in the store. Of course, it wasn't about the *candy;* it was about the *math.* I thought he was going to drive himself crazy over those jelly beans. He wouldn't eat or do anything else that night except check and recheck the numbers, sure that there was a rational explanation for how he could have been so far off.

The next day, he found out there *was* a rational explanation. The teacher had put a giant wad of aluminum foil in the center of the jar. Maybe she didn't want to spring for so many jelly beans, or she didn't want to send so much candy home with one kid. Whatever the reason, she'd rigged the game so that Jake's equations hadn't worked – unintentionally, of course, because who on earth would suspect that a first grader was going to use an equation to figure the cubic volume of a guess-the-jelly-bean jar? But Jake was completely undone.

The jelly bean incident, as it came to be known in our house, was when I came up with an intervention that I've used ever since with my own kids and all the kids I've worked with. 'I know you're upset,' I told Jake, 'but there's a scale. When someone you love dies, that's a ten on the scale. When something's a ten, you are entitled to flip out. You're actually entitled to do more than that. You can crawl into bed and stay there, and I'll be right there holding the tissue box.

'But then there's the other end of the scale, and that's where you'll find that jarful of jelly beans. It's not someone breaking a bone or losing an arm; it's a jar filled with candy we can buy at the drugstore. That's a two, and you respond to a code two event with a code two reaction, not a code ten.'

I use this intervention to help kids, particularly autistic ones, get some perspective. 'Someone crashes his car / Your shoes feel scratchy. Which one's the ten?' I ask. 'When it's time to go code ten, by all means, go code ten. But you can't waste code ten on the way the label in your shirt itches your neck.'

Sometimes Jake needed a little reminder to respond to a code two event with a code two reaction. But in general, having a rule-based check on his social behavior helped him respond appropriately. It was so effective that people began to ask me whether Jake had been cured of his autism. He hadn't, of course, and he never will be. Jake's autism is something he copes with every day. There's always some event that has the potential to make him go 'full Rain Man,' as we say in our family. But Michael and I keep trying to give him the tools he needs to make appropriate choices, and in general he does.

We went to Barnes & Noble most Saturday afternoons. Wes and Jake were allowed to choose two books a week, whatever they wanted (although I was still steering them toward the bargain section), and then we'd all get a snack at the café and look through what we'd bought. I don't care how many books I've read, there's always something special about opening a brand-new book and having a whole afternoon to get lost in it. It gave me real pleasure to share that feeling with my boys.

Jake, unsurprisingly, always went straight for the reference books. If it was filled with time lines, maps, graphs, and charts, Jake wanted it. A history of great scientists was one favorite, and *Timechart History of the World* was another. But nothing trumped the college textbook on environmental science.

I came to understand that Jake memorized facts as a way of calming and comforting himself. Reading lists of facts had the same effect on him that watching a half-hour sitcom or flipping through a gossip or fashion magazine had on one of my friends. Just as my experience with my sister, Stephanie, had helped me see talents and gifts where other people saw deficits, observing my husband's quirks helped me understand what soothed Jake.

Michael also memorizes trivia to relax. Ask him who starred in some obscure movie from the 1970s or who played first base for the Cardinals in 1983, and he'll tell you without hesitating, and then he'll update you on whatever that actor or first baseman has done since. When he worked for Target, they called him 'the Mike.' During the summer he spent unloading freight, he learned every SKU number in the store. So later, if a price tag was missing, instead of price checking it at the register, other employees would get on the walkie-talkie and say, 'Mike? Suave coconut shampoo?' To my tremendous annoyance, I have never seen him miss a question on *Jeopardy!* and I have flat-out refused to watch it with him ever again until he goes on the actual show and wins. So seeing Jake curled up with a list of exoplanets or asteroids didn't seem as weird to me as it might to another parent.

Jake's interests were wildly varied, too. He read every book about American history he could get his hands on. Jake's hunger for information seemed limitless, and his memory, as far as we could tell, was inexhaustible. Jake could tell you that poor, obscure James Buchanan was the fifteenth president of the United States, as well as provide you with the dates he served, the date he was born, whom he married, and when he died. He knew what state Buchanan was from and what percentage of the electoral college vote he had received.

He couldn't stay away from any textbook that had a test in it. (He's still like that. I must be the only mother on earth who needs to console her child when an exam is canceled.) I remember the day he discovered the section in the bookstore for test preparation. ACT! PSAT! SAT! MCAT! GMAT! LSAT!

Here were pages and pages of numbered problems, and lots of them were math! He looked at me reproachfully, as if I'd deliberately been withholding this wonderful treat. His favorite book in first grade was a GED preparation manual. He wasn't interested at all in the language sections, so I can't say for sure that he would have passed the test in its entirety, but by the end of that year, he regularly got perfect scores on the math tests.

Weirdly, people at school didn't seem to notice all these crazy things Jake was doing. If they did, nobody said anything. At the beginning of first grade, the kids were given a big workbook of math problems, a full year's worth of work. Jake filled in the entire book during the first two days of class. The teacher knew what he'd done, and she told him he could sit in the corner and read a book during class.

What he did instead was to create his own visual-based math language, which he still uses to tutor other kids. This language uses colors and shapes to represent numbers and combinations of them to represent equations. Imagine an abacus colliding with a kaleidoscope, and you're close. He layers transparencies in different colors and shapes on top of a light box now, but back then he had thousands of pieces of construction paper, meticulously cut into shapes that could be laid on top of one another so that he could do complex calculations. But nobody, including Jake, ever mentioned the fact that he'd essentially skipped a grade in math to me or Michael.

Going through old papers, I found some of Jake's work from those days. (I hadn't remembered, but when other kids were drawing a square with a triangle on top to represent their houses, Jake was using his crayons to draw models of more efficient hydroelectric plants.) In one of those old boxes, I found Jake's first-grade journal. The teacher had given them a week-long assignment: What would you do if you were president?

One of Jake's entries from that week reads, 'If I were President, I would tell people to aband New Orleans. Also If I were president I would build New Orleans some where else. I would even tell an argetect to draw and build an amusement park. When he or she was done, I would go to the amusement park. I would have a fun time.'

At the time, I thought I'd never seen anything quite as adorable as the 'he or she' in that sentence. A few pages later in that first-grade journal, there's another entry: 'If I were president, I would go to Florida and warn people from hurricanes.' We didn't think anything of this either. It was hardly news to us that Jake was obsessed with climatology and climate change. His preoccupation with the weather is still a joke in our house. We always say that Jake won't remember what he got for Christmas last year, but when he's eighty, he'll still remember how much snow there was on the ground. (He can't remember the name of a single kid in his kindergarten class, but he can describe, in vivid detail, the torrential rainstorm that required him to take shelter in a stairwell while he was waiting for the bus on his very first day.)

Of course, what pops out at me now is that the journal is dated January 2005, seven months before Hurricane Katrina devastated the southern United States.

# A Boy Cave

By second grade, Jake was humming right along in school. But I always saw his autism as a shadow in the background that had the potential to creep forward and snatch my child back if I let it. So, just as I would have gotten Jake tutoring help if he was falling behind in math or reading, I felt that it was up to me to make sure that he had friends. To do that, we needed a little help.

Now, I am *into* Halloween. I love it. Michael's always teasing me about the lengths to which I go (and the lengths to which I make him go) in order to make the holiday special. It is widely acknowledged in our neighborhood that if you stay still long enough, I am going to decorate you or put you in a costume. For Jake's first Halloween, for instance, not only did I sew him a full-body pumpkin costume, but I also made our little red wagon into a pumpkin float. I put Jake in his little pumpkin suit into the pumpkin wagon, threw a jack-o'-lantern and some pretty squashes in next to him, and dragged the whole shebang all over the neighborhood.

The year Jake was in second grade, I drove out to a nearby farm to pick up some pumpkins so that we could carve them into jack-o'-lanterns with the kids in the daycare. Driving back, I passed our neighbor's house and felt a little pang seeing her boys – she had seven of them – out in the yard playing football with some of the other kids on the street.

When I got to our house, I cut the engine and sat quietly in the driveway, watching Jake. He was outside, too, but the contrast between our house and our neighbor's was stark. One of Jake's favorite activities that year was to create multidimensional math shapes – cubes, spheres, cylinders, cones, and, of course, his beloved parallelepipeds – out of items he found around the house. Spent paper towel rolls, Lincoln Logs, Q-tips, and craft sticks – everything was fair game. That evening, he was busy arranging some of the shapes on our porch, lining them up neatly all along the front railing.

I got out of the car, went into the house, and put a pot of water on to boil for pasta. Then Jake and I spent a companionable few minutes in the fading autumn light decorating the porch together – he with his multidimensional math shapes, me with my spiderwebs and gourds (and maybe a fog machine and a shrieking ghost or two). When I heard my neighbor calling her kids in for dinner, I had an idea.

I wanted Jake to have friends, but I knew I couldn't send him out to play football with the neighbor boys. That wasn't going to work. Jake's physical delays made him clumsy and slow, and I'm not even sure he knew the rules of football at that time. (I'm quite sure he didn't care.) We needed to find some common ground.

What if I made our house – specifically, Jake's room – the kind of place that a boy couldn't help but gravitate toward, so that those other boys would come to him?

The next day, I went shopping. As always, we didn't have much money, but I saw it as an investment in Jake. I bought him a loft bed and got cool fuzzy rugs and beanbag chairs for the area underneath it. I had Mike and a neighbor push our big-screen TV upstairs, even though it left us with just a little one in the den, and I bought Jake a PlayStation, as well as the videogames the teenager behind the counter told me he'd choose for himself. I bought every kind of flavor-blasted Doritos they had in the store, and made a big batch of chewy homemade cookies with extra chocolate chips. In short, I created the ideal kid hangout – a boy cave – and then I opened the doors.

Jake was a little baffled by my redecorating, but as long as he could have pictures of the solar system up on the walls, he didn't care about the furniture. The new setup also played to Jake's strengths. Because of his incredible visual-spatial skills, Jake was (and still is) amazing at videogames. He's been known to attract crowds at Circuit City by playing the expert level of Guitar Hero with the game controller behind his head.

The kids came, and they stayed. In fact, Jake is still close with a lot of the boys he got to know that year. One of them in particular, Luke, is still a good friend. Luke's mom and I had an unspoken understanding. She always hoped that Jake's love of academics would rub off on Luke, and I secretly hoped that some of Luke's football cool would stick to Jake.

The moms were my secret weapon, especially a couple of days into winter break, when their own boys had gone completely stir-crazy. They loved Jake. 'Please, Kristine, rescue me. They're trashing the joint! Can Jake come over to play?' Whenever another boy's mom would drop Jake off after a playdate, she was always quick to compliment him: 'He is so incredibly polite! I don't know how you got him to have such lovely manners!' But I don't think Jake actually had any more decorum than most other seven-year-old boys. He was just quiet. I would have been thrilled to hear Jake yell 'Tickle torture!' when Wes provoked him, so I had my fingers crossed that if he spent enough time with his friends, he'd learn to be just as boisterous as they were.

Similarly, while the other mothers we knew were rolling their eyes at the language their kids used, I practically jumped with pride the night Jake told me the movie he'd seen that afternoon was 'wack.' I tried not to make a big deal out of it, but as he was clearing the table, I couldn't help grinning at Mike. It was his very first piece of slang.

Sometimes Jake and his buddies would play chess together,

Grandpa John, building his beloved sailboat. He was never too busy to take us fishing.

My Grandpa John and Grandma Edie on their wedding day.

We both had big dreams for this little boy.

Jake could spend hours watching the play
of light and shadows.

No cereal box was safe. How could we know he was learning to calculate volume?

I couldn't tear Jake's attention away from the reflection on this apple long enough to get a good picture.

An elaborate pattern Jake made on the carpet with Q-tips. These designs gave me a peek into his mind.

Therapy was boring . . . but Little Light wasn't.

The children at Little Light successfully achieve circle time by popping bubbles with their toes. Jake is pictured on the right in his beloved plaid shirt.

That first year, we thought we were going to lose Wes.

Jake and Christopher shared a real connection,
one I hadn't seen Jake have before with a friend.

Jake after class with his first mentor, Professor Pehl at IUPUI, who helped me to see Jake as a scientist.

There's always a lot of work, but there's *always* time for fun. That's what brothers are for! Here on the family hammock: Jake, Wesley, and Ethan.

Jake 'at home' in the honors college, surrounded by his peers, takes the lead working through an equation.

Jake writing an equation on a window with a view of the Chrysler Building.

$$\sum_{n=1}^{\infty} a_n \text{ divergent if } \int F(x)dx \text{ is divergent}$$
$$a_n = F(x)$$
$$\text{and } \sum_{m}^{\infty} a_n \text{ convergent if } \int F(x)dx \text{ is convergent}$$
$$a_n$$

Jake presenting his research.
He looked so small in his suit.

Jake and Igor at the famed Barnett Academy, home of the Fighting Moose.
The roses are from Mike.

The whole family.

but mostly they watched movies or battled with their light sabers and ate every chip in the house. When the *Star Wars* prequels came out, Jake memorized every line. But for the first time, he wasn't the only one. Nearly every boy his age could recite those movies by heart. I was so happy to see him hanging out with his friends, I kept the chips and videogames coming, and I didn't fuss too much when someone took out one of the living room lamps in their pursuit of Darth Maul. Sometimes I'd have to give Jake a little nudge: 'Hey – maybe it's time to stop talking about math now?' But in general, he adapted incredibly well, and those kids became real friends.

By now, the daycare was completely integrated into our lives. As before, projects often spilled over from the garage into the house. Most of the time, the project was so much fun that everyone got involved. For instance, we spent two weeks creating a wall-sized mural out of thousands of jelly beans in every color you could possibly imagine. It was hard work! But we were all together, singing songs and telling stories, and it was beautiful when it was done. The immense size of it gave the children a real sense of accomplishment. I'm also pretty sure that we ate as many jelly beans as we glued onto the wall.

Around that time, a new mom came to see me. She was going back to work the next week. Her baby was at that age where separation anxiety kicks in, and it seemed that she was even more upset about leaving her baby than the baby was to be left. I completely understood, of course. I'd been there myself. So I went to sleep thinking, *What can we do to make this little girl's first day as special as possible?*

The next day, I put the kids in the daycare to work – all twelve of them, including Ethan, and when they got home from school, Wesley and Jake, too. Together we made huge butterflies out of strips of crepe paper, in every color they had at the party store.

Then we glued them together, and I had Mike hang them from a frame attached to the ceiling. 'Go big or go home,' he teased me, not for the first time. The effect of all of the butterflies together, covering the entire ceiling and fluttering in the breeze from an open window, was breathtaking.

The kids I took care of were doing activities and projects that others would have considered wildly out-of-bounds for children their age. But I never understood why you would hold a child back. If they could do something, and they wanted to, why wouldn't you let them? Every day, I was astounded by their native strengths. I could never be an electronics whiz like Elliott or artistic like Claire.

My grandparents had always given my sister and me little jobs to do, even when we were tiny. We loved organizing the art supplies in the Sunday school, for instance – a real job, and we did it as soon as we could walk. Stephanie and I were put in charge of organizing the tea service at church, too. Each tray needed to be washed and polished, then set with a full creamer, a sugar bowl, and a small glass full of polished spoons. Nobody ever worried about us breaking a glass, and I don't remember that we ever did.

We learned at my grandmother's knee to cut ordinary paper into intricate pieces of art before most kids were allowed to handle safety scissors. We learned how to sew our own clothes as soon as we were old enough to hold a needle. My grandmother's precise stitches were barely bigger than the weft of the strong cotton fabric she sewed, a sign of her experience. One of my earliest memories is of hiding underneath the big quilting frame my grandmother would set up in the front room whenever someone announced an engagement or a baby on the way. I was free to play under the frame after I had proudly contributed my own carefully embroidered square to the quilt. I was three.

I'd learned to bake from my grandmother as well, and not from a recipe, but by feel. Stephanie and I could tell when the bread had risen enough by the strands of gluten that pulled away from the bowl. We knew when to check cookies for doneness by the smell. This wasn't when we were teenagers, but little girls, still using a stool to reach the countertop.

Perhaps it came naturally to me to give the kids in the daycare, and my own children, a lot more responsibility than other people might have. For example, as a toddler Ethan loved pasta. He'd always been interested in cooking and baking, so I bought him an inexpensive hand-cranked pasta maker. The first few batches he made were not great, but he stuck with it. After a month, four-year-old Ethan's linguine was delicious.

Noah loved math, so I built him an abacus by stringing giant beads onto wooden dowels, and he taught himself to multiply. Claire loved to sew, so she made little animal-shaped pillows out of felt, and we took them to the children's hospital as gifts for the patients. In my experience, independence and the opportunity to be creative never went to waste if the children were allowed to do what they loved.

# Who Am I?

'I hope next year I'll be able to learn.'

That was Jake's response to his second-grade teacher when she asked him what he was most looking forward to in third grade. Jake was starving for knowledge, craving it, longing for it, in a way that was a little frightening at times.

Michael and I were no longer surprised by the depth and breadth of his interests, by his endless memory, or by his ability to see patterns and connect them. But we were finding it hard to keep up. We supported his voracious appetite as best as we could with our trips to Barnes & Noble and lots of time on the Internet, but it was never quite enough.

Mike said it best: Jake was like Pac-Man. If there was something in front of him he could learn, he'd gobble it up and be energized by it. When he hit a wall, he'd just reverse course and find something else to learn. Heather, who helped me with the daycare, was in her sophomore year of college when Jake was in third grade. It was Heather who rediscovered Jake's facility for languages, hints of which Michael and I had seen when he'd taught himself Japanese from DVDs as a baby. She had to take a Spanish class to satisfy her language requirements. One night she forgot her Spanish-to-English dictionary at our house, and the next day she discovered that Jake had taught himself a bunch of Spanish words.

Soon after, she brought in a beginner's textbook for him, because she was curious to see what he'd do. Two weeks later, he could conjugate verbs, and he did the same thing with Chinese when she brought him a starter book she'd found in a secondhand shop down by the college. I have to confess, I didn't encourage Jake to actively pursue other languages. I was more interested in helping him to become conversational in English. When he was chattering away in Spanish, I couldn't understand a word he said. English was quite enough for me.

Heather worked for me on and off for a long time, so she knew Jake well. She told him once, 'Someday you're going to win a big award, and your mom is going to make so much noise celebrating that she's going to get you all kicked out of the restaurant.' Jake found the idea of me whooping it up in a fancy restaurant incredibly funny, so it became a running joke between them. When Heather arrived for work, she'd always ask, 'Hey, Jake, has your mom gotten you kicked out of that restaurant yet?'

In some ways, Heather was more his peer than the kids in his third-grade class. When she was studying for her exams, Jake would curl up with her and study, too. When I asked if he was a distraction, she'd say, 'No, he's helping!'

Watching them together, I could see that he was. 'Don't forget this,' he'd remind her, his little finger pointing to a fact on a chart.

'He'd do better on this final than most of the kids who are going to take it,' Heather told me one night as she was putting on her coat to leave.

The fascinating thing was what he did with the information he memorized – the way he assimilated, integrated, and manipulated it, as well as the conclusions he drew. For instance, he had become obsessed with geology and would talk endlessly about plate tectonics, fault lines, geothermal vents, earthquakes, and volcanic islands. The interest itself may have been narrow, but the way he implemented it was not.

One Sunday afternoon when he was in third grade, he took over the dining room table, covering every inch of it with textbooks, tidily lined up edge to edge. When it was time to clear the table for dinner, Mike called me over in a hushed voice. One enormous book was open to a diagram of the Wabash Valley Fault, the seismic zone that runs through Indiana, and next to that was a 3-D image of the fault. Another open book showed a reconstruction of a hunting camp used by the Clovis culture, the nomadic Paleo-Indians who occupied the area during the prehistoric period. Yet another showed an illustration of a Native American guiding a French explorer through Indiana in the early 1700s. A fourth was open to a geographical and statistical map of the state dating back to 1812. And a topographic map drawn by the U. S. Army in the 1940s sat neatly next to an up-to-date ASTER satellite image of the state.

In a notebook, Jake had calculated the precise longitude and latitude of our house, as well as the corresponding celestial coordinate system. Nearby, there was a book of star maps, open to the constellations that would be most visible from central Indiana that evening.

It was astonishing: a cross section of our place and time, a multilayered, historical snapshot, spanning from prehistory to the present, and from the earth's very core to the farthest reaches of the solar system. I didn't doubt for a second that not only had Jake memorized every fact that I could see in those open books, but that he was also working on a synthesis of what he'd learned, a woven tapestry that would bring together all those random details from multiple disciplines, a theory much more than the sum of its parts. It gave us a peek into the complicated matrix that made up the beautiful universe of Jake's mind.

Michael and I stood together, taking it all in. Then I had to yell down to the basement to get him to come upstairs and put all this stuff away so I'd have someplace to put the lasagna. Sometimes I think that if I'd stopped to totally comprehend what I was seeing, it would have been harder to be a mom to him. 'It's just Jake,' Michael and I would say to each other. We never stopped to think about how truly beyond belief his capabilities were at that time, and I think that was probably a good thing.

I don't really know when Jake first became aware of himself as a prodigy, but eventually he came to understand how different he was. He always liked to lie under the trees in our backyard. On occasion, we'd hear him giggle and say, 'Four thousand five hundred ninety-six,' or some other large number. That was the number of leaves on the tree. It wasn't that he was counting the leaves, at least not one by one, the way you or I would. The number was just obvious to him. If one came wafting down, he'd adjust the total: 'Four thousand five hundred ninety-five.' When Jake started to realize how unusual these behaviors were, he became a little more self-conscious about them. 'Okay, that was kind of two hundred forty-six toothpicks,' he'd say with a chuckle, referring to the iconic scene in the movie *Rain Man*.

I hated his self-consciousness, not wanting him to feel embarrassed about the gifts that made him special. But third grade was hard. At age eight, boys tend to group together by their favorite sport. You have the baseball boys, the football crew, and the soccer kids. Jake still had a lot of physical delays. He was a slow, uncoordinated runner, and swimming was a struggle. So when the school sent the sports sign-up sheet home, he didn't put his name down for any of them.

He did sign up for the chess club, a group that met for matches before school. Most of the players were still learning how the pieces moved, so Jake didn't have a lot of serious competition. He kept things interesting for himself by sacrificing a number of his important pieces – his queen, one of his bishops, and five of his pawns – early in each game, leaving himself with only weaker pieces with which to defend his king. None of the children ever noticed that this was deliberate, even though he gave up the same pieces every time. While the other kids were learning the game, Jake was honing important social skills, such as how to be patient while someone else takes a turn and how to give and take in relationships.

He got a lot out of the friendships he made with kids at school and in the neighborhood, but he was also socially aware enough to know that he was somehow different from his friends and from all the other kids in his class. After school, the other kids wanted to shoot baskets or watch sports on TV. Jake did those things, too, but he really wanted to spend time working on advanced math or updating his political map of the United States.

There was a fundamental part of Jake that he couldn't share with the other boys. Gerrymandering or soil chemistry or whatever his preoccupation was that week generally didn't interest them, and his passions only underscored the difference between him and them. By that time, Jake found it easier to slow himself down, to sit there and pretend that it took him twenty minutes to get through a times-table worksheet, like it did for everyone else. Getting along socially meant that Jake had to keep part of himself – a big part – a secret.

One of the prodigy experts we talked to pointed out that when someone with Jake's IQ concentrates on doing anything, even if it's just acting like an ordinary third grader, he's going to knock the ball out of the park. Yet the double life he was leading also caused him to have a kind of identity crisis. He had to find out who he was, because he didn't really know.

Jake and I spent a lot of time online looking at videos of autistic savants and child prodigies. Many of the child prodigies on YouTube are musical, which had the unexpected side benefit of inspiring Jake to play music. Jake would listen to a few minutes of a piece of classical music, press Pause, sit down at the piano, and instantly play what he'd just heard, more or less perfectly. This was amazing to watch, and it seemed to be relaxing for him. Jake has never been a morning person, but playing the piano for a few minutes in the morning became one of his favorite ways to wake up.

We found videos of Kim Peek, the autistic megasavant on whom Dustin Hoffman's character in the movie *Rain Man* was based. Peek was known for calendar calculation, among other things. He could tell you, for instance, not only the date of Winston Churchill's birth but also on which day of the week Churchill was born, based on the year of his birth.

'Really? *That's* a big deal? I can do that,' Jake said, as we watched the video clip.

'You can?' How could I not have known about this? Admittedly, a skill like that doesn't generally come up in conversation.

'So what day of the week was I born?' I asked.

'In 1974, April seventeenth was a Wednesday,' he said, without looking away from the screen.

He was, of course, right.

I also had no idea how good his visual memory was until we saw another documentary online about the artist Stephen Wiltshire. Wiltshire is an autistic savant who has been called 'the Human Camera' for his ability to draw a nearly perfect rendition of a landscape he's seen only once. For the documentary we saw, the filmmakers hired a helicopter to fly him over Rome. After a single aerial pass, Wiltshire was able to draw the city, down to the most minute architectural details, such as the number of columns in the Pantheon.

'That's how I see, too,' Jake said, surprised that there was someone else out there who saw the world the way he did, and also by the fact that *everyone* couldn't accurately remember how many windows there were in a skyscraper they'd seen only once. Jake didn't have Wiltshire's artistic ability, but he, too, could remember accurately how many cars there'd been in the Best Buy parking lot we'd passed at fifty-five miles an hour, and how many of them had been silver, along with hundreds of other minute details.

Seeing other autistic savants on YouTube was a relief for Jake, but it wasn't a solution to the alienation he felt in his everyday life. In some ways, knowing that other savants and prodigies were out there actually intensified Jake's feelings of loneliness.

There's a big difference between knowing you're not alone because you've watched someone on YouTube and feeling like you're not alone because you have someone to talk to as an equal. Jake could tell me all about his interests, but we weren't having a conversation. I wasn't suddenly going to have an insight about pyroclastic flows that would engage him. The best I could do was listen and ask questions, and at a certain point that's not enough.

At Jake's urging, I got in touch with Dr Darold Treffert, Kim Peek's doctor, and one of the world's leading experts on autistic savants. At that time, Dr Treffert's website featured profiles of a number of savants, and Jake felt an immediate sense of connection. For someone who had been asking the questions 'Where do I fit in?' and 'Where do I belong?' Dr Treffert's site seemed heaven-sent. So I called.

In the world of autism, it can take a year to get in touch with an expert in your state. I was shocked to find that Dr Treffert answered his own phone. I told him about my unusual son, and he was immediately interested. After we'd talked for a while, he made a comment that I think about almost every day. He said, 'Wait and see. Your son will surprise you.'

At the time, I didn't fully understand what he meant. 'Oh, he already surprises me plenty,' I said, laughing. 'He surprises me every day.'

It was true. After all, I hadn't had the slightest idea that he could do calendar calculation, had I? But in the years since that conversation, I've come to realize how truly wise that prediction was. Dr Treffert knew that we'd only seen the very tip of the iceberg. He understood that Jake's capabilities would increase exponentially as he got older and that they would expand past anything we could have predicted.

During that first call, I told Dr Treffert about the loneliness Jake was experiencing. In response, he offered to introduce Jake to another eight-year-old prodigy. The two boys were gifted in different areas, but they shared many of the same interests and had similar development patterns. Dr Treffert thought that they might get along and be able to relate to each other in a way that neither could with others their age. I could barely wait to get off the phone to call the other mom, but it turned out she didn't want to make a date for the boys. Her son, she explained, was too busy to make new friends. His music practice and touring schedule simply didn't permit it.

I was shocked. Nobody knows better than I do that a gifted kid is self-motivated. I never once made Jake do math or learn physics or astronomy, and I'm sure that other kid's mom never had to force him to practice his instrument. I'm the biggest proponent out there of allowing children to do what they love; it's the cornerstone of everything I do. But in all things, there has to be a balance.

'Physics will be there tomorrow,' I always tell Jake. 'That math isn't going anywhere.' The same is true for chess or music or art. I'm sure that nobody was forcing Bobby Fischer to play chess every waking minute when he was a child; that's probably what he wanted to do more than anything else in the world.

But when that's the case, I believe it's a parent's job to close up the chessboard and send the kid outside to play. A child needs to have friends his own age; he can't discover who he is in a vacuum.

Despite all our efforts, the loneliness and boredom of third grade eventually got to Jake. He was desperate to learn, and school seemed only to be getting in the way. He'd stay up until all hours reading in bed, no matter how many times we went and turned out the light. Then in the morning, he didn't want to go to school. The compromises we'd asked him to accept between what he had to do and what he loved to do no longer seemed in balance. The vivid, engaged, excited child who chattered about asteroids from the backseat of the car – that was *my* Jake. The kid I was kissing goodbye at the bus stop every morning seemed like his shadow.

When he got home from school, instead of playing with his friends in the neighborhood, eight-year-old Jake would squeeze himself into one of the cubes in a bookshelf we had in the daycare. When parents arrived to pick up their kids, they'd find him crammed in there. Some of them even thought it was amusing.

But there was nothing funny or cute about it. I was deeply concerned. This was true autistic behavior. I felt as if I was losing him again.

# Saved by the Stars

I called Stephanie Westcott, the psychologist who'd first given us Jake's autism diagnosis. She listened as I told her what was going on, and she didn't mince words: 'It sounds like he's bored, Kristine. You have to engage him. Has he expressed an interest in anything recently?'

That was easy. Jake had been pestering me about algebra for more than a year. Unfortunately, third-grade math meant multiplication tables and long division, not the algebra he was so desperate to learn. I couldn't help him. By third grade, he'd blown way past any math I'd ever learned. As the math and science he loved had gotten more and more complex, Jake had left us behind. The only help I could offer was to listen while he wrestled with the problems and tried to work them out himself.

So I called the school. Teaching was what they did, and Jake needed a teacher. Maybe there was a gifted math class he could join? They invited us to come in for a meeting to discuss some options.

Warning bells went off as soon as I saw how many people were assembled there. Why did the school psychologist need to be in the room when we were there to talk about math?

The meeting started civilly enough. Michael and I explained how desperate Jake was to learn algebra, and we shared our frustration that we couldn't help.

'He'll have plenty of time to learn that material when the gifted program starts in fourth grade. But in the meantime, we might be able to get him some extra assistance if we reopen the IEP.'

I was dumbfounded. An IEP? I thought we'd left that conversation behind in kindergarten. Jake's desire to learn was not an expression of a need for services. This wasn't a kid who needed extra help because he couldn't sit in a chair. Jake was a straight-A student.

'But he doesn't need assistance. He needs resources.'

'An IEP might be the way to get him those resources.'

I still didn't understand. 'Why are we talking about special ed? Is Jake disruptive in class? Is he not able to communicate? Is he not playing with his friends at recess?'

'No, no, of course not. He's a model student, and he's got lots of friends. There's been no problem with Jake at all.'

'Does he need occupational therapy? Physical therapy? Speech?'

Again the answer was no.

'Then what is it? Why are we talking about an IEP?'

It was the alphabet cards all over again. I had come because my son had been begging me, for two years, to learn more about a school subject that I couldn't help him with. He needed resources to learn, and I'd come to his school to get those resources, but they were saying that to get them, we'd have to put Jake back in the special needs box.

'I think we're done here,' I said. 'Excuse me.' And I walked out of the room.

Michael came running after me, utterly shocked. 'Kristine! Come back in and finish the meeting.'

'I'm not going back in,' I told him. 'We're done. I don't want anything to do with any conversation pertaining to my son and special ed. That's not why I'm here. I'll meet you at the car.'

I didn't blame Jake's school or the teachers. In fact, I was grateful to them for their work and dedication. They were trying to do the right thing for Jake. But in my heart, I knew that opening up an IEP was not the way to go. I knew that I might be making a mistake, just as I had known that when I pulled him from Life Skills. Even though I do believe the mother gut is always right, maternal intuition doesn't come with warning lights and buzzers. In this case, however, the path was clear to me.

I hired my aunt, a high school math teacher, to teach Jake algebra. When he quickly surpassed what she could comfortably teach him, I realized that a little math tutoring wasn't going to solve the bigger problem. Stephanie Westcott was right: Jake was bored. He needed something or someone to truly capture his imagination, to encourage him, to challenge him. The advanced astronomy lectures at the Holcomb Observatory had worked to bring him out of his shell before, so back we went, the whole family this time, with Wesley and baby Ethan in tow.

The change in Jake was dramatic. Those were beautiful days that the five of us spent together at the planetarium. The boys would eat peanut butter and jelly sandwiches on a picnic blanket on the grounds, and then we'd attend the presentation of the week. I'd bring as many car sticker books as I could fit into my bag to keep Wesley and Ethan busy, but Jake was engrossed. We'd always end up back at the giant telescope at the top of the building, with Jake looking out at the stars.

Those trips to the observatory became a new family tradition, exactly the kind of happy, ordinary childhood experience I wanted the boys to have. Ethan was a bit young, but Wesley was quickly engaged. The more he learned, the more interested he became, and it wasn't long before he and Jake would spend the drive home talking about issues in advanced astronomy as if they were at a professional conference. *Seriously*, I'd think, catching Mike's eye, *who* are *these people?*

Wes and Ethan were happy, but Jake – well, we felt as if we'd *saved* Jake. Almost immediately after we resumed our visits, his social life picked up again. After school, he happily headed out to ride his bike or play tag with his friends. I'd learned my lesson. As long as Jake could get a good dose of serious astronomy, he could keep up with the social end of things in school. As I had seen so many times with the typical kids at the daycare and the autistic kids at Little Light, as well as over and over with Jake himself, all of his other skills would come along naturally as long as he was doing what he loved.

Then, right when we were back on track, the observatory closed for the winter. There had to be another way to kindle Jake's interest. We couldn't lose the gains we'd just made. Watching the PBS series *Cosmos* and hanging out on the NASA website wouldn't be enough; Jake needed to be completely immersed. So I searched for another planetarium.

Indiana University–Purdue University Indianapolis (IUPUI) was right down the road from Butler University, where the Holcomb Observatory was located. Although IUPUI didn't have a planetarium, it did offer astronomy courses. And so I soon found myself on the phone with Professor Edward Rhoads, who taught a freshman course on the solar system there.

I would never have been brave enough to ask a favor for myself, but because I was advocating for Jake, I was fearless. I told Professor Rhoads that I had an autistic son who loved astronomy and that we'd had a lot of success with him socially and in other areas when he was able to engage in the activities he loved. Would he consider allowing Jake to sit in on his class? I explained that this wasn't about academics or furthering Jake's education, just that I thought this class would make him happy, and indirectly help his social skills.

I knew how crazy my request sounded. This was a university course, after all, and Jake was eight years old. But I also knew that getting permission for him to attend this five-week class was my best chance to keep him out of the bookshelf. At one point in my conversation with Professor Rhoads, I even suggested that perhaps we could sit in the hall outside his classroom and eavesdrop on his lectures. That didn't turn out to be necessary. In an extraordinary act of generosity, Professor Rhoads agreed to allow Jake to sit in on his freshman course on Saturn, on the strict condition that I would take him out of the classroom at the very first sign of any disruptive behavior.

It was an afternoon class, which meant that I had to pull Jake out of his last third-grade class about twenty minutes early. Fingers crossed behind my back, I told his teacher that he had a series of doctor's appointments, hoping that she wouldn't ask for a note. In the car, Jake said, 'Well, he *is* a doctor.' It was almost a joke, a rare foray into humor for Jake, who hadn't quite tapped into that part of himself yet. I took it as a good sign.

IUPUI is a commuter college, and many of the students are older part-timers. As Jake and I made our way into the small classroom where the course would be held, I suspect that most of the attendees assumed that I was a student whose child care arrangements had fallen through. Although I felt sure that I was doing the right thing for Jake, I was still nervous about how the afternoon would unfold. Jake might fidget, drag his chair across the linoleum floor, or somehow otherwise make too much noise. If he did, there was nowhere to hide. So my heart was beating hard when Professor Rhoads took his place at the front of the classroom. He was slightly disheveled, introverted, and passionate about his subject – the very picture of the absent-minded professor. He reminded me a little of Jake.

Thankfully, as soon as Professor Rhoads began to speak, I could feel Jake's body relax, and when I looked over at him, I could see that he was the happiest I had seen him in months – concentrated and intent, but peaceful.

Professor Rhoads had a deck of slides, mostly Hubble Space Telescope pictures of Saturn, which were mesmerizing in their beauty. While clicking through, he asked the class to interpret what they saw.

'What is this black dot in front of Saturn?' he asked the class. Nobody answered.

Jake scribbled in the margin of his notebook and pushed it over to me: 'If I know, can I say?'

'If nobody else answers,' I wrote back. 'And *raise your hand*.'

Jake waited a moment, and then his hand went up. The professor turned to him and nodded. 'It's Titan's shadow,' Jake said.

The other kids in the class exchanged glances. I was a little taken aback myself. I was surprised not that Jake knew the answer (by that point, nothing Jake knew surprised me), but by his manner. He wasn't nervous or the slightest bit self-conscious to be participating in such a discussion in a university classroom. He seemed totally self-possessed and confident. He seemed like he belonged there.

During that first class, he answered one or two other questions, always waiting to make sure that none of the enrolled students wanted to try. I could tell that Professor Rhoads was beginning to understand that this was more than whimsy on my part and that Jake was more than a little kid who'd caught a few episodes of *Nova*.

The Jake I went home with that night was a completely different kid from the one in the bookshelf. The days we had class were the only days I didn't have to try twenty times to wake him up in the morning. 'We've got class tonight' worked better than any alarm clock. As we drove to class, Jake would physically lean forward in his seat as if he couldn't wait to get there.

Toward the end of the second class, Jake scrawled a note to me in the margin of his notebook: 'I have a question.'

I wrote back: 'Save it until the end, and make it a good one. Don't waste the professor's time with something we can look up at home.'

After class was dismissed, Jake waited patiently until the rest of the kids had asked Professor Rhoads their questions. When it was finally his turn, I couldn't help noticing that he was dancing a little, shifting his weight from foot to foot in a gesture immediately recognizable to every mom. It had been a long lecture, and he'd had a Coke in the car on the way there.

Fortunately, I wasn't the only one who noticed, and there may even have been the faintest trace of a smile on Professor Rhoads's lips when he said, 'Science is important, Jake. But there are some things that are even more important than science. If you'd like to use the restroom, I promise that I'll be here to answer your question when you get back.'

Jake's question concerned the low gravity on Enceladus, one of Saturn's moons, and what that meant for the possibility of life there. I didn't know then that Enceladus is considered one of the most likely spots in our solar system for life to exist (it has an ocean), but I could tell from the way Professor Rhoads responded to the question that Jake had done what I'd suggested and made it a good one.

By the third class, Jake's participation had become a kind of shared joke. If nobody's hand went up when Professor Rhoads asked a question, he'd wait a few beats and then turn to Jake with an eyebrow raised. More often than not, Jake was right, and by the time the semester was over, he was openly participating in the class. Jake has never been a particularly big kid, but he'd never looked smaller to me than he did up at the whiteboard next to those college students.

When the professor announced that the class would be breaking up into groups to come up with a final presentation, everyone was clamoring to work with Jake. He took the presentation seriously – he did all the research and put together a killer PowerPoint presentation. This was his first exposure to college students, though, and he started to get anxious when he realized that his partners weren't putting any work into the assignment. He didn't understand what was going on. It fell to me to explain that in the best-case scenario, they were probably leaving their own work to the very last minute.

'And in the worst?' he asked.

'Well, honey, they can see that you've done a good job with that PowerPoint presentation and that it's all ready to go. They probably think that they don't have to do much at all.'

Jake thought about that for a minute and then decided to tell his fellow students that they could have his PowerPoint slide deck, but they'd have to do the research themselves to figure out what it meant, because he wasn't going to participate in the presentation. He wrote Professor Rhoads an email explaining why he wouldn't be there. It was an impressive show of ethics, and I smiled a little to myself. I suspected it wouldn't be the last time that overwhelmed, sleep-deprived college students would try to hitch a ride on Jake's coattails. Maybe the next group would have better luck.

# Pop-Tarts and Planets

They had strawberry Pop-Tarts in the vending machines at IUPUI. Munching a Pop-Tart while waiting for his astronomy class became the highlight of Jake's week.

When Professor Rhoads's class was over, Jake took another freshman survey course, this one on the solar system, taught by Dr Jay Pehl. I liked him immediately. He had a kind, friendly face and hands covered with chalk, and he was known for carrying a handkerchief packed with candy in his pocket. Dr Pehl's class was much bigger than the one Jake had taken with Professor Rhoads and took place in an enormous auditorium. I emailed in advance to ask if we could attend. Dr Pehl responded by saying that as long as we didn't disturb anyone, he probably wouldn't even notice that we were there.

After the first class, Jake was hooked. Unfortunately, we couldn't get to the next couple of classes because Michael had to work. But I knew how important it was to Jake, so the following week I brought all three boys with me and took the two youngest for a walk while Jake sat in. It was weird to watch him walk away from me into the lecture hall. He was physically dwarfed by the other young people swarming around him, and I could see that his shoelace was untied. I'd never left him anywhere before, except at elementary school or a friend's house, and this seemed very different to me. I was there ten minutes early to pick him up at the auditorium door.

Jake didn't talk at all during those early classes with Dr Pehl, but he was eager to sign up for the next class in the astronomy curriculum, Stars and Galaxies, also taught by Dr Pehl. Early on in the second class, Jake raised his hand. It's well-known, he said, that binary stars exchange gases; the gas from one star transfers to another and causes changes in the second star. But since the second star gets bigger, Jake asked, is it possible that some of the gases could go back to the first star and cause even more changes there?

Dr Pehl looked thoughtful. 'You know, I've never thought about that,' he said.

The answer wasn't in any of the textbooks either. Later, Dr Pehl helped me to see that this tendency to take a well-understood concept and build on it is the engine behind Jake's tremendous creativity. He is always pushing a theory or concept he's read or learned about one step further.

Jake took all the quizzes and all the tests in those early classes with Dr Pehl, and he aced them all. (I remember Dr Pehl telling him whom to write to after he'd found an error in the textbook.) When Stars and Galaxies was over, Jake signed up to take the first course on the solar system again. He'd exhausted the astronomy courses offered by IUPUI.

To keep himself occupied while he was waiting to ask Dr Pehl his inevitable questions at the end of class, Jake would move slowly through the rows of desks in the enormous auditorium, picking up discarded coffee cups and wadded-up pieces of paper. He'd put the abandoned Coke cans into the recycling bin or stick a student's forgotten calculator into his backpack, holding it for the person until he saw him or her the next week. It was as if IUPUI had hired the world's smallest janitor. By the time he'd made his way down to the lectern, the other students would be finished asking their questions, and he'd present Dr Pehl with his.

After he'd been taking classes for a year or so, Jake floated an idea, an alternate theory he'd been thinking about. Did Dr Pehl think it could work?

'I don't have the slightest idea,' Dr Pehl said. He sat down in the front row and tossed Jake a whiteboard marker. 'Here's a marker; there's the board. Go ahead. See if it works.' For the next fifteen minutes, the two of us sat and watched as Jake blazed through equation after equation.

This was the first of many after-class sessions, but it represented a turning point for me. With a real sense of shock, it occurred to me that I'd never seen Jake talk about the things he was most passionate about with someone who actually knew what he meant. Here, finally, was someone who could parry with him, question him, correct him, challenge him, and truly appreciate him. Here, finally, was a conversation.

I saw how quickly Jake picked up the material and how his scary speed with the math worked to his advantage. I recognized how Dr Pehl's direction could focus Jake's voracious mind. There was a lot of math he didn't know. After all, he was only nine. But that represented only a temporary stumbling block for Jake. Unlike the other students, he could make a note, go home, learn what he needed to learn, and then start from there the following week.

'Every time I turn around, he's jumped up another level,' Dr Pehl told me once, shaking his head.

Jake had a million ideas, and the university environment fed them. At the end of any given class, he'd run through ten theories on the whiteboard while Dr Pehl sat in the front row and watched him do it. Better than most people at seeing patterns, which are fundamental in math and science, Jake was not afraid to draw associations between them even if they occurred in unlikely places. If he saw any connection at all, he'd run with it, and if it turned out to be wrong, he'd just move on. Dr Pehl encouraged his daring. 'Nobody's going to remember a mistake you made when you were nine, Jake,' he'd say, laughing.

Watching Jake at the front of that classroom, I was impressed once again by his confidence and how resilient he seemed to be.

If Dr Pehl pointed out a potential problem with one of his ideas or asked him how he'd resolve a discrepancy, Jake didn't take it personally. There was no ego involved, no 'Back off; this is *my* theory.' Instead, it was more like 'Another puzzle! I'll have to think about that for a second.'

I genuinely appreciated Dr Pehl's support. He was as shocked as I was that people had been so ready to give up on Jake. Every once in a while, he'd turn to me, eyes wide, and say, 'And this is the kid nobody thought would ever read!'

Nor was he quite ready to give up on me. After I'd been coming to class for a while, Dr Pehl insisted on giving me the day's quiz. 'Come on, he's got to be getting this talent from somewhere,' he said.

'Whatever it is, it skipped a generation. I promise you, it's not from me,' I replied.

It wasn't as if I was spending my days in some kind of heady intellectual pursuit. I'd spent most of my professional life singing 'The Wheels on the Bus.'

But Dr Pehl persisted, and so I took the quiz. I got one of the four questions right. For those of you as pathetic as I am in math, that's 25 percent. I'm not one to make excuses for myself, and in this case I didn't have to, because Dr Pehl was only too happy to do that for me: 'You weren't expecting a quiz. Pay close attention next week, and we'll try again.'

I didn't know how to tell him that I had been paying attention! But I was up for a challenge, and the next week I buckled down. I took notes and thought I had at least a rudimentary grasp of what was going on – until I took the quiz. This time, I didn't get *any* of the questions right. Zero percent. Even I could calculate that.

'Anyone can have a bad day,' Dr Pehl said, still encouraging me. 'Let's see what happens next week.'

So the next week, I gritted my teeth and concentrated so

hard my head hurt. By the time the quiz landed on my desk, I was sweating through my blouse. The questions swam in front of me. Just when I was about to give up, I heard a compassionate voice in my ear: 'B. The answer to number two is B.'

I thought Jake was the culprit and was gearing up to deliver a lecture on academic honesty and the importance of letting other people make their own mistakes. But Jake wasn't even paying attention to me. He'd finished his own quiz in a matter of seconds and was reading ahead in the textbook. My rescuer was, in fact, Dr Pehl, who was smiling and shaking his head. He'd seen that it was hopeless and had taken pity on me.

Once, when I thanked Dr Pehl for taking an interest in Jake, he made a remark that stuck with me: 'A great mind is just a great mind, and I try not to worry too much about what package it's in.'

I had cause to think of that comment when an older woman leaned over during a break in class to compliment me on how well behaved my little boy had been during the lecture. It gives you some idea of how far we'd come that for a minute I genuinely didn't know what she was talking about. Jake had spent the class filling a notebook with equations tangentially related (as far as I could tell) to the topic Dr Pehl had been lecturing on. I'd been looking forward to hearing what Dr Pehl had to say about Jake's many thoughts after class. But all that woman saw was a smallish nine-year-old with a not-so-clean face, wearing Crocs and drawing in a notebook.

That moment, I realized that I no longer saw Jake as a little kid or a student. I'd begun to see him for what he was – a scientist. We had finally found a place where Jake could just be Jake.

# Two Pies

After Jake had settled into attending astronomy courses at IUPUI and most of the kids at Little Light had been mainstreamed, I began skill development classes at night for the lowest-functioning kids. I felt a huge responsibility to help parents see what their kids could do so that they wouldn't give up on them.

The first time Katy, a severely autistic nonverbal seventeen-year-old, walked into my house, she made a beeline for the kitchen. She opened every cabinet, looking at all my pots and pans, and when she got to my mixer, she caressed it as though she'd been reunited with a long-lost pet. She also had a sweet tooth, and her mother always kept a pack of strawberry wafer cookies for Katy in her purse.

Reminded of Meaghan and how much she'd loved our play dough projects, I whipped up a quick batch of white icing, brought Katy a spreader, and showed her how she could ice her cookies before she ate them. The next day, I greeted her with a giant bowl of that same white icing, as well as a couple of boxes of food coloring. That week, Katy learned that yellow added to red makes orange and that the more yellow you add, the lighter and brighter that orange becomes. Over the course of the next two weeks, we made every color we could with the limited palette available to us.

The next week, I gave Katy a pastry bag so that she could create stars and flowers with individual petals. As the weeks went by, I watched as her decorations got more and more sophisticated and ornate. Eventually, I went to a special baking supply store and got a much wider range of food coloring and pastry tips for her to work with. There were beautiful jewel tones and pastels in the color kit, but they paled in comparison with the shades Katy made, colors with names I know only from the catalogs: dusky violet, carmine, cyan, cerulean, gold-enrod, fawn.

Eventually, Katy and I began making cakes to decorate together. I'll never forget the wedding cake she copied from a magazine, with sugar pansies so real I was afraid to put them in my mouth. I was so pleased when her father called me a couple of months after we'd started working together to tell me that she'd gotten a job working in the bakery department of a super-market in our community. Like the parents of so many autistic children, he'd been worried that Katy would be dependent on her mother and him for the rest of her life. She'd gone all the way through the special ed system, and they'd had very little to show for it. Of course, my goal hadn't been to get her a job, but to find an activity that she could enjoy doing during the day. It had worked so well and so fast because she loved it.

'Katy has been in this world with you since you had her,' I told her dad. 'She's been to every party you've taken her to. She's heard every conversation.' I believed that, just as I believed that Jake had been with us at that party so long ago with Clif-ford the Big Red Dog. When he was a toddler, he got lost in his alphabets because he couldn't handle the social requirements. Since he couldn't tell me what color balloon he liked or what kind of cupcake he wanted, he hid behind that book. But he'd been there all along.

I began acting as an advocate for a number of Little Light children in the public schools. I went to their IEP meetings with their parents, bringing with me a portfolio of the work we'd done together. I remember one meeting for a little boy named Reuben, who had joined us in our second year at Little

Light and had done some skill development classes with me. Reuben was obsessed with boats, so we'd spent months learning about yachts and schooners and catamarans. We'd classified boats, written reports about boats, and made models of boats, just like the ones I used to watch my grandfather piece together in his garage for the grandchildren to play with at the lake.

During this time, Reuben had learned to read. He'd been motivated by a sumptuously illustrated book about the luxury liners of the early twentieth century. His handwriting and fine motor skills also had improved immeasurably due to the tiny lettering he'd used to write names on the sides of the boats we'd built together.

Everyone related to Reuben's therapy and education had gathered around a big table for his IEP meeting. His physical, occupational, and developmental therapists were there, along with his mainstream classroom teacher, his special ed teacher, and the school psychologist. Everyone took his or her turn giving an up-to-date evaluation of Reuben's abilities, and then the group used those to determine what percentage of the day Reuben should spend in a mainstream classroom.

When the group's conclusion was declared to be 20 percent, I cleared my throat and opened his portfolio. His occupational therapist, for instance, had said that he couldn't draw a circle – but there was an *o* and an *a* in 'boat,' and I could prove that he could write that word beautifully. Reuben could do a lot more than they thought he could. We went through the whole folder together, and we were able to get that percentage up significantly.

Rachel's son, Jerod, had been coming to my skill development classes, too, and he'd made a lot of progress as well. Rachel and I had become friends, and it drove her crazy that I wouldn't accept money for the work I did. I tried to explain to her that it was simply the way I'd grown up. When I was little, Grandma

Edie baked two pies every morning. The family would make short work of one of them at dinner, and there was always someone in the community – a recent widower, a family with a loved one in the hospital, or a couple with a new baby – who was grateful and happy to receive a gift of the second pie.

The truth is, that second pie didn't feel like a 'good work' to us. Doing charity was so much a part of our lives that we almost didn't think about it. After all, it wasn't much more work to make two pies when you were already making one. Helping other people who were going through a hard time, supporting the other members of our community – these weren't lofty ideals that we spent a lot of time talking or thinking about; they were just what you did.

That model was my template for Little Light. I felt lucky, to be honest. How many people go through life wondering what their purpose is? I'd never had to wonder. I'd known that I had been put on earth to help children since I was a child myself. Between the daycare and Little Light, I got to be who I was and to do the work I loved. It was hard work, yes, but it was also incredibly fun. I felt filled up every day, knowing that I was contributing to an ideal bigger than myself. And I didn't even need to leave the house! The doorbell rang, and there the kids were, my life's work. What could possibly be more important than those children?

Since I wouldn't take any money from her, Rachel would bring me sandwiches. Five pounds later, I cried mercy and was ready to listen when she asked if there was another, more meaningful way that she could help. Was there a program I wanted to do, for instance, that she and I could set up?

Yes, there was something that I felt was missing from the choices available to families with autistic children. The program I was thinking of would give these kids a place where they were celebrated while also helping them to establish a network of friends. It would allow them to have the ordinary childhood experiences that other kids took for granted.

Michael and I had both continued to prioritize happy childhood experiences for our own kids. We wanted them to make memories they'd think back on fondly their whole lives, little traditions they'd be able to pass along to their own children. For instance, we liked to go fishing at the lake, just as I had when I was a child. We caught frogs (actually, *I* caught the frogs while the boys made faces like they were going to throw up). We played laser tag and went to the community swimming pool. I planned epic Easter egg hunts with live rabbits, handmade chocolates, and hundreds of hand-painted eggs. We took homemade cookies in our picnic basket to the Holcomb Observatory grounds and made s'mores together in our backyard. Yet one crucial aspect of childhood was missing for Jake, an essential ingredient in a wholesome childhood, and that was sports.

I first had the idea of setting up a sports league for autistic kids back when Jake was two. At that time, other kids his age were attending movement and music classes, and even though he was still very much locked in his own world, I took him to a trial class at one of those toddler gyms. I thought he might like the giant padded-vinyl tunnels, the squishy ladders, and the cushioned obstacle courses. He did. What he didn't like was sitting in a circle to sing songs at the beginning and end of class. We had only recently begun Little Light, and Jake hadn't yet learned about circle time, so he kept wandering off to visit a giant inflatable ball they kept in one corner. The behavior wasn't disruptive, however, and as soon as the children were allowed to leave the circle, he would rejoin the group.

While Jake bounced on the trampoline, I struck up a conversation with an older boy of six or seven, who was waiting with his mom for his little sister, who was in the class. He was wearing a handsome karate uniform, and when I complimented him on it, he puffed out his little chest with pride, making sure I saw the yellow belt at his waist.

By the end of the class, Jake was obviously having a great time, and I was very pleased by the progress he'd made. Still, when I told the instructor we'd like to sign up, he told me after an awkward silence that he didn't think Jake was ready to participate. 'If he can't stay with the group, he can't stay in the class,' the instructor said.

It might sound naïve, but that was the first time I realized that Jake's autism meant he wouldn't be able to participate in sports. Maybe it wouldn't have hit me so hard if I hadn't just met that little karate kid, but as I held Jake's hand to cross the parking lot, I was really upset. Would my son never know what it felt like to shout 'Gooooaaaaal!' or to douse the kid who'd pitched the winning game with Gatorade? Would he never know how it felt to slide into home plate, seconds ahead of the tag? Did his autism mean that Jake would never make a touchdown or get grass stains on his soccer uniform?

Five years later, my fears in that parking lot remained valid. Jake had successfully been mainstreamed into regular public school and had lots of friends there and in our neighborhood, but mainstream sports were still largely off-limits to him, as they are for many autistic children. Gym class was the only place where Jake's autism still tripped him up. When they were playing dodgeball, he made for an easy target, and he often felt bullied when his classmates ganged up on him. The idea that he'd agree to participate in a team sport with kids his own age was completely unrealistic. Even Little Leaguers (and, very often, their parents) really want to win. They can be cruel when a kid fumbles the ball or forgets where to run – especially an autistic kid who has physical delays or auditory processing glitches.

I knew from other parents' stories that Jake's experience wasn't unusual. Still, all the things that make sports hard for autistic kids are also why they're so important. Sports are an opportunity to give autistic kids the chance to know how it feels to *play*. Making or missing a goal, catching a fly ball, nailing a free throw – these were all childhood experiences I didn't want Jake to miss. I hadn't thought about sports much until Rachel's question about a program I'd like to do. Then I couldn't stop.

# A Chance to Play

In 2005, with Rachel's help, I decided to start a sports program for autistic kids. But our plan for Youth Sports for Autism almost didn't get off the ground because I couldn't find a suitable meeting place. We couldn't do sports in the garage daycare area because there was barely enough room in there for five little kids and their parents, and our backyard was much too small. So I opened the phone book up to the letter *A* and proceeded to call every church and town hall I found within a sixty-mile radius to see if they had any space to rent.

Every phone call was a variation on the same theme. Oh, yes, they had a room. Of course, they'd love to rent it out on Saturday mornings. But as soon as the word 'autism' was introduced, the person on the other end of the line would say, 'Oh, I didn't realize it was for kids with special needs. We don't have the liability insurance,' or 'We're not wheelchair accessible,' or 'I'll need to run this by our board of directors.' I'd leave my name and number, but I'd never hear from them again.

We didn't need wheelchair access, and we weren't any more of a liability than an Alcoholics Anonymous meeting or a mommy and me music class. And I'm sure that if I'd been calling on behalf of a Girl Scout troop, we wouldn't have needed board vetting. But what could I do?

I'd almost given up when a flyer came in the mail announcing a spring carnival taking place at a nearby church. There were going to be outdoor games and a bouncy house, and it occurred to me that if they had room for all that stuff, they had room for sports. Taking a deep breath, I picked up the phone and gave it one more try: 'Hi, I need a home for a sports program for a group of kids with autism. Would you let me rent some space?'

After months and months of hearing people say no, I almost didn't trust my ears when the building manager said yes. And when I drove into the parking lot, I could barely believe my eyes. If I'd made a wish list of everything I could possibly want or need for sports with these kids, Northview Christian Life Church would have fulfilled every item on the list. Behind the enormous, modern church, there was a long, low outbuilding with two rooms, one with a rudimentary kitchen and a couple of couches where parents and younger siblings could hang out, and a large, empty room that could easily accommodate a group of active kids. Outside, a gently sloping hill led down to a soccer pitch, a track, and a baseball diamond, as well as a couple of basketball courts. Best of all, there was plenty of grass with no designated purpose at all. There a child could lie on his or her back and make a whistle out of a fat blade of grass or pick animals out of the clouds. There were buttercups in the baseball field, enough open space to run fast and far, and nothing but big, beautiful, blue Indiana sky above. It was perfect.

That spring, the church would allow us to come only once a month. My plan was to do a different sport, modified to make it autism accessible, every session. I'd spend the week buying whatever I needed for that week's sport. When our alarm clock sounded at 4:00 a.m. on Saturday morning, we were off. I'd load up the van with the materials for the day's activity and drive over to Northview, where I'd meet Rachel, who would help set up the room. Around nine, the kids would start arriving, and we'd stay most days until the daylight was gone.

As with Little Light, parents had to stay with their kids. Youth Sports for Autism wasn't a drop-off activity (most of the kids weren't independent anyway), and nannies couldn't substitute. This had to be an activity the whole family did together.

For the first time since I'd started working with children, I saw *dads* – dads in sweatpants and baseball caps, playing with their kids. This was an experience many of them thought they'd never have.

I made one thing clear to the families: After a week of non-stop occupational, physical, developmental, and speech therapy, Saturday morning was a time for fun. This was our time to play and be silly, to do all the weekend activities that ordinary families take for granted. Suspicious, parents would show up and ask, 'Really? We're just going to play? No therapy?'

'No therapy,' I'd say. 'We're just going to play.'

When you have a kid with autism, it's not your calendar that needs to be cleared of serious work; it's theirs. Sometimes what you *don't* do is as important as what you do. I'm not sure that I would appreciate that as much if I hadn't grown up in Indiana. We joke about living in the middle of a cornfield, and it's almost literally true. (There's one a block away.) There aren't a lot of parties where we live, but there are a lot of bonfires. And barring the occasional cow or pig, there isn't much to see except sunlight and sky and grass. That's what makes Indiana so special.

And so on those Saturday mornings, we had only one goal: to celebrate our kids and their achievements, no matter how those achievements looked to the outside world. There weren't any expectations for performance, and there was only one rule: When a child took his or her turn, everybody had to cheer, no matter what.

These certainly weren't the fastest kids, or the most athletic. But even if a kid brought a single bowling pin down while holding her dad's hand, we'd break out in cheers. If a low-functioning kid such as Max so much as picked up a bat, we'd run around screaming and high-fiving as if our team had won the World Series. And when Jerod made a touchdown, even if there wasn't another kid anywhere near him to intercept the ball, we'd lift him up on our shoulders as if he'd just won the Heisman Trophy.

The very first day, I came up with an obstacle course that everyone could do. The kids had to pick their way through five hula hoops lying on the ground; cross a mat by stepping on four giant, brightly colored 'feet' that I'd cut out of felt; and then pick up an extra-large beanbag (actually a buckwheat neck and shoulder pillow) and bring it back to the group. I'd bought bags of cheap gold medals at Walmart, the kind you'd put in a little kid's birthday party goody bag. I made sure I had enough for everyone. So even when a child stepped on every single hula hoop and none of the giant feet, he or she got a medal.

A few weeks in, I noticed that Adam, a nonverbal thirteen-year-old, was always clutching that medal in whichever hand his mom wasn't holding. The medals weren't very sturdy to begin with, and his was beginning to look a bit worse for wear, so after class I slipped a couple of spares into his mom's purse. Turning to thank me, she had tears in her eyes. 'You can't imagine how much it means to him to have a medal,' she said. 'He sleeps with it.'

Many of the Little Light graduates participated, but a lot of families we didn't know came, too. Without realizing it, I'd hit on a universal need: Families seemed to have been yearning for a program like this one.

One of the kids who came was a six-year-old boy named Christopher. He was a year younger than Jake (though at least a head taller) and was already a really good basketball player. The two of them clicked instantly. That first week, after his class was over, Christopher didn't want to leave. Later, we learned that he was getting bullied at school. Jake had to stay because he was waiting for me to finish the rest of the classes, so the two of them spent the afternoon together, playing hide-and-seek and mucking around with whatever sports equipment was strewn about from the earlier classes. By the time we were loading all the balls and mats back into our van, the two of them were already fast friends.

Saying our goodbyes, Christopher wrapped his arms around me again and again. He must have hugged me goodbye eight times. It was pretty extraordinary behavior for a kid with autism, and it showed me right away how much this program meant to these kids.

By the end of the month, Jake and Christopher were inseparable. That alone would have made the work we put into the program worthwhile. With his interactions at the university complementing his hang-out time with the kids he knew from the neighborhood and from school, Jake was much less isolated than he had been. But with Christopher, there was a real emotional connection, a bond he didn't have with any other friend.

After a few weeks, I opened the sports league up to all age groups. Many of the kids who showed up were much older than Jake, some of them in their mid- to late teens.

My goal was that every child who came would feel as if he or she was part of a team. To achieve that, I had to make some modifications. Mike commented once that I wasn't making sports autism-friendly so much as I was reimagining sports. With hockey, for example, ice was out. Fine, we'd play hockey on the carpet. But we couldn't use real hockey sticks, or we'd have more casualties than players. Maybe brooms would work. How do you get an autistic kid to like the feel of a broom handle? You wrap it in foam tape to make it squishy. We used a ball instead of a puck, made the goal the kids' height, and painted the posts colors they found appealing.

Mike and I certainly didn't have a lot of money to work with, but as usual my creative, resourceful grandfather served as my inspiration. This was the guy who had welded together a totally watertight, operational submarine for his kids in his driveway.

(My grandmother, terrified that someone would drown, called the scrap metal dealer and had it hauled away while my grandfather was out fishing. But I'm sure it would have been amazing!)

'If God has a job for you, he's going to give you everything you need to get that job done,' Grandpa used to say, pulling his truck over to the side of the road to pick up some discarded timber or metal from someone's trash pile. I often thought of him saying that when I was trawling Walmart or Target for items I could repurpose for sports. I bought huge rolls of Astroturf and cut it into pieces to make miniature golf greens. In the beginning, the kids golfed with balloons. And every holiday – Halloween, Valentine's Day, Christmas – I'd decorate those greens in an appropriate holiday theme.

Bowling is fun, but bowling alleys are incredibly loud, which makes them nightmarish for many autistic kids. Strips of wrapping paper from the dollar store became color-coded bowling lanes. One week Mike and I loaded a case of Mountain Dew into his car so that his co-workers could drink it and get the empty bottles back to me before the weekend. The green empties made for a nice contrast with the clear two-liter bottles that we had already discovered made great bowling pins.

Some people were concerned about my expenditures. 'What about your kids and their college funds? What about your own retirement?' But I'd found my calling, and I always had faith that the money we needed would come in due time. Neither Mike nor I had grown up with much. We never even thought we'd own our own home. Everything we had seemed like a gift, and it felt like a further blessing that we could fight misconceptions about autism and help the families who were living with it. Thankfully, Michael was not only on board but also incredibly good-natured about it. We'd be at the hardware store, and he'd say, laughing and shaking his head, 'I guess my bonus is going toward Astroturf!'

I called in every favor I could from friends in our community. We had the soccer coach from the high school come to teach the kids soccer. Again, we used balloons for balls at first so that the kids could learn how to pass and make a goal. When it became clear that broom hockey was a hit (Jake was the goalie!), we got members of the U. S. Hockey League's Indiana Ice to come and play on the carpet with the kids.

When we finally moved out to the baseball diamond, I maxed out my credit card to buy different-colored T-shirts with the team names on them, so that the kids would know how it felt to be on a team. For many of the lower-functioning kids, sitting in that dugout was the first time they'd been apart from a parent or caregiver. But they were fine, because they were with their teams, and, of course, their parents were cheering them on like crazy from the bleachers. By that time, we all felt like one big, happy family.

I'd learned a lot from Little Light. I knew that the activities had to be attractive to the autistic brain, so I created lots of visual rules. Twenty different colors of duct tape created boundaries on the mats. Almost everything we did had a sensory component. There were inflatable balls, squishy mats, and balloons. I scattered those sensory toys all over the silky parachute covering the floor so that the children would be enticed to sit there with me.

It's true that all these things were designed to make the activities appeal to autistic kids. But I also believe that it's through our senses that we heal, and that's true not just for autistic kids and other people with special needs, but for everybody.

Before Jake was born, I had a sweet little girl in the daycare named Rose whom I grew to rely on as a role model for the other kids. When her father Jim's life partner was diagnosed with cancer, Jim completely fell apart. He was so focused on taking care of his partner and Rose that he didn't have any time to take care of himself. He was such a mess, I worried that he'd lose his job. One morning I sat him down and covered the dark circles under his eyes with concealer from my makeup bag.

Not surprisingly, Rose began to be affected by the strain. She seemed listless and cranky, and she wasn't taking a leadership role with the other children anymore. I grew concerned: Rose was my responsibility, and she was not flourishing.

When Jim dropped off Rose one day, his hands were shaking so badly that he couldn't get Rose's lunch out of his briefcase. I put my hands on his shoulders, looked him in the eyes, and said, 'You are not okay, and if you keep going this way, your family is not going to be okay. You need to heal your own spirit so that you can take care of the people in your life.'

'I'm not sure I know how,' Jim said, distraught.

'Please, may I make some suggestions? On your way home from work tonight, buy a chicken, along with some rosemary and sage.'

'But I don't know how to cook a chicken!'

'Turn the oven on to three hundred fifty degrees, put the herbs inside the chicken, and smear some butter and a little salt on the outside. Cook it for an hour and a half. While the chicken is cooking and all those wonderful smells are wafting through your house, take the softest blanket you have and put it in the dryer for ten minutes. Then wrap that comfy blanket around yourself, turn on some music you love, and look at a family photo album. Don't get up until that chicken is done. When it is, sit down with your family and have dinner.'

I then sent him on his way with a pair of my own fluffy chenille socks.

Jim needed to reconnect with his senses. I firmly believe that we experience life through them. But when we're too busy or going through a traumatic situation such as Jim was, we neglect them. We don't think about the way that cashmere scarf keeps us warm when we're frantic to get to an appointment on time. We don't take the time to search the radio for a fun eighties station before we pull out of a parking space. Instead, we're wound up too tight to feel much of anything at all.

The Jim who came to drop off Rose the next day was a different man – rejuvenated, and more rested and peaceful than I'd seen him in months. Yes, the rest of that year was still very hard for him and his family, but Jim had a rescue remedy he could use whenever he felt depleted, overwhelmed, or depressed. He could make himself physically warm and comfortable. He could make his house smell like a home. He could nourish himself and his family with a home-cooked meal.

Indulging the senses isn't a luxury, but a necessity. We *have* to walk barefoot in the grass. We *have* to eat clean snow. We *have* to let warm sand run through our fingers. We *have* to lie on our backs and feel the sun on our faces.

That was why the kids who came to the sports program didn't have to do anything but play. A lot of people were skeptical about this approach, and some of the families who'd been with us at Little Light left to use that time for more therapy. A lot of people were concerned that Jake wouldn't get what he needed because of my single-minded focus on play and ordinary childhood experiences. Compared to more formal practices, my strategy didn't seem like much: 'Hit a ball to your friend, and I'll cheer.' What kind of therapy was that? But I was like a broken record about it: 'You don't have to do anything. Just *play*.'

And it worked. I began seeing improvements right away. Activities that had seemed completely out of the question when we started, such as relay races, became not only possible but fun. In the pictures from that first year, you can see most of the kids wandering around, totally lost in their own worlds. In the ones we took around Christmas, though, you can see that they'd started to get it, sitting in their spots on the parachute, facing me and paying attention.

Once a month wasn't enough; we needed to meet weekly. The church said that we could, as long as we cleaned the buildings we were using before we left. I had to laugh. Twice a week when I was growing up, my sister and I would help my grandmother clean the interior of the church that she and my grandfather had built. She'd put a kerchief over her hair, load her bucket of supplies into the car, and drive my sister and me over there so that we could push the sweeper, wipe off the hymnals, and dust and wax the pews. For my grandmother, this was a type of community service.

In a similar way, Youth Sports for Autism was community service for me. Mike and I had stopped going to church in the years after Jake's diagnosis. (This is very common among families with autistic children.) One Sunday morning, there had been an incident at church. While I was standing in the lobby with Jake, the mother of a girl I'd gone to high school with spotted me. Shrieking with delight and trailing perfume, she swooped toward us, her brightly colored shawl sailing out behind her. As she grabbed my face to plant a kiss on my cheek, Jake completely flipped out. He lay flat on the ground, screaming at the top of his lungs. When I tried to pick him up, he kicked at me, grabbing and ripping my silk dress.

It's one thing when your child loses it in Target, but it's another thing altogether when it happens in church. I was completely humiliated. Everyone stopped to stare at us, and someone even made a joke about sprinkling holy water on him. We finally made it down the hallway into the restroom, where I sat him up on the counter between the sinks, rubbing his back and wiping his eyes, trying to reassure him that everything was okay. Eventually, he loosened his grip, releasing sweaty handfuls of my dress.

I believe that tantrums aren't a symptom of autism, but a

symptom of the failure to understand autism. It wasn't that Jake didn't *want* to go to church; it was that he *couldn't* go. The experience was just too much for him. If I had forced him to go, I would have only ended up with a miserable child and another torn dress. And if he couldn't go to church, then – for a little while anyway – neither could I. I picked him up off that counter, and with the whole church watching, I walked back through the lobby and out the door. Then I put Jake in the car, and we left.

Although we were back in regular church attendance, I found that doing service through sports brought me a tremendous sense of peace and community. I thought of my grandfather often on those Saturday mornings. He had instilled in me a sense of play and an understanding of its importance. He'd also taught me to see my own misfortune as an opportunity to create a community rather than closing myself off from one. It was through his example that I'd learned that helping others means you are never alone.

The families of these autistic children hadn't taken joy in anything for a long time. The parents were exhausted and demoralized, and their wonderful children had been told over and over they were worthless. Hadn't it been practically impossible for me to find a place that would even allow them on the property? Bringing these families together and helping to put some joy back into their lives meant everything to me. In a way, Youth Sports for Autism was my church.

Our whole family loved it. Wesley was in his element. He could do even more extravagant running flips than usual on the mats we used to cover the church floors. Ethan was growing up around all different kinds of people, and his steady, calm demeanor made him a favorite with the older autistic kids. And I could see Jake starting to shine.

When people ask me today how Jake can be so social and at ease with people despite his autism, I tell them that we owe a lot to sports. On those Saturdays, we weren't training him for the Mathematical Olympiads or taking him to the science fair. Instead, we were out on the soccer field or the baseball diamond or the basketball court, prioritizing friendship, social interaction, community, teamwork, and self-esteem. In sports, Jake wasn't a prodigy or an autistic kid with physical delays. He was a kid standing in the outfield, scuffing the rubber sole of his sneaker into the sunburnt grass, exactly like thousands of other kids all over America.

Very quickly, sports became more than just sports. Christopher had started a trend by sticking around after class. Every week, I noticed that more and more families were hanging around, too. They'd spill out onto the soccer field, lazily kicking a ball around or throwing a Frisbee. They'd bring lunch, and many of them would stay until the sun went down. In the winter, people would bring sleds, and the kids would shoot down the hills over and over until a steaming mug of hot chocolate with marshmallows was the only thing that could thaw out their little hands and cheeks.

We started a Facebook group. Every few days, someone would post a story of triumph, always with the same coda: 'Take that, autism!'

It had been a long time since a lot of these families had laughed together, since they'd felt hopeful, since they'd teased one another and hung out without worrying. I loved seeing the moms sitting on the bleachers, hands wrapped around a cup of coffee, gossiping with their friends, while their husbands played horse on the basketball court with the kids. A lot of these people had forgotten the importance of childhood, of simply having fun.

I understood that. For a while, Michael and I had forgotten it, too. But then we had remembered, and now we could help these families learn to have fun again, too.

# A Dream Come True

Most couples share dreams about the future that they discuss at night when they're lying in bed and the rest of the house is quiet. For some people, it might be a luxurious cruise to the Caribbean or winning the lottery. For Michael and me, our dream was a little closer to home.

In 2006, I won a GasAmerica Hometown Hero Award for Youth Sports for Autism. The prize was quite a bit of free gasoline, which we were excited about. But the word 'hero' embarrassed me. On the news, I saw soldiers leaving their families to fight for freedom and democracy in Afghanistan. Our next-door neighbor is a firefighter. Every day he goes to work, he faces the possibility of risking his life to save someone else's. Those people are the real heroes, not a mom in capri pants making miniature golf greens.

It was Michael who helped me gain perspective, and galvanized by the award, I was determined to go even further. We'd seen that sports could be transformative for autistic kids. How much more amazing would it be if we had a permanent home for these activities? We'd had to move Jake and Wesley into one bedroom so that we could keep the storage bins crammed with sports equipment in the other one. We'd jerry-rigged the church space to make it work, but we would be able to do incredible things if we had a place of our own.

Sports had exposed us to older children with autism, which meant that we could see into the future for some of the younger ones. Being a teenager is hard. Being an autistic teenager can be *really* hard. We understood that there would be a time when

Jake and Christopher and their friends would be in need of a respite from whatever social difficulties they might encounter at school. In that respect, the search for our own sports space felt a bit like a race against time.

Little Light and Youth Sports for Autism had become a safe haven for Jake and his friends. Michael and I wanted to take this a step further and create a recreation center where autistic children and teenagers could play sports or watch movies, get help with their homework, or play a game of tag without anyone trying to 'fix' their autism. Many years before, when we'd needed an official name for the charity behind Little Light, Melanie had suggested that we call it Jacob's Place because it sounded friendly, not like a hospital or a treatment center. We'd only ever used that name on our tax returns, but it was the perfect name for a recreation center. Making Jacob's Place a reality became our dream.

The sports program had grown so rapidly that the church space we were using was badly strained at the seams during the winter months. Instead of cutting back, we chose to see this as an opportunity to grow. In the summer of 2008, we sold one of our cars, cashed out Michael's 401(k), and went looking for Jacob's Place.

We had to look in the country. I had my heart set on a whole building, but our budget was laughable. One real estate agent actually did laugh when she heard what we had to spend: $15,000 for the building itself and another $5,000 for whatever improvements or equipment we'd need. That wasn't nearly enough money to buy anything close by, even in Indiana.

At the time, Michael had to drive all over the area for his job, and he kept an eye out for anything that looked promising. One day he called home and said, 'Kris, you have to come. I think I've found it.'

We'd bought a beat-up Ford Bronco for $500 to replace the

car we'd sold. It was a noisy eyesore, with more rust on it than paint. The kids loved it because you could see the road passing underneath the car through the holes in the floor – sort of like the car the Flintstones drove. I trusted it only to get me back and forth to the grocery store, so I was a little nervous when I looked at a map and saw how far away the building was. But I clunked along and finally made it to the tiny town of Kirklin, Indiana – blink and you'll miss it – about an hour from our house.

Transportation anxiety aside, the drive there was beautiful, much of it on single-lane gravel roads through real farm country. I imagined this trip could be a kind of therapy in itself for stressed parents and kids.

When I got there, I saw Michael's car parked at the end of the main street, which seemed mostly to be made up of abandoned storefronts. He was standing in front of the most dilapidated brick building I'd ever seen. It looked old. I mean really old – like nineteenth-century old. You could plainly see that it hadn't gotten any love or attention since at least the middle of the twentieth century. There were no intact windows, and the back wall had caved in and was falling down. There was no sidewalk outside, except for the occasional chunk of concrete sticking up between the weeds.

Keeping my game face on, I tried the door to the side entrance. 'That door's not so good, actually,' Michael said.

Once I got it open, I could see what he meant. There was nothing behind it but a gaping black pit. One more step would have sent me plummeting fifteen feet into the debris-filled basement. (I had nightmares for months about falling into that hole.) It got worse. The entire second floor in the back of the building had sunk and collapsed, so that it hung like a suspended bowl over the first floor. There was no way you could step in there without the threat of the whole second floor collapsing on you. Peering into the darkness with our flashlights from the safety of the doorway, we could see a bunch of creepy antique medical equipment and furniture left over from the building's time as the town doctor's office.

The place was filthy, it was in the middle of nowhere, and it was obviously unsafe. But there was a lot of history there, and more to be made. When I closed my eyes, I could see it filled with the families we had come to know and love so much through Little Light and Youth Sports for Autism. In my mind's eye, I could see the moms hugging one another, relieved to have a place to relax and share their worries after a long week. I could see groups of kids in beanbag chairs watching movies, and others paired off over chessboards and card tables. And where that bowed second story hung so precariously in the back, I could see Jake and Christopher alternating free throws from the half-court line of a big, beautiful, newly painted basketball court.

I looked at Michael and smiled. 'This is it,' I said. 'This is the rec center.'

Jake and Christopher were inseparable by then. I had also become close friends with Chris's grandmother Phyllis, who was raising him. That summer, the two of us would hang out by their swimming pool and talk while the boys swam. Those were rare moments of relaxation for me, and I treasured them. Their family owned a car dealership and lived in a huge home, complete with outdoor and indoor basketball courts, a pool, and an elevator. Of course, Jake loved to go there. But Christopher loved to come over to our little house, too, to roast hot dogs and make s'mores in our backyard. He was incredibly fun to be with, the type of person who can turn even a disappointing situation like a rained-out picnic into a grand adventure.

Christopher and Jake had bonded over the fact that they didn't always fit in. It can be difficult for an autistic kid to distinguish between kids laughing *with* him and those laughing *at* him. When Christopher told a joke and the boys at school laughed, he couldn't always tell what it meant. Had the joke gone over well, or was the laughter unkind? Jake's years in elementary school and all our efforts to bring friends into his life had helped him. By the time he met Christopher, he felt more comfortable socially and could help his younger friend navigate his way through the awkwardness of that age, the uncertainty of never quite knowing what other kids thought or felt. There were no walls between them.

Jake's mentoring came to be a big part of their friendship. Jake was always saying, 'Here, learn this. You need to know this weird little skill, or it's going to be hard for you to get along.' On the very first day they met, Jake taught Christopher to hula-hoop. It seems like such a small thing – people don't need to know how to hula-hoop. But there was an element of urgency to it, because every skill that a kid like Christopher has is one less thing he can be teased about, one less thing that sets him apart.

Christopher also helped Jake. He was much bigger than Jake and had more natural skill at basketball. Jake's skills got a lot better under his tutelage, and he came to understand the pleasure of practicing a sport.

Christopher was also obsessed with magic. Jake loved to write letters to Christopher in code that he would have to decipher, and Christopher delighted in learning obscure tricks and demonstrating them for Jake, who would then have to figure out how they worked. Christopher's dexterity and mastery of the principles of magic improved, and the tricks he did got harder and harder. The harder they got, the happier Jake became: It was rare for someone his own age to present him with a puzzle that truly challenged him. Sometimes the two of them would collaborate on an illusion together. For example, Jake helped Christopher design an elaborate trick that required a number of mirrors to be set at precisely the right angles, an activity that was right up Jake's alley.

They went to different schools, but they saw each other every Saturday at sports and again the next day at church, and they called each other on the phone every night to talk about sports. I'm strict about everyone sitting down for dinner together, but I was so glad to see Jake have such a good friend that I'd often make him a turkey sandwich and cut up some veggies for him so that he could eat while he and Christopher talked on the phone.

Michael and I quickly realized that we'd bitten off more than we could chew as far as the rec center was concerned. The $5,000 we had left over to pay for repairs to the building was all we had in the world. I remember Michael looking at our bank statement, shaking his head, and saying, 'If our furnace blows at home, we're in for a cold winter.' Mike's father is a carpenter, and he was genuinely alarmed by the scope of the work. The first time he walked into the building, he said, 'You cannot afford to get involved in this. Seriously, don't walk away from this – *run*.'

We didn't listen. Like a lot of people in America at the time, we'd taken advantage of the credit bubble. Michael had been promoted a number of times, and the daycare was booming. I had visions of expanding it, maybe even creating a little school out of it. With Ethan's arrival, we'd also badly outgrown our little house. At one point, I realized that the whole family couldn't actually fit in the living room together unless one of the kids was perched on the arm of the couch or sitting on the floor at our feet. If we couldn't comfortably watch a movie together, we needed more space.

The original plan had been that we'd live in the rec center and fix it up at the same time, but the town wouldn't run electricity or water into the building until it was up to code. I don't mind roughing it, but raising three young boys in a tent inside an uninhabitable building seemed a little extreme, even for me.

So we took out a mortgage and put money down on a house being built in a new subdivision in Westfield, a middle-class suburb carved out of the farmland north of Indianapolis. Without exaggeration, the new house was my dream home, a place I never in a million years could have imagined living in, let alone owning. There was enough space for all of us – even more than we needed. In the plans, the kitchen, dining room, and living room were open to one another, so we could all be together in the same space. Nobody would need to be banished from the kitchen so that I could get dinner on the table. Ethan was very interested in cooking and baking, and at four he could even make some basic meals by himself. When I looked at the plans, I smiled to imagine the feasts he'd soon be able to produce.

The new house would also have a huge garage, which could easily accommodate more daycare children and an assistant. Michael and I agreed that even though it would cost us a little money, we'd hold on to the old house until we moved into the new one. I wanted there to be minimal disruption for the daycare kids as a result of the move.

As we watched the house being built over the spring and summer, we came to know our new neighbors. We'd stop by to see what progress the builders had made and then have a picnic in the little playground on the banks of the pond situated right across the street from our lot. While the kids swung and climbed, Michael and I talked to the other people who'd come by to see the progress on their own homes.

The day we moved in, I honestly felt like a burglar. I'd grown up in a poor neighborhood on the east side of Indianapolis, and I kept waiting for someone to come along and tell me I didn't get to live in this gorgeous house after all. Parts of my house still make me smile every day. The fact that Mike and I each have our own sink in our bathroom makes me feel like the queen of England.

It became clear within the first day or two that the open kitchen–dining room–living room area was where we were going to spend most of our time. Friends who stopped by with housewarming presents would walk in, plop down on a couch, and end up staying for dinner.

We'd been right about the community, too. I didn't have any choice but to meet our next-door neighbor, Narnie, and neither does anyone else who crosses her path. (While out shopping with her recently, I overheard her introduce herself to someone while I was in the changing room. In the time it took me to try on two dresses, Narnie had found out everything about this woman's upcoming wedding, her fiancé, and which of her emotional needs he did or didn't meet. *There she goes again*, I thought.)

As soon as our moving truck pulled up to the house that first day, out bounded Narnie from the house next door. And would you believe that she started unpacking the truck? Completely unself-conscious, with a wide-open face and a deep, full belly laugh, she had my closet in order by the time I'd introduced myself, and I hadn't known her an hour before she was doing my dishes. There's no such thing as privacy around this NRA-card-carrying, yoga-practicing grandmother, and that's a good thing, because when she comes into your life, she will be there for you when you really need her, every single time.

Having a neighbor who would come over for a cup of tea every afternoon (cocoa on Wednesdays) made it official: I had everything I'd ever wanted. Our new home was filled with the people I loved, and slowly but surely we were building the rec center we'd talked about for so long. I told Michael, 'Okay, I'm done. This is it for me. I have every single thing I've ever hoped for.'

Then the recession hit, and suddenly the rec center was the very least of our concerns.

# Dark Times

The entire state of Indiana was hit hard by the recession, and fast.

Michael was an early casualty. One night while I was in the kitchen making dinner, I heard something on the local news about a Circuit City closing. I was halfway across the room, still drying my hands, when I heard Wesley ask, 'Hey, is that Dad's store?'

It was. The two of us stood there and watched Michael lose his job on TV.

That store was more than a job for Mike. He'd come into a difficult situation there. It was located in a very run-down neighborhood and was notorious within the company for having lost more merchandise to theft one year than it sold. But Mike saw a lot of potential in the staff. He promoted the hardest workers, got rid of the bad apples, reorganized the store, and provided incentives. Most notably, he promised to do a backflip in front of the registers whenever anyone exceeded his or her sales quota.

Within six months of his arrival, it looked and felt like a completely different place. The next year, everybody who worked there celebrated Thanksgiving together. Mike had been so successful at turning the store around and had created such a dynamic sales force that Circuit City had begun to talk to him about developing a staff training program that he could take to other stores.

And then it was gone. People who are worried about losing their jobs don't buy television sets. So the store was shut down.

The community Mike had fostered, so close it felt more like a family, was disbanded. For a few weeks, Michael worked for the liquidator, systematically dismantling the store he'd built and selling it off piece by piece, a sickening experience. When that work was over, there was nothing more for him to do.

I'd gotten a little money from my grandfather that we'd used for the down payment on our house. Because of that, we were able to stay there. But not everyone in the neighborhood was so lucky. One by one, the houses around us went up for sale. Every time I left the house, I'd see a new For Sale sign flapping in the breeze, telling me that another one of the wonderful families I'd met that summer was losing its dream.

Michael and I were in financial trouble, too. Between the rec center and the new house, we'd spent every single penny we had. Nobody could get a loan, so any idea we'd had about selling our old house went out the window. That meant we had to carry on with two mortgages on one income. Then we had to support two mortgages on *no* income, because as more and more families in our area were affected by the economic downturn, the numbers in the daycare shrank, too. It seemed like every day, another parent, face white and tense, would come in to break the news that he or she had lost his or her job.

Daycare had always been steady work. Since I'd opened my doors, there had always been more kids who wanted to come to the daycare than I could take, and that was never more true than after the success of Little Light. But during the recession, neither my reputation nor the success we'd had with the kids was relevant. If you don't have a job, you don't need someone to watch your children. And in working-class Indiana in 2008, it seemed as if nobody had a job anymore. I hung on with one or two kids for a while, and then those kids were gone, too. When I closed the door behind the last one, I was, for the first time, truly afraid.

When Mike had lost his job, I'd found ways to cut corners, including making big pots of chili for the family. (Jake and I looked it up: Chili was invented during the Great Depression of the 1930s as a way to stretch a little bit of meat.) When the daycare numbers dwindled and I couldn't even afford to make chili anymore, I would put a big pot of water on the stove and throw five packs of ramen (three for a dollar) in so that we could still have a family dinner together. To make it fun, we'd ask the kids three trivia questions, with Michael imitating the Soup Nazi from the sitcom *Seinfeld*, wiggling his eyebrows and making faces and berating the kids in a crazy accent if they got the questions wrong. 'No soup for you!' he'd thunder, making them laugh until they were about to wet their pants. Both of us were determined to keep the mood light for the kids, no matter how scared we felt.

That winter was one of the coldest on record in a state notorious for unforgiving winters. A lot of the time, we couldn't afford to heat our house. To stay warm, we'd pile onto the big couch under a load of blankets, watching movies and cuddling with one another. Many people around us burned old tables and chairs for heat. A lot of people didn't have electricity, and the people who did weren't using it. Every house was dark. There were no lights on anywhere. I remember walking through Walmart, the aisles cleared of everything except necessities: camping gear, coffee, fire logs, lighter fluid, water, cheap electric blankets for those without heat – and beer. The store didn't bother to stock anything else. It looked like an army surplus store.

Then I got a call from my brother, who had been living in our old house. He'd lost his job working construction, and there was no hope of another one. There were lines around the block for those jobs. He'd been taking care of my dad, who'd had some health issues, including open-heart surgery that winter.

When it became clear that nobody was going to buy the house, Ben had offered to move in with some of his friends and fix it up in the hope that we could find someone to rent it. But they didn't have enough money to heat it, and one particularly cold night – with a windchill of minus thirty – while my brother was sleeping somewhere warmer, a pipe burst, and the equivalent of an Olympic-sized pool's worth of water rushed through the house.

It was a catastrophe. The entire house was gone, just gone, on the inside. There were no walls left, the ceiling was on the floor, and the stairs went up into nowhere. Everywhere you looked, there was dripping water overlaid with ice. The drywall still standing bulged with moisture. When I opened the door and saw the damage, my knees gave way.

Like everyone else, our insurance company was in serious financial trouble and didn't know if it was going to be able to stay in business. At first the company disputed that we were insured, but even when we'd had to eat ramen to survive, we'd always managed to pay our bills. Still, the company sat on our claim, and sat on it, and sat on it, while our flooded house slowly rotted from the inside out. I was frantic. With every passing week, the house became more uninhabitable, but we didn't have a single cent in the bank to fix it.

At that point, I was babysitting for a lower hourly rate than I'd charged when I'd first opened my daycare sixteen years earlier. I let everyone know that I was available anytime – nights, weekends – for anyone who needed help. Moms I knew from Little Light and from sports would bring their kids to me if they were still employed. That was the unspoken code: If you had a job, you looked out for those who didn't. To avoid feeling like charity cases, we baked for one another, or sewed, or cleaned one another's homes. I watched people's kids. Still, there wasn't much money to go around.

For the first time in my life, I was hungry. I bought vitamins for the boys because I could no longer regularly afford meat. If there was meat, I would pretend to have a stomachache and push my plate away so that they would have more. New winter clothes were out of the question, and every piece of clothing we had was mended within an inch of its life. Wesley, my little kamikaze, looked the worst. There were patches on top of patches on his pants. It made me sick to watch the boys heading down for the school bus with an inch of wrist showing between their parka sleeves and their gloves, but I knew too-small coats were better than none, and a lot of people had none.

By Christmas, we were barely making it, and the false cheer of holiday decorations going up in the empty stores only highlighted how desperate and frightened everyone felt. We're not big on Christmas presents in our family. Christmas is a religious holiday for us, and we tend to focus on charity. But when our church gave us a box to fill for the poor, we had to write a note saying that we had only prayers to send. Our pastor understood. We certainly weren't the only ones with nothing to give that year. But without question, that was the hardest thing for me to do.

Still, we had our own little miracle. First thing Christmas morning, when Mike went out to shovel the driveway, he popped his head back in the door and called quietly for me so that the kids wouldn't hear. A bright red sack sat on our snow-covered porch – a Santa sack. I looked at him, and my heart dropped into my stomach. What had he done? I knew for a fact we had $32 in our bank account, and there was no money coming in for a while. If that was gone, there would be nothing for groceries.

But Mike was looking at me the same way. 'Oh, no, Kris,' he whispered, 'what did you do?'

I shook my head, and then the answer hit us both at the exact same time: *Narnie*.

Inside the sack, there were three brightly wrapped presents, and they were the perfect presents: a Lego set for Ethan, a skateboard for Wesley, and a telescope for Jake. And when Narnie brought her cup of coffee over later as she usually did, innocently asking us how our Christmas morning had been, I wept with gratitude in her arms. It remains the single kindest gesture I have ever known, and it sealed Narnie as an unofficial member of our family.

That was a bright spot, but it was short-lived. Once so empowering, Facebook only brought news of more suffering. Everyone was broke and afraid. Every night on the news, there was another plant closing, another factory shutting down, signaling disaster for another family we knew. The President visited, and when the president comes to Indiana, you know you're in trouble. I heard at one point that half the state was unemployed, which seemed like a conservative estimate from where I was sitting, maybe because everyone we knew was working-class like us. Nobody had anything, but we had to keep our chins up, and so no matter how bad the news got, I'd always post, 'Any of you are welcome over for a pot of ramen anytime!!!!'

By January, it looked as if our worst fears might come true. My sister, Stephanie, and I stayed up late talking on the phone, seriously considering what we would do if we lost our homes. The threat was real, and it was happening to people we knew. One of my daycare moms had lost her house and had ended up on the street with her kids. She had been taken in by friends, but nobody was sure how long the arrangement would last, as the other family was struggling, too. Stephanie and I figured we could always take our families out to the church my grandfather had built and live up in the unused choir loft for a while. I was calm during the conversation, but after we hung up, I started shaking and couldn't stop. The prospect of being homeless, of our children being homeless, terrified me.

The weather was unrelenting. Christopher, Jake, and Wes spent every weekend building complicated tunnel systems through the snow covering our yard and developing elaborate spy games to go with them. Because it was so cold, the igloo safe house they constructed became a permanent part of our property. The moms I knew were all worried about the driving conditions, but the schools got paid for lunches, and so they stayed open, even though we couldn't even get down to the end of our own driveway without falling. (Wesley flattened a cardboard box so he could 'surf' down the icy hill.) More than once after I saw the bus fishtail down the road toward our stop, I told my boys I didn't care about their attendance records and brought them right back home with me.

Our Super Bowl party was a brief bright spot in that horrible winter. The Super Bowl is always a big deal in our house. Michael loves football, and so do our boys. Every year, I put on a big feast – wings and potato skins and cupcakes decorated to look like footballs – and people come over to watch the game with us. That year, the feast was just a bowl of pretzels, but I was grateful anyway. At least we could all be together. We made a party out of it, cheering and screaming at the television, and the boys competed to see which one of them could make up the silliest cheerleader-style dance.

Even Christopher was there – sort of. Phyllis hadn't been able to drive him over as planned, so Jake called and put him on speakerphone, and he stayed on the phone with us all day. He and Mike pretended to high-five through the phone, and Christopher even opened a bag of pretzels on his end. After a while, I forgot that he wasn't actually there. That was a great day.

Soon after, I received an official letter from the town of Kirklin containing more bad news. Our rec center building was a hazard, the letter said, and the town had no choice but to demolish it. I closed my eyes and saw a wrecking ball swinging through the basketball court we'd hoped to build. The kicker? Not only were they going to destroy our building, but they expected us to pay them for the privilege of doing it. As I stood there with the letter in my hand, my eyes still closed, I thought, *It can't get worse than this*.

A week later, I'd have given everything to take that thought back.

# Jealous Angels

Late in February, I picked up the phone to hear my friend Rachel's voice telling me to turn on the TV. I rolled my eyes and said, 'Don't tell me. More bad news?' expecting to see another factory closure, heartbreak for somebody else we knew. But the bitter joke died on my lips when I heard nothing but a sob on the other end.

I switched on the television to the local news station and watched as the words 'Breaking News: Spring Mill Elementary Student Struck and Killed by School Bus' went by on the crawl. Even after I saw his name, even after they'd flashed his school picture up on the screen, I still didn't believe they could be talking about Christopher.

His school bus had dropped him off in the school parking lot, not at the curbside spot where Christopher was used to arriving. In a story that will be nauseatingly recognizable to any parent of a child with autism, Christopher was disoriented by the change and tried to make his way between parked cars over to the building entrance he knew best. While doing so, he ran into another bus lane and was hit by another school bus.

I don't remember the rest of that day at all. I was in shock. How were we going to tell Jake?

When he got home, there was a group of women from the neighborhood and from the sports program in our living room, all standing in a horseshoe around the television. Narnie was crying and rubbing my back, but I was still too stunned to move or speak.

'Was there a bus accident?' Jake asked, scanning each of our faces for clues. Almost as if in answer, Christopher's school picture came up again on the screen. I watched Jake's face as comprehension hit, and then he threw himself on the couch and made a noise I have never heard another human being make, a noise I hope to God I will never hear again.

He stayed there, squashed underneath the cushions of the couch, for hours. Eventually, Mike and I got him out of there, and Jake and I drove over to see Phyllis. We were close enough that I didn't even knock before going into her house. I found her sitting motionless in the living room, still in the bathrobe and slippers she'd been wearing that morning, while the phone rang and rang. Jake took one of her hands, and I took the other, and the three of us sat there together without speaking for the better part of the night.

Jake's grief over the loss of his best friend threw his autism into high relief. His sorrow was so intense, so all-consuming, that I think he simply didn't have the emotional resources to navigate socially the way he could most of the time. He had room for only one emotion, grief, and the fact that other people could operate on a wider bandwidth was beyond his comprehension.

He was genuinely shocked, for instance, by the behavior of the other mourners at the wake. The mood in the room was one of complete devastation, of course. But there was also a buffet, as there usually is, and people were making themselves plates and sitting down and eating together. To me and almost everyone else there, this was a welcome signal of community and fellowship, of people embracing life even in the face of this horrifying tragedy, but it was incomprehensible to Jake. The idea that anyone had room for anything other than grief – that a person could feel this tremendous loss and also eat a piece of chicken, or ask a question about how someone's grandkids were getting along at school – was inconceivable to him. He sat in the receiving line with Phyllis for most of the afternoon, accepting condolences like the family member he'd become.

On the car ride home, Jake said, 'I didn't think angels got jealous.'

I didn't understand. 'What are you talking about, honey? Angels don't get jealous.'

'I think they do,' he said. 'They came and got my best friend because they wanted to play with him.'

After we buried Christopher, it was like a hush fell over the world. I couldn't wrap my head around the idea that such a happy, gentle spirit was gone. It seemed impossible, a violation of every principle in nature. When I opened my eyes in the morning, for a few precious moments I would forget that this light had been put out. Then I would remember, and the hurt would start again.

A few weeks later, I came home to a message from a man named Chip Mann. He was interested in restoring some of the older buildings in Kirklin, he said, and he wanted to talk to us about ours.

I was numb as I drove out to meet him. The rolling landscape that had always brought me such peacefulness and joy now seemed barren and ugly. I understood what people meant when they said they felt dead inside.

I pulled up in front of the building. As soon as I stepped out of the car, a tall, commanding man with gray hair and piercing blue eyes strode up, hand extended to shake mine. I handed the keys to the building to Chip without meeting his eyes. 'You can go in, but I can't walk through it with you. I can't bear it,' I told him.

Watching his disappearing back, I thought, *There it goes. This is the end of the dream for these kids.*

'I'll give you a thousand dollars,' he said decisively when he came out. It was a fraction of what we'd paid and put into it, but what choice did I have? A thousand dollars was better than paying the town to tear it down, and our own finances had been so dire for so long, even that pittance seemed like a fortune.

Suddenly, I started to cry. Standing in the middle of the street in front of a man I'd met minutes before, tears streamed off the end of my nose. Without meaning to, I blurted out all our plans for the building. Through my sobs, I told Chip how Mike and I had talked for years about building a recreation center for autistic kids such as my son Jake, and how we'd put every penny we had toward it. I told him how we had wanted to make Jacob's Place a safe place for them, a place where they could be themselves. I told him we'd recently lost one of those kids, a really special one.

'I'm sorry,' I said finally, wiping my face as best as I could. 'I guess I'm not in a very good place in my life right now.'

Chip looked at me for a long time, and then he took my arm and started walking toward another old commercial building directly across the street. There had been a fire in there, and it was almost as dilapidated as mine was.

'I own this building, too,' he said. 'Are you telling me if I put a basketball court in here, you'll find kids to play on it?'

Still sniffling, I nodded.

'Okay, then. We're going to do this. I'm going to build Jacob's Place.'

Chip was a successful entrepreneur, bringing the same acumen he'd used to create a series of thriving businesses to revitalizing Kirklin. For a long time, I didn't completely believe he was real. This was a prayer answered. The construction crew got started that spring.

In March, Michael got a job with T-Mobile. We all breathed a sigh of relief. At least we could put food on the table. Then, after months of refusing every single contractor's bid we'd gotten, the insurance company finally sent us a check for the damage to the old house. It was drastically less than it should have been – the amount the adjuster authorized would barely be enough to repair the floor – but we didn't have any choice in the matter, and it felt as if we were at least on the right track.

That terrible winter wasn't done with us yet, though. The contractors we hired claimed that they'd have to move into the house in order to do the work for so little money. They did, along with their terrifying dogs, so we could never get in to see how it was going. They ended up stealing the first two payments we made to them and taking off with everything in the house they could remove: light fixtures, door handles, radiator covers, the cabinets we'd bought to replace the ones lost in the flood. They set a fire in the garage, and then they were gone.

It was a devastating blow, especially when we'd thought things were starting to look up. By that time, summer was officially starting, and as the weather heated up, the mold in the house took over. Michael and I decided that we had to try to do the work ourselves. We'd buy the cheapest materials on a Lowe's card and get by as best as we could. Michael put the word out to all of our friends on Facebook: 'Please help. We have to fix the house. If you have any skills at all, please come and lend a hand.'

The next Saturday, hundreds of people showed up, almost all of them the parents of kids I'd helped over the years through the daycare, Little Light, and the sports program. It was like an old-fashioned barn raising. People brought their own tools and anything they'd been able to find in their basements or garages that we might be able to use: cabinets, lights, paint. Some of them brought friends with them ('This is my next-door neighbor, Al, and he's going to do all your grout.') They stripped the walls and put up new drywall. They brought new carpeting and laid it. As this amazing community of people rebuilt my house, I cried and passed out slices of pizza and coffee and doughnuts.

A couple of months later, I drove over to Kirklin to check the progress on the rec center, and I ran into Chip on the street.

'You've got to come over to see your old building, Kris. You're never going to believe what we found in there.'

He took me over to show me the work he'd done. I could hardly believe my eyes. The entire second story, which had been hanging like a bowl over the back, had been completely restored. It was amazing. I'd owned that building for a year and a half, and I'd never even gotten back there; it was too scary. Chip had to jump up and down to show me it was safe to walk on the floor.

All the wood, though damaged, was very old and very beautiful, and so he'd made the decision not to tear down the second story, but to restore it. He'd hired workers to salvage all those warped pieces of wood, then rebend and sand them to bring them back to their former glory. And do you know what they found when they started sanding all those layers of varnish off of those old floors? Painted lines. At one time in the building's history, that room had housed a basketball court.

I was so stunned, you could have pushed me over with a feather. Chip told me that when he'd seen them for the first time, he'd fallen to his knees. 'When I saw those lines, there wasn't any doubt left in my mind. It felt like a sign – a sign that I was supposed to be making a rec center for these kids in Kirklin.'

I smiled then, more widely than I'd smiled all winter long, as I headed back to the other building across the street. It did feel like a sign – like Christopher was up there in heaven looking down on us, telling us he wanted his friends to play.

# Bold *and* Underlined

'Cheetos or chips?'

The good thing about a ten-year-old boy is that no matter how obsessed he is with the electromagnetic physics lecture he's attending, he will always give serious consideration to what kind of junk food he's going to share with his mother during the break.

By the time Jake was in fifth grade, a question about snack food was the only kind I was capable of answering for him. He'd run through all the astronomy classes at IUPUI, and he'd taken some of them, including Dr Pehl's, a number of times. When we all realized it was time for him to move on, Professor Rhoads suggested that he might be interested in taking a class in electromagnetic physics.

He *was* interested – fascinated, in fact – but I was completely lost. The professor, Marcos Betancourt, began the weekly class with a lecture. Then the students would split up into small groups to work equations on the whiteboards lining the walls, and at the very end the class would reconvene for a closing lecture. It was an evening class, and I suspect breaking the class up in this way encouraged the students to stay awake. Unfortunately, the strategy didn't work for me. The most basic concepts eluded me during the lectures, and the equations on the boards were even worse. With apologies to Dr Betancourt, I started bringing a book to class. Eventually, I stopped attending altogether. Jake was in heaven, and I felt confident he wasn't going to misbehave.

About two weeks before the end of the class, Dr Betancourt

mentioned to me that Jake's participation had begun to drop off. He was no longer paying rabid attention to the lectures, and he was not joining the others at the whiteboards during the recitation portion of the class, electing instead to stay in his seat, reading intently. Whenever he could, he'd pepper Dr Betancourt with questions. Apparently, he had gotten sucked into one of the concepts they were studying, and he didn't seem to be able to move on. All his questions had to do with light and how it moves through space.

When he'd exhausted the specific knowledge (and perhaps the patience) of the professors at IUPUI, I had to broaden his field of inquiry. Once more, I found myself on the phone, advocating for Jake by way of a crazy request. I got in touch with Dr Alexei Filippenko at the University of California, Berkeley, and Dr Philippe Binder at the University of Hawaii at Hilo. Both calls began the same way: 'Please, please, don't hang up, but I have this ten-year-old . . .'

You have to understand how far out of the realm of the ordinary this was for me. I had no experience with world-class astrophysicists. Yet there I was, buttonholing these renowned scientists because Jake had a question his own professors couldn't answer. Even more remarkably, they became friends and among Jake's most encouraging supporters. Their answers seemed to temporarily solve whatever problem Jake was struggling with, but our Pac-Man was running out of dots to gobble.

Early in 2009, I received a call from Dr J. R. Russell at IUPUI, wondering if we could meet.

The special-needs kids in the daycare made it hard for me to find someone who could take over if I needed to get away. Some of the kids were intensely compromised. For instance, one of the little boys, Ty, had a feeding tube that an assistant had to be trained to change.

In addition to the daycare, we'd opened our home to a number of seriously disadvantaged children through a program at our church called Safe Children, a free foster arrangement for families in temporary distress. We fostered a little girl for a single mother who needed surgery and a brother and sister for a family that had lost its home in the recession and didn't want the kids to go into a shelter.

Fostering was Mike's idea. We'd finally been able to sell the old house, and he was so grateful to be back on our feet again financially, it seemed natural to ask how we could help people who weren't quite there yet. I was behind the idea 100 percent. We had so much love to give, and fostering made me feel as if we were putting our big, beautiful house to good use. Only after we started to take in children did I truly feel as though I had the right to live there, and I was finally able to paint the living room the girlie peach color I'd picked out when I was a child.

Fostering was an amazing experience for all of us. It meant a lot to Mike and me that our children would know what it felt like to give to people in need, and it was wonderful to see my sons in this new context. Jake's patience, Wesley's openheartedness and generosity of spirit, and Ethan's sweet, serious peacefulness weren't news to us. But seeing how easily our children gave of themselves and how much pleasure they seemed to take from it made me a thousand times happier than anything we could have bought.

Some of the children who stayed with us came from the kind of poverty we couldn't have imagined before we'd met them. I remember the whole family turning away in horrified silence, our hearts breaking, as one little boy who had never seen indoor plumbing before opened the sliding door in the kitchen and used the backyard. (He was a love, though, and caught on quickly.)

So between daycare and the foster kids, simply getting out of the house during that period took some major planning. But the morning of my appointment with Dr Russell, I scrambled to rearrange things, remembered to put a clean blouse and some lip gloss on, and drove down to the university.

Honestly, my first reaction was anxiety. We'd been attending a lot of classes at IUPUI, and we hadn't paid for any of them, relying instead on the benevolence of the individual professors. They hadn't seemed to mind having Jake (and me) in their classrooms. Quite the opposite, in fact. But who knew? One thing was clear: We couldn't afford to take these classes if we had to pay for them. We were in better shape financially than we'd been in a while, but we were still a long way from being out of debt, and there was no way we could afford to pay for a university class going forward, let alone the classes Jake had already attended.

But I'm a naturally positive person, so by the time I was halfway there, I was thinking happier thoughts. *Maybe they want to give him credit for that last astronomy class*, I thought. After all, he'd taken the tests along with the other kids. *Wouldn't that be a kick if this ten-year-old had three college credits under his belt?*

As I parked the car, I thought, *Well, this is either going to go really well or really badly.* Whichever way it went, I knew we would find a way to get Jake what he needed.

As it turned out, Dr Russell ran a program called SPAN – Special Programs for Academic Nurturing. He'd heard from the professors at the university what Jake had been doing, and he thought that his program, which allows exceptionally talented high school students to enroll in university classes, would be a good fit for Jake. 'We'd like Jacob to apply to IUPUI through the SPAN program,' he said.

When all I could muster was a blank stare, Dr Russell clarified his offer. Would we consider pulling Jake out of elementary school and sending him to college?

Part of me thought the whole thing was a prank. I wouldn't have been surprised to see someone pop out from behind a bookshelf with a video camera. Yes, I had been convinced for a while that elementary school wasn't necessarily the best place for Jake. And yes, Jake had been attending these college courses. Still, I thought of them more as a hobby, the way some kids are serious about ballet or gymnastics or soccer. To me, the time we spent at the university was simply a pastime, albeit an unusual one.

'You know he's ten, right?' I couldn't help asking.

Dr Russell laughed. 'Yes, we know very well how old he is.'

My mind was racing while Dr Russell explained the application process to me. If we were interested, there was quite a bit to be done. First, Jake would need to have some formal testing, starting with an evaluation of his current academic achievement. We'd need to be able to document that Jake was capable of sitting through a lecture without assistance, and we'd have to collect letters of reference from professors he'd already taken classes with.

I apologized to Dr Russell for being dazed as he ushered me out of his office. There was a chair directly outside his door, and I sat down. I needed to think about how to break this to Michael.

The two of us had talked about pulling Jake out of elementary school before. Or, rather, *I'd* talked about it. Every time I saw how bored Jake was or noticed any signs of regressive behavior, I'd start talking to Michael about home-schooling Jake. Clearly, Jake wasn't getting what he needed, and I felt that we owed it to him to explore other options. Didn't it make more sense for him to learn during the day instead of staying up all night reading?

I can be a force when I feel strongly about something, and I didn't marry a rubber-stamper. I'd seen plenty of couples argue over things such as which kind of plastic sandwich bags to buy. Michael and I never bickered unnecessarily about small stuff, but that isn't to say we didn't disagree. On the topic of school, Michael was adamant and unmovable. He prided himself on being able to give his kids the kind of childhood he'd dreamed about when he was young, and pulling Jake out of public school and home-schooling him wasn't part of that vision. More specifically, he felt that Jake's ability to make and keep friends would suffer. Jake was going to stay in elementary school, and that was that.

With every passing year, however, it became clearer that elementary school wasn't an ideal environment for Jake. Still, I understood that Michael wasn't ready to make a change. Now it looked as though we were going to have that conversation again.

It wasn't as though I was wholly convinced myself. My knee-jerk reaction to agree with Mike. Absolutely not, no way. This wasn't just home-schooling; this was *college*. The idea of Jake attending university seemed ridiculous. The place where we live isn't a college-driven area. Most people get married right out of high school, and the majority of them go to work in a factory or in the automotive industry. Although Michael and I both went to college, we work in the service sector, as do most of our neighbors.

To add to my confusion, while I sat at a red light on the way home, I watched an aggressive shouting match between two homeless men, reminding me that I hadn't yet considered how we'd make sure Jake would be safe. I couldn't have my baby hanging around alone between classes on a downtown college campus.

But I couldn't close the door completely on the possibility either. I had no intention of telling Jake about the opportunity yet. I knew that he'd snap at the chance to go to college. But Michael and I had to agree on the best course of action first.

That whole day, I went back and forth. When Michael came home that evening, the two of us sat under a blanket on our porch, watching the boys play with some of their friends in the playground across the street. Jake's friend Luke was there. Luke's a football kid, and the contrast in size between the two of them only reinforced how crazy it was to even consider Dr Russell's offer.

'It's ridiculous, right?' I asked Mike.

'Completely. They're insane. A ten-year-old does not go to college.'

I agreed. 'Look at him. He's not even as big as a regular ten-year-old. That kid can't go to college.'

Of course, his size wasn't the main issue; his social development was. How would he make friends? What would it mean for the friends he already had? And, most important, what would it mean for his childhood? The more I thought about the idea, the crazier it seemed. Yes, Jake was smart. But shouldn't he have the chance to participate in all the usual high school activities? It's one thing to skip one grade, but *seven* of them seemed extreme.

It might sound silly, but the idea that Jake wouldn't have a prom was hard for me to accept. One of the bitterest pills I'd had to swallow when Jake was so lost in his autism was the realization that he might never find someone to love and support him, someone to share his life with, the way Michael and I had found each other. I knew from my friends that having romantic relationships wasn't always easy for autistic teenagers and young adults. (Not that it's easy for neurotypical people either!) Since Jake had emerged from his isolation, I'd hoped that he would be able to find satisfaction in that part of his life, and for some reason I had a sentimental attachment to the idea of him going to the prom. I'd always imagined snapping a picture of Jake and his date (wearing the corsage he'd bought to match her special dress, of course) before they headed off to the dance.

Michael's mind was made up: Jake should stay in elementary school. Part of me agreed with him, but at the same time I kept having a vision of Jake crammed into our bookshelf. I knew that auditing university classes had pulled him out of that space. I'd watched him on too many afternoons twiddling his pencil and staring out the window while the school friend he was helping labored mightily over a page of fractions. I couldn't help contrasting that listless Jake with the dynamo who'd joust and parry with Dr Pehl at the end of every astronomy class. Going to college at age ten wasn't what other kids were doing, but Jake wasn't like other kids.

I couldn't accept that Michael and I were at cross-purposes. Folding socks while Jake did math sitting next to me in a pile of still-warm laundry, I wondered whether I felt so strongly because I spent more time with Jake than he did. Michael wasn't there those afternoons when Jake was begging to learn algebra. He wasn't at the university when Jake was making those professors' jaws drop. Because of what I'd witnessed, I understood that our son was a scientist, while to Michael he was just a little boy.

We were never going to get out of this limbo without help. It was time to get an objective evaluation. So in August 2009, I took Jake in for a battery of achievement tests with Dr Carl Hale, a neuropsychologist.

As usual, I went to the appointment with Jake, but I drastically underestimated how long the tests would take. In all, I sat in the empty waiting room for about four and a half hours, long after I'd finished the book I'd brought with me, as well as the magazine I'd found at the bottom of my bag.

Looking out the only window, I could see a gas station two long blocks away. A few hours in, I found myself staring at it wistfully, fantasizing about going over there to get a cup of coffee and another magazine. But I couldn't leave. I didn't know how much longer they were going to be, and I didn't want Jake to come out to find me gone.

When he finally emerged, he looked like he'd had a grand time. Dr Hale said that he would provide us with a formal report in about a week, but he was deeply impressed. Jake's scores were off the charts, particularly in math and science.

Then Dr Hale did a curious thing. He asked me about my own experience in the waiting room. I made a little joke about the padding on the chairs, but he was serious. He wanted to know what it had been like for me, waiting all those long hours in that empty room. When I finally admitted how bored and uncomfortable I'd been, he said something that changed my mind forever.

'Now you know what it's like for Jake in a fifth-grade classroom. Being in regular school is like staring out a window, wishing your heart out for a cup of gas-station coffee. The worst decision you could possibly make is to keep your son in regular school. He is deeply bored, and if you keep him there, you will stifle every iota of creativity he has.'

I was horrified by the idea that Jake's school days bore any resemblance to the mind-numbing hours I'd spent in that room. Instinctively, I knew that Dr Hale was right, and I will always be grateful to him for having gone to such creative lengths to make his point. His waiting room wasn't ordinarily so bare, but knowing that we were struggling with the question of whether to send Jake to college, he'd stripped it of magazines and other diversions before we arrived.

When Dr Hale's report arrived a week or two later, his recommendations were crystal clear. Jake had scored 170 on the

Wechsler Fundamentals: Academic Skills achievement test, which measures broad skills in reading, spelling, and math. The normal range is between 90 and 109, superior between 110 and 124, and gifted between 125 and 130. Scores above 150 fall into the category of genius. Furthermore, Dr Hale believed that Jake's numerical operations score, which measured his math computation skills, was probably higher than 170 but could not be measured due to 'ceiling effects': One hundred seventy points is as high as the test can go for a kid Jake's age.

Dr Hale's conclusion: 'It would **not** be in Jacob's best interest to force him to complete academic work that he has already mastered. Rather, he needs to work at an instructional level, which is currently a post-college graduate level in mathematics, i.e. post master's degree. In essence, his math skills are at the level found in someone who is working on a doctorate in math, physics, astronomy, or astrophysics.'

There it was, in black and white. This wasn't my opinion, but an objective evaluation made by an expert. Jake belonged in college. (Actually, Dr Hale seemed to be recommending that he proceed directly to graduate school, but this wasn't the time to split hairs.) I took a deep breath and brought the report in to show Michael.

'**Not** in Jacob's best interest. That's bold *and* underlined,' Michael read aloud, his eyebrows raised. I nodded. He was still shaking his head, but there was a look of resignation on his face, and I knew that, thanks to Dr Hale, the door had opened a crack.

After the report arrived, we finally told Jake about Dr Russell's offer. As we knew he would, he lit up like a Christmas tree and said, 'Can I go to college? Please, Mom? Can I go to college?'

Michael was now open to a conversation, but he was far from convinced. I argued that going to college early couldn't damage Jake's chances for the future; it could only improve them. He was way ahead of his class, even in the elementary school's gifted program. Even if Jake went to college and failed, if he didn't learn a single thing or make a single friend, he could come right back and do junior high like everybody else. Ironically, the fact that Jake was so young also tipped the odds in his favor.

'I'm so far out of my comfort zone, I can't even see it from here,' Michael grumbled. But he didn't protest when Jake and I went ahead with an application to the university through SPAN.

# Skipping a Grade – or Seven

From that point on, everything accelerated. Once I really understood how bored Jake was, that we'd unknowingly put his brilliant, active, growing mind in a box too small to contain it, college seemed like the only option.

Convincing Michael had been a significant hurdle, but the application itself was another. Dr Russell wanted to know that Jake was capable of sitting through a longish lecture without acting out. Jake had been attending university classes for two years without a single issue, but I'd usually been in the seat next to him. Jake would have to do this on his own.

One of the deans at our high school had brought his kids to daycare when they were little, so he knew our boys. When I told him about this challenge, he offered to let Jake sit in on a math class, a review session to prepare the students for their calculus final. I wasn't sure how it would go. Jake was good at sitting still, but he'd never had any formal math instruction past fifth-grade fractions, and they'd be covering an entire semester's worth of work from the hardest math class in the Indiana public school system.

The class was scheduled two weeks out. I explained the situation to Jake: 'Don't worry; you don't need to know calculus. All they're watching for is your manners. You just need to be able to sit nicely through this class.'

Jake looked at me. 'I'm not going to sit there if I don't know what's going on,' he said.

I sighed. Of course not.

He wanted textbooks, so we bought them for him. Then he

sat on the porch in front of our house in the spring sunshine and learned the formal language of geometry, algebra, algebra II, trigonometry, and calculus. He did it all by himself and all in two weeks. As we subsequently discovered, Jake had already figured out the fundamental principles of math on his own. Just as you can understand the principle of addition without knowing what a plus sign is, Jake had already developed his own private system for calculus. He simply didn't know yet how to write it down so that other mathematicians could understand it.

Jake took that calculus final along with the rest of the kids and aced it. In fact, he was the only one in the class able to answer the extra-credit question – a question so hard that the teacher asked him to come up and write the explanation on the board. The day I picked him up from the final, I found him surrounded by admiring high school students, all of them towering over him.

Even with that hurdle cleared, there was a lot to do to complete the SPAN application.

Jake told me one night at dinner that he'd found Indiana University High School online. 'I want to enroll in AP U. S. History,' he said. We told him that was okay, and a couple of weeks later he came to us with another request. There was a computerized testing center down at the university where he could take a CLEP (College-Level Examination Program) exam, designed to help college students test out of subjects they were already familiar with, thus allowing them to earn college credits without having to waste time and money on taking the course. He wanted to try to test out of the U. S. History course he'd taken online.

The next weekend, we drove down to the campus. The woman behind the counter at the CLEP office asked if she could help, and I said, 'Yes, we'd like to test out of AP U. S. History, please.'

'We?' she asked, confused.

'Well, my son, actually.'

'I'm sorry, ma'am, but he has to be here to sign up for the test. You can't do it for him.'

We looked at each other, both baffled, and then a little voice said, 'Down here!'

She stood up and peered over the edge of the counter, where Jake was laughing and waving his hands at her. 'Oh! Hi!' she said.

Jake didn't have any photo identification, such as a student ID or a driver's license ('Does my library card count?' he asked), so the woman had to call her manager in to assign him a log-in number. It took a while to get the system to allow him to take the exam, but she was obviously charmed by the idea of this little kid taking the test alongside the older students, and she figured it out. I remember looking up to check on him and seeing his little legs swinging under the chair as he clicked through the questions. The computer grades the exam while you wait, and sure enough Jake tested out of U. S. History that morning. The whole staff of the CLEP office cheered as if they'd known him his whole life.

That lit a fire under him. He went online and started taking every course he could find. And then every weekend, he'd want to go to the university so that he could test out. Eventually, I had to have a talk with him. It cost about $75 to take a CLEP exam. That was a mere fraction of what the course would have cost, but we flat out couldn't afford for him to take a test a week. We settled on a compromise: one test every two weeks.

The astronomy exam was particularly funny. He used only fifteen minutes of the two hours he had to take it and ended up with an almost perfect score. The people in the CLEP office, friends by then, were truly shocked by that one.

Once we had completed all the items on Dr Russell's checklist, I submitted Jake's reports – the IQ test and the assessment from Dr Hale, notes from the professors whose classes he'd audited, and all his CLEP scores – as well as a note from the high school calculus teacher, vouching that yes, Jake was capable of sitting through a class. A few weeks later, Jake received his acceptance letter. He jumped up and cheered. Shortly afterward, Dr Russell called us in for a brief welcome interview.

On the day of the interview, I put Jake in charge of bringing some change for the parking meter, as he liked to put the coins in the meter. In his excitement, he brought way too much money, so he had lots of coins in his pockets. When he sat down in the chair in front of Dr Russell's desk, all the coins fell out onto the floor. Jake couldn't concentrate until he'd picked them up and stuffed them back into his pockets. The second he sat down again, all the coins tumbled out, rolling everywhere and making an appalling noise. Not to be deterred, Jake began scooping coins off the linoleum into his baseball cap. Of course, they immediately fell out through the hole in the back of the cap.

This disastrous business with the coins went on and on and on, like a never-ending Three Stooges routine. It would have been funny if it hadn't been my son's college interview. Dr Russell kept trying to hand him a baseball cap and a backpack with the SPAN logo, but he couldn't get Jake's attention, because Jake was chasing runaway coins around his office. Eventually, after Jake got most of the coins under control, Dr Russell gave him the backpack and cap, as well as a triangular IUPUI Jaguars flag for his wall. Still trailing coins everywhere, but now wearing his SPAN cap, Jake headed off down the hall.

The interview had been a complete disaster. When Dr Russell put his hand on my arm, my heart sank.

'Based on what we've seen here today, I think we should start slow the first semester, with three credit hours,' he said. 'Let's be fair to Jake and give his social skills and his height a chance to catch up.'

The news that Jake could take only a single class that first semester was devastating, not least because we'd pulled him out of elementary school. I blamed myself. We usually do a practice run for any new situation, but who could have predicted an overflow of parking meter coins? Jake, of course, was distraught. He could see the promised land, but they wouldn't let him in. Even acknowledging Jake's lack of maturity, I wasn't sure holding him back was fair. He still looked like a little boy, and he hadn't exactly aced the interview, but three months wouldn't make much of a difference in his height or anything else.

Nevertheless, he signed up for the one course he was allowed to take, an introductory course in multidimensional math. The first time I flipped through the textbook, I was stunned. Here were the geometric shapes Jake had been obsessed with since he was a toddler. It's surreal to open a college textbook and finally have a context for your young child's preoccupations. In my mind, I had always put Jake's shapes in the same category as Legos or Lincoln Logs (which he sometimes used to build them): funny little toys that clogged up the vacuum cleaner and hurt when you stepped on them with bare feet.

By the third session, Jake had set up a study group and was tutoring the other kids in the class. The professor also wanted him to participate in a math club for high school students he ran on Saturday mornings, a training camp for the Mathematical Olympiad. I took Jake there one Saturday so that he could see what it was like, thinking maybe he'd meet some kids he got along with. Warning bells went off when the professor showed me the coffeemaker and pointed out the way to the college bookstore. Five hours later, I realized that this math club would mean that Jake would have to give up every Saturday to sit in a stuffy basement classroom with a bunch of kids doing math.

I *love* our weekend traditions. The whole family goes out to a little brunch place for pancakes, and then we go to the rec center or the pond across from our home, or to our neighbors' for an afternoon barbecue. When it's cold, we go to the bookstore and treat ourselves to new books and hot chocolate with whipped cream at the café, or we make cookies at home and invite friends over to play a board game. This time seemed especially important to me once Jake left elementary school. Maintaining the friendships he'd made there was our highest priority, and those kids were free on the weekends.

So when I went to pick Jake up, I steeled myself to tell him that he probably wouldn't be participating again. He beat me to the punch. Getting into the car, he said, 'That was cool, but I don't think I need to do it again.' He'd found a sample Mathematical Olympiad problem set online the night before and had stayed up until two in the morning blowing through it for fun. It hadn't been a challenge for him, and he didn't want to take a win away from any of the kids who'd been studying so hard to get into the competition. 'They're all trying really hard, Mom. It's not fair.'

I was so proud of him at that moment, prouder even than if he'd won the Fields Medal, the most prestigious math prize in the world. Jake knew he'd have his own victories in the world, and he understood that this one wasn't for him.

# An Original Theory

Because he was restricted that first semester to three credit hours and an introductory math class, Jake suddenly found himself with a big chunk of time. Mike, still unsure whether we'd thrown Jake's whole future away, would find us sitting at the breakfast table together while Wesley, Ethan, and all the other kids in the neighborhood were getting dressed for school and trudging down to the bus stop. He couldn't resist needling me a little: 'Rigorous program you're running here, Kris.' Then he'd turn to Jake and say, 'Shouldn't you have your backpack and a notebook or something?'

'Michael, he's eating his breakfast. He doesn't need a backpack to eat his breakfast,' I'd say.

'People don't wear fuzzy frog slippers to school,' Michael would mutter as he left the room, shaking his head.

Eventually, I'd turn to Jake and say, 'So what *are* you going to do today?'

Jake would say something like, 'Um, supermassive black holes?'

I wasn't worried. Mike knew as well as anybody that Jake's mind never stopped running. Even while relaxing with his brothers at the pool, he'd be thinking about fluid mechanics. His education had also gotten a rocket-fueled boost thanks to iTunes U, a series of video podcasts available through iTunes. These free lectures featured professors from top universities such as Stanford, Yale, Harvard, MIT, UC Berkeley, and Oxford, speaking on hundreds of topics ranging from languages to Shakespeare to philosophy. There were lectures on relativity, special relativity, string theory, quantum mechanics – anything, in other words, an astrophysics-obsessed elementary school dropout could want.

Jake was hooked. As soon as breakfast was done, he'd hit the computer. His attitude was, 'They're not going to let me go to IUPUI? Fine, I'll go to MIT.'

The question of how light moves through space, the concept that had captured Jake's imagination during Dr Betancourt's class, had begun to percolate. Jake was already familiar with relativity and special relativity, but the lectures supplemented his own research and enabled him to delve more deeply into those topics than he had before. His hunger for knowledge was like a gigantic engine, driving him to search out and voraciously cram in as much information as he could get his hands on. It was as if he couldn't bear to waste even a second of this precious time. Once again, I had to remind him to eat, to bathe, and to play. The question wasn't how I could make him do the work, but how I could get him to stop.

He wanted more than anything to share his tremendous excitement about all the things he was learning. I'd be watching *Ellen* and tidying up the kitchen while the daycare kids took their afternoon nap, and Jake would come in, commandeer the television, connect his laptop, and physically drag me over to the couch so that he could show me the lecture he'd watched that morning. 'It's math and science story time with Mommy!' he'd say.

'Oh, no honey,' I'd beg. 'Not organic chemistry. Can it be anything but organic chemistry?' (As if string theory would be better.) Sometimes he'd get so wrapped up in watching, I could sneak away to unload the dishwasher, but mostly I was stuck sitting there, my brain hurting, while Jake scribbled furiously away in his notepad.

I liked to tease him about torturing me, but the truth is,

I treasured those afternoons together. I was struck by how natural it was for him to assume the role of teacher. Jake loved nothing better than to stand at his little whiteboard and teach me what he was learning. 'Tell it to me like I'm a cheeseburger, Jake,' I'd say, and he would, going through each of the incredibly complicated ideas slowly and clearly until I understood. Even though I had little or no talent as a student, he had an endless amount of patience for the process. You could see how much he loved it.

One of the kids in the daycare at the time, a boy named Noah, thought the sun rose and set on Jake. Noah loved nothing more than to lie on the floor at Jake's feet, his legs up in the air, watching Jake do math. Even when I had to beg Jake to take a break to eat a sandwich or take a shower, he would always find time to show Noah the difference between acute and obtuse triangles, or how to measure the circumference and the diameter of a circle. Watching Jake with Noah helped me to see what motivated Jake to teach. It was his passion for the subject, pure and simple.

It's hard for many people to relate to, but Jake genuinely thinks math and science are the most beautiful things on earth. The way a music lover thrills to a crescendo, the way a lifelong reader catches her breath in delight over a perfectly crafted phrase, that's what math is like for Jake. This is a boy who dreams of tesseracts and hypercubes. I have come to understand that numbers and numerical concepts are like friends to Jake. His iPad password right now has twenty-seven characters, comprising numbers and formulae he likes. Every time he types it in, it's like he's high-fiving one of his buddies. I always tell him, 'Jake, you don't understand. Math scares people. It scares me.' I think this is why he's so dedicated to stamping out what he calls 'math phobia' wherever he finds it. He honestly believes that if I'd been taught differently, I'd love math as much as he does.

When I'd get tired, my head spinning from the numbers, Jake would talk to the dog. Since I'd had no idea what the experience of leaving elementary school would be like for Jake, and because I'd wanted him to know he had someone (besides me) who'd be there for him all the time, I'd gotten him a puppy, a St. Bernard he called Igor. By choosing a St. Bernard, I'd signed on for much more than I'd expected. Igor ate like a garbage disposal and grew and grew until he was bigger than Jake. Every day, I'd vacuum up a whole dog's worth of hair. 'How is that creature not bald?' Mike would ask, changing the vacuum cleaner bag yet again. In the spring, when it rains a lot in Indiana, I'd mop my kitchen floor, and then five minutes later, I'd have to mop it again.

Igor and Jake were inseparable, and I came to accept the giant dog as a permanent fixture in the kitchen, where Jake liked to do his math. Igor would sit there watching, head cocked and an intelligent look on his face, as the equations poured out of Jake. I was so grateful for the dog's loyalty and attention, I didn't even mind the drooling. Narnie always got a kick out of the scene. 'In this house, even the dog is doing astrophysics,' she'd say. We both thought that Igor was probably absorbing more than either one of us was.

Jake's affinity for teaching wasn't a surprise to Narnie, who, thank heaven, could be relied on to interrupt those epic teaching sessions with a pot of hot chocolate. 'His whole life, he's had to explain to people how he thinks,' she once said. 'What's the difference between that and teaching?'

As always, she was right. But I also thought Jake's drive to teach was motivated by the same thing that had brought us to the university in the first place: He wanted a conversation. Math is a foreign language to most people, and Jake was starved for conversation. His solution was to try to teach the people around him to 'speak' math. The lectures he downloaded may have satisfied his tremendous need to learn, but unless he could make these concepts understandable to others, he'd never be able to talk about them.

Unfortunately, he was stuck with Igor and me, and as he got deeper and deeper into the material, it became ever more clear that he needed a lot more in the way of conversation than we could give him. One night Michael and I were flipping through the channels, and we stopped on a movie called *I Am Sam*. In it, Sean Penn plays a developmentally disabled adult named Sam, who is the parent of a typical five-year-old girl. In one very moving scene, the daughter is reading Dr Seuss's *Green Eggs and Ham* to Sam, and they both realize that she has surpassed him intellectually. When the scene was over, I found I'd been gripping Michael's hand so hard my fingernails had left marks in his palm. I could relate to what Sam felt in that scene: an odd, bittersweet mixture of pride and abandonment.

I was so proud of Jake and his achievements, and we'd been having so much fun together, but now here we were again in a situation where he couldn't talk to me. This time, of course, it was for a good reason. Although I wouldn't have traded my brilliant son for anyone in the world, there was a part of me that felt a little cheated by Jake's accelerated academic schedule.

All those progressive steps kids take toward separation and independence – their first sleepover, learning to drive, their first date – prepare their parents for the inevitable separation, too. I was experiencing some of those steps with Ethan and Wesley, but I hadn't experienced any of them with Jake. Instead, it had happened all at once. That's why it was so wonderful for me to sit next to Jake on the couch while he was watching a lecture by a professor at Princeton or Harvard. Even if I couldn't understand the most basic concept under discussion, I could rub my son's curly head and spend some time with him. I might not be able to engage in the conversation, but for a short time at least, I could be a mom to him.

The semester off was truly an astonishing period intellectually for Jake. He had time to explore everything he wanted, as deeply as he wanted, with only his rich curiosity as a guide. It was as if we'd given a powerful racehorse permission to run free after years of reining him in.

'Slow down, guy, there's smoke coming out of your ears,' Michael would tease him. But sometimes it almost seemed as though we could hear the synapses firing as Jake experienced epiphany after epiphany, each idea igniting the next one. He was on fire, and everything he watched or read or learned served as kindling.

A lot of Jake's ideas were equations that had already been developed and proved. Some were original, although many had flaws he'd expose two or three days later. There was no frustration or irritation associated with these false steps. In fact, he'd move on so easily that the setbacks didn't even seem to register. He might have been following a path only he could see, but for him it was clearly marked.

This creative fugue state was his primary reality, while the stuff of everyday life seemed more like an afterthought. Without warning, he'd throw himself off the swing set at the playground across the street and run home as fast as he could, barely able to contain the equations spilling out of him. After fleeing the dinner table one night without a word, he gouged a whiteboard with a fork: He hadn't taken the time to trade it for a marker. The ideas came so fast and so furious, I gave him a notebook to carry around so that he could keep track, a strategy that met with only limited success. Invariably, while he was writing one idea down, another would occur to him, and he'd be off in another direction entirely.

That semester, Jake was as focused as I'd ever seen him. Always, though, his intensity was mediated by a sense of enjoyment, an excitement that felt like play. When the equations he was working on grew too extensive for paper, he began using whiteboard markers on the windows of our house. I'd often stand quietly in a doorway, watching him work. The math flowed out of him so easily, and so quickly, that it seemed more like he was taking dictation than actually thinking about what should come next. The only limit seemed to be how fast he could write.

I was reminded of watching him and Christopher shoot baskets, which they'd happily do for hours, breaking only for a sip of soda or a handful of pretzels. Some of their shots would go in; others would not. Sometimes they'd talk; other times the only sound besides the bouncing ball would be the squeak of their sneakers on the floor. But as he did math on the windows, there was an easiness, a sense of relaxed pleasure, about the activity, something I was seeing for the first time since Christopher's death. 'He's having *fun*,' Narnie said, watching him in wonder.

One morning I was having a cup of coffee in the sunny little room where we sometimes had breakfast. Jake came in, ignored the fruit plate, grabbed a croissant off the table, and sat down with his feet in my lap.

'Mom, I need you to listen to me,' he said. 'It's math, but if you listen carefully, I'll explain it so you can understand. I've found a pattern.'

Jake always had a preternaturally acute ability to detect patterns, and this, of all his gifts, was the attribute the professors he'd been studying with always singled out as the key ingredient to his success.

What he told me was truly astounding. I really had no idea what Jake was working on. I had enough sense to trust that he was moving forward on something important, but for all I knew, 'something important' meant a crash course in college physics, an impressive enough achievement for an eleven-year-old boy. But it turned out to be more than that.

Jake's theory, which was in the field of relativity, was both elegantly simple – clean and clear enough for me to understand – and superbly complex. If he was right, he'd be creating an entirely new field of physics, just as Newton and Leibniz had revolutionized math by inventing calculus.

The first breathless words out of my mouth surprised even me. 'Jakey – it's *beautiful*.'

The smile Jake gave me at that moment was beautiful, too.

Jake had started with a picture. Now he needed the mathematical notation to describe what he was seeing. I've come to understand that math is really a language, a way of describing what people like Jake see. He had all the rudiments already, but a concept of this complexity required a vocabulary he didn't yet have.

I think it's fair to say that at that point, he became obsessed. All the lightheartedness I'd admired earlier disappeared, as he struggled to put the picture he saw so clearly in his mind into the mathematical notation other scientists could understand. He began making models of space-time and dimensional models of space, and the equations on our windows grew longer and longer.

He stopped sleeping. He had always been a committed night owl, but this was different. Now he wasn't sleeping at all. Michael would go into Jake's room to wake him up in the morning, and he'd find Jake sitting upright where he'd left him eight hours before. 'Jake! Did you forget to sleep again?' Michael would ask. He would nod off at breakfast and in the car, but at night he would be wide-awake, reading and doing math.

We took him to the pediatrician, who shared our concern

and suggested that we enroll him in a sleep study. Jake spent one night in the hospital, bristling with wires and tubes and electrodes. The study confirmed what we suspected: Jake wasn't sleeping. But there was nothing physically wrong with him. The only thing keeping him up was the math.

Ultimately, he became so wrapped up in this gigantic equation, I became concerned. I was leaning against the doorjamb, watching Jake as he scribbled furiously on a window, filling the panes with mathematical symbols I couldn't even begin to understand. Meanwhile, through the window I could see kids his age playing in the park across the street, chasing each other and hanging upside down on the swings.

He seemed lost in the equation. It occurred to me that maybe he was stuck. Perhaps he didn't have the information he needed to move on to the next step. Maybe he needed to consult with someone who had a better handle on this material, someone who could see if he'd taken a wrong turn. I didn't care one bit about the equation. All I knew was that it was insanely long and taking up too much of his time. But helping him fix it seemed like the best way to get him off the window and into the park.

'Jake, we can't go on like this,' I said. 'Let's get you some help. Someone else may be able to see where you're stuck.'

He looked at me, trying to figure out what I was talking about. 'But I'm not stuck, Mom. I'm trying to prove I'm *wrong*.' That was what he'd been doing with that equation, checking and rechecking his work, searching for the flaw or the hole that would mean the whole theory was garbage.

I persisted. At least we should find out if there was any validity to the theory before he dedicated another six months to it. Jake conceded that it might be helpful to talk to someone, and he knew immediately whom he wanted to get in touch with: Dr Scott Tremaine, a world-renowned astrophysicist at the Institute for Advanced Study, in Princeton, New Jersey, where

Einstein had taught until his death. So I called Dr Tremaine, who listened when I told him about my unusual eleven-year-old and his theory. The last thing I wanted to do was waste his time, so I emphasized how efficient we'd be if he'd take a fast look at this equation and tell Jake what areas he thought needed work. I stressed that I was making the call not because of the science, but because of Jake's autism. I needed to get him off that window.

Dr Tremaine said that he would look at a short video, which we could send him by email. Before we got off the phone, he made sure to tell me that original theories are rare in a field as crowded with researchers as physics. I'll be honest: I was relieved! If this was already well-covered ground, I thought it would be relatively easy for Dr Tremaine to see where Jake was going wrong.

We'd all been so caught up in Jake's work that it was almost a surprise to get his exam results from his first official college course. As predicted, Jake had aced Multidimensional Math. His score on the final exam was 103. Nobody but his father was surprised.

'He got an A in college math, Kristine,' Michael told me in a tone of complete amazement, waving the transcript at me. 'This is incredible!'

I tried not to laugh. 'Babe, this is not news. What is it exactly you think we've been doing down there? I told you he was answering questions nobody could answer and running study groups and acing all the quizzes.'

'But an A, Kris – an A! In college math!'

Michael was so proud, he emailed everyone he knew. He even posted Jake's results on Facebook. Now, when he came down in the morning and found Jake and me at the breakfast table, he'd clap his hands together and ask, 'How is everything going at the famed Barnett Academy, home of the Fighting

Moose?' (I can't believe I'm making this public knowledge, but Igor's full name is Igor von Moosenflüfen. With an umlaut.)

Michael's surprise helped me have an even greater appreciation of the tug-of-war we'd gone through to arrive at the decision to allow Jake to leave elementary school. We were two strongly opinionated people, united on one principle: There was nothing more important than doing the right thing for our kids. We had pushed and pulled at each other, trying to figure out what the best decision might be for Jake, and we'd gotten there. I felt almost as proud of us as I did of Jake.

Although Jake's performance in that first college class could not have been better, SPAN informed us that he would be restricted to just six credits the following semester, and they had to be prerequisites. That eliminated the Modern Physics he was so desperate to take. When we got the news, Jake didn't say anything, but I saw his face fall, and Mike and I watched as he went upstairs very slowly, then quietly closed the door to his room.

I looked at Michael. 'This is ridiculous,' I said. 'We jumped through all the hoops to put together this application package. He got in with flying colors, and now they won't let him go? We're not doing this for the bumper sticker. What's the point if he can't take classes?'

I stewed some more, and then the lightbulb went off. 'If he's going to be a college student, maybe we should go ahead and enroll him in college.'

Once we'd thought of it, it was the simplest solution. There was a bonus, too. If Jake applied to IUPUI through the usual channels, he'd be eligible for a scholarship. There wasn't any financial aid offered for the SPAN classes, and SPAN kids didn't qualify for the state assistance that college students could get. Scraping together enough for tuition and books for the multidimensional math course had required us to make some sacrifices, and that was only one course. I felt bad that we weren't in a better position financially, but realistically who has a college fund ready for an eleven-year-old?

So I started putting together a real college application for Jake. I'd already assembled a good package for Dr Russell, but now I took the project really seriously. I wanted to make it clear – maybe even to myself – that this wasn't my opinion, a proud mom saying, 'Look at my gifted son!' Instead, I was going to compile unassailable evidence of what I had come to understand was true, which was that Jake belonged in college and that he wouldn't be okay unless we provided this opportunity for him.

I had no idea what a college admissions office would want to see, so I threw everything in *plus* the kitchen sink. If I thought of it, we did it, which is why Jake joined Mensa, the international high-IQ society. (Narnie loved to go through Jake's mail, which always included newsletters from Mensa and from another, more exclusive high-IQ group called Intertel. 'I swear, this kid gets the most interesting junk mail I've ever seen,' she'd say.)

Jake, with Wesley tagging along, would sometimes get together with the local Mensa chapter on the weekends and participate in its projects. One time, the group was asked to help a couple decide whether a fallen tree was on their property or that of the local nature conservancy abutting it. The conservancy usually insisted on a surveyor's report from someone with an engineering degree but had agreed to accept whatever the Mensa group said. So that weekend, Jake, Wes, and some Mensans, using only a homemade compass and a protractor, went out to survey the property, which included a heavily wooded ravine. (Wesley, who doesn't understand why anyone would walk when they could jump, climb, rappel, or parasail, was totally in his element.)

Jake stepped forward and took a leadership role. He developed a formula on his scratch pad and led the way. At his direction, the Mensans marked off the area with string and ruled on the boundary dispute. The couple had been right, and the fallen tree was the conservancy's responsibility. It was interesting to see that the conservancy accepted the opinion of a group led by a ten-year-old and his eight-year-old brother as gospel.

Later that week, as I was driving Wesley and a friend of his to get some ice cream, I overheard Wesley describing how he'd spent his weekend: 'There's this group that needs my brother and me to help out sometimes.' I turned away so they wouldn't see me smile. When the Mensa chapter asked me to contribute a piece to its newsletter, the Mensans were quite surprised to see that I'd written an essay about how important it is to play.

Dr Tremaine got back in touch. He had taken a look at Jake's equation, and he sent Jake an email with a list of books to get and things to think about, all of which were completely over my head. But he also wrote me an email. In it, he confirmed that Jake was indeed working on an original theory, and he made it clear that if Jake's theory held, it would put him in line for a Nobel Prize. He closed his letter by encouraging me to support Jake in whatever way I could, because he believed the work Jake was doing would be important for science.

One of the most illustrious astrophysicists in the world had not only reviewed my son's theory but had validated it. That, I can tell you, was a chicken soup moment in a class all its own.

Soon after our correspondence with Dr Tremaine, we got another piece of good news. Jake had been formally accepted as a freshman at IUPUI. In addition, he was the recipient of a Chancellor's Scholarship, which would cover his tuition.

Jake was going to college, this time for real.

# A Home Away from Home

'This isn't going to work.'

Jake was standing in the living room next to the backpack we'd bought that morning. It was filled with all the math and science textbooks he'd need for his first day of college. I'd been a little worried that they wouldn't all fit, especially when I saw his physics textbook, the size of two telephone books put together, but Jake had gotten everything in there. Now all he needed was someone to carry it for him.

Jake, being Jake, was trying to calculate what kind of fulcrum he'd need to actually get the thing on his back, but dragging it around by the straps seemed to be the best he could do without assistance. I wasn't much help, so we called Mike to lift the bag onto Jake's back. Mike and I stood and watched as poor Jake – all eighty pounds of him – staggered briefly under the load before losing the fight and his equilibrium, toppling sideways over onto the couch.

Mike and I looked at our son, his head buried in the cushions as he struggled ineffectually to right himself. (Jake, it should be noted, isn't above hamming it up a little.)

'I think he's right. We may need to do something different here,' Mike said thoughtfully, as the exaggerated flailing and muffled hollering from the couch became ever more dramatic. Wesley, never one to ignore a clear advantage, took the corner at top speed and executed a flying leap to land on top of the backpack already squishing his older brother.

Ethan, reading nearby, ignored both of them. I decided to do the same and planted a kiss on my husband's face. 'Something different?' I said. 'Here we go again.'

That was how Jake became the only kid on campus to use a rolling suitcase to transport his books from one class to another. Eventually, he'll be big enough to manage a backpack. Unfortunately, we're pretty sure it won't happen before he graduates.

Solving a little problem like finding the right luggage for Jake's books seemed like child's play, considering I'd spent the summer worrying about the reality of an eleven-year-old wandering around a downtown campus alone.

Jake likes to say that he didn't come with common sense, but the truth is that his autism can still get in the way of his ability to take care of himself. (It's a gray, sleeting, snowy day in Indiana as I write this. This morning I had to send Jake back upstairs to change out of shorts and flip-flops before going outside.) As book-smart as he might be, he isn't yet street-smart. Out where we live, he's never had to be. But even back then, before there was any media coverage of him, he attracted more than his fair share of curious looks and impromptu conversations, and I knew the scrutiny would be even more intense when he was alone. As a result, I had real concerns for his safety.

We'd thrown technology at the problem with some success. Jake would have his own phone, so he'd be able to call me when he left class, meaning we could 'walk' together, even as he crossed the campus alone. We got into the habit of using iChat, so I could actually see him and feel connected to him (and remind him to stop for a sandwich). But from my perspective, the real problem was that there would be nowhere for him to go when he had time between classes.

When Jake was taking only a single class, Mike or I could easily drive him down to campus, walk him to class, and hang around answering emails or reading until he was done. But we knew that wouldn't be realistic if he was attending the university full-time. He'd have hours between classes and study sessions, with nowhere to go. As hard as I tried to banish them from my mind, those homeless men fighting on the street corner kept surfacing again and again, and as I lay awake at night, I came up with much worse scenarios as well. 'College is not PG,' I kept telling Mike, over and over.

When Jake is nineteen, I'm sure that he will get into all sorts of high jinks. I'm not naïve; I know *Girls Gone Wild* will be in his life at some point, whether I like it or not. But Jake was only eleven, and I didn't want him exposed to anything he wasn't emotionally ready for. My worst fear was that someone would haze him or play a prank on him. What if someone thought it was funny to see what would happen if they gave the little kid in the library a six-pack of beer?

Wandering through the house one night, anxiety gnawing at my stomach, I realized that this safety issue could actually be the deal breaker. If I couldn't find a place for Jake to hang out, he might just have to learn at home.

So I tried to find someplace on campus – a comfy corner, a little lounge, a common area – where Jake could go and be safe, somewhere he could work and study or chill out. That safe haven eluded me, though, and by the end of the summer, I began to feel really unsettled. I was about to give up when, on my final recon mission, one of the women who worked in the library struck up a conversation with me.

'I've seen you down here a few times,' she said. 'What is it that you're looking for?'

I explained, and she told me about the Honors College, a brand-new college at the university that prioritized independent research and real-world field experience for the brightest students. Not only did the program sound as though it would be a perfect fit for Jake, but it also had a home, a suite of offices deep in the basement of the library, accessible only to honor students with a special key card.

It sounded too good to be true, but the reality of the Honors College completely blew me away. Students can see into the offices lining the corridors, and the administrators and educators can see out. There are places for the kids to work and study and laugh together, as well as places for them to retreat and curl up by themselves. There are state-of-the-art touch screen Smart Boards in the lounges and unlimited hot chocolate in the kitchen. It's a think tank, a student union, and a home away from home, all rolled into one. At the center of this amazing place is Dr Jane Luzar, the founding dean of the Honors College and its resident guru and angel, who spends her days making the program the best it can be. The kids don't call her Dean Luzar, but Jane – and often, Mama Jane.

Finding Jane and the miraculous space she's created for these kids was such a huge relief to me as a mom, we never seriously thought about Jake going to school anywhere else. I knew we'd made the right decision the very first day Jake was down there. My phone rang, and it was Jane. 'He's on the move,' she reported. Jake had left the Honors College.

Jane told me that she would watch out for Jake, and she has. It's not because he's so young either. I've seen her scold a twenty-year-old for skipping lunch.

Jane also looks out for Jake academically. He has to satisfy a number of requirements in order to graduate, which can be boring for him. He was not thrilled about the algebra-based honors physics requirements he had to take that first year, for instance. Rather than doing the problems using the classic, easier, and less precise Newtonian physics, Jake used the quantum approach, which requires several pages of equations and delivers a much more accurate result – at least until the professor asked him, for the purposes of the class, to stick with the simpler way. Jane knows that he's restless in those classes, so she stays on him, asking what he might do outside the classroom with the material they're covering

Jane also understands that Jake isn't on a normal trajectory. There's no rule book here, no guidelines for how to proceed. We're all making it up as we go along. So when Jake expressed an interest in taking master's-level classes in physics, Jane made it possible for him to sit in on a 600-level class. Yes, it was unusual for a freshman, but she believes in him, like she believes in all the kids.

Other universities, including some very prestigious ones, have come forward to court Jake. But we haven't been able to find an environment that would work as well for us and for our family. Administrators at one East Coast Ivy League school told me they'd love to have him, and the offer was tempting. The financial aid they offered was outstanding, and of course the facilities and the professors he'd have access to would be unparalleled. It's one of the best schools in the world. But there was a sticking point, and for me it was enough to put the whole conversation to bed. To attend, Jake would have to live in a dorm.

That was so absurd to me, I couldn't even process it. Maybe it's my background: Traditionally, Amish people don't even have old-age homes. You raise your kids, and then you help to raise your kids' kids, and then when you're old, your children and their children take care of you. I don't live with my mother and sister, but I do talk to them a couple of times a day. So the idea that I would send my eleven-year-old off to the East Coast to live in a dormitory by himself wasn't one I was comfortable with.

'He's part of a family,' I protested. The admissions officer was unmoved. Our family would be welcome to find an apartment close to campus, he told me, but Jake would have to live in a dorm with all the other incoming freshmen. I looked over at Jake, who was stealing a big chunk of brownie out of Ethan's sundae, and I thanked the admissions officer for his time. It was a lovely offer, but it wasn't for us.

Eventually, we may have to go elsewhere. But for now, we're at home.

Dr Pehl always used to say that the other kids in his class were there to do their work, but Jake was there to learn. He's like a sponge, soaking it all up, always hungry for more math, more astrophysics, more concepts. We often have to put the brakes on him: 'Hold up, dude. Let's eat some dinner.' But I don't ever question that he's doing the right thing, or that we did the right thing for him.

I still have some anxiety about Jake being alone on campus. But by now, so many people know him that I don't feel as if he's ever completely alone. I'm down there a lot, in part because Ethan and Wesley have been accepted to SPAN, too. Jake has to take chemistry to graduate, Ethan has to take it as a prerequisite for the microbiology he wants to do, and it's required for the meteorology that has captivated Wes. So all three of them may take a chemistry class together, which will be funny to see. When I'm not there with his brothers, Jake calls me when he's walking around the campus.

The rest of the time, he lives a normal student life. Normal for Jake, that is. Last year, he went to get a chicken sandwich from the student union, where he stumbled upon a contest in honor of Pi Day (March 14 – get it? 3/14?). The student who could recite the most digits of pi would win a pi T-shirt.

He called me. 'I'm going to try,' he said. 'I know pi out to forty digits.'

'You do?' Yet another surprise. 'Well, okay. Good luck, and don't forget about lunch.'

Another call when he was done. 'How did it go?' I asked. 'Did you get a sandwich?'

'I did it forward and backward, so they counted it as eighty digits.'

Then he had to hang up. He'd been reciting pi when he should have been eating his lunch, so he was going to eat his sandwich (no pickles, thank you very much) on the way back to class.

That night, Narnie stopped by for a cup of tea. She sat at the counter with Jake, and I told her he'd won a T-shirt for knowing pi out to forty digits and back again.

'I know it out to two hundred now,' Jake interrupted.

I was startled. 'What? When did that happen?'

Apparently, the organizers of the Pi Day contest had given everyone who participated in the contest a little business card with two hundred digits of pi printed on it in a tiny font. Worried that eighty digits wouldn't be enough to secure the T-shirt, Jake had memorized the rest on his way back to class. Four hundred digits – backward and forward – would do it, he was sure.

Narnie and I both laughed at the image of Jake heading across campus, memorizing four hundred digits of pi, while dragging a rolling suitcase with one hand and eating a chicken sandwich with the other.

The next day, we ran into Narnie in the driveway. 'Hey, Jake, how's the pi?' she asked.

'Good. I haven't memorized any more, though. Mom says it's a waste of time.'

I had, because it was. Jake could keep going and going until the end of time – but why? The synesthetic autistic savant Daniel Tammet memorized pi out to fifty thousand digits and recited it to raise money for an autism charity, which was a wonderful thing. (Ultimately, the recitation took him more than five hours. He used chocolate to get through it. That, at least, I could relate to.) But even Daniel Tammet talked more in his book about the challenges of managing his social anxiety and the physical difficulties of the recitation than any particular intellectual challenge.

Narnie came right back at Jake, with the world's most innocent look. 'What?' she said. 'No, silly. I was talking about cherry pie.'

Jake cracked up, shaking his head as he got into the car. There's no chance of him getting a fat head as long as Narnie's around.

I laughed, too, but something was nagging at me. Halfway down to the university, I looked at Jake in the backseat in my rearview mirror. He was playing Angry Birds on his iPad.

'Hey, Jake,' I said. 'Why did you stop memorizing pi at forty digits?'

'I didn't stop at forty. I stopped at two hundred.'

'But before. Why did you stop at forty?'

'It was forty including the three. Thirty-nine decimal digits, actually.'

'Okay, but why did you stop there?'

'Because with thirty-nine decimal places, you can estimate the circumference of the observable universe down to a hydrogen atom. I figured that was all I'd ever really need.'

# Lucky Penny

One of the first things I noticed about the Honors College was Jane's expectation that her students become meaningful citizens of the world. They are actively expected to devote time and service to helping others.

Jake's own form of service began with tutoring in the math lab, which he began doing as soon as he got to campus. The kids he tutors usually make one joke about his age and then get down to the nitty-gritty of whatever it is they don't understand. That talent for teaching I first saw in our living room has blossomed, something you can see every time he helps someone understand a new concept and the light of comprehension dawns.

When I see Jake, I can't help thinking about Grandpa John. Math and science are so electrically charged for him, so vibrant and beautiful, that he wants everyone to be as passionate about them as he is. When one of his most labor-intensive tutoring students (a fairly desperate case, by her own admission) passed Calculus II, she and Jake both cried with relief. He also seems to have inherited my grandfather's patience. 'You'll get it; take your time,' he encourages the kids he tutors. And then he just sits back and watches, munching away on some Crunchy Flamin' Hot Cheetos, while they work their way through a new problem. He also runs study groups, some of which are standing room only. Again like my grandfather, he has a unique gift for creating communities of people who can support one another. Nobody knows better than he does that you can't do it alone.

Jane has pointed out that Jake's facility at tutoring gives the rest of us a window onto how he sees math. If one approach to solving a problem doesn't seem to be working for the student he's tutoring, he'll come up with another way, and another, and another, until one finally clicks. His dexterity is evident. Whereas even someone quite gifted in math can usually only grind out one or two ways at most to arrive at the right solution to a problem, for Jake all the many different roads one might take to get there pop up instantly. Watching him teach, you can see that he's having fun. In return, the students he tutors have taught him things such as eating peanut butter with a spoon straight from the jar. (Thanks, guys.)

I'll confess that when we were thinking about college, it didn't occur to us that Jake would make real friends with the kids there. But Jane expects all the kids in the Honors College to form a community and to nurture one another both academically and emotionally, and Jake has become an important part of that. The age difference isn't as pronounced as we expected. There's a 'little brother' quality about the way the other kids treat him that I find very endearing, and he enjoys it, too. As the eldest in our family, it's a new experience for him. Jane told me recently about walking into the kitchen and overhearing a group of kids talking about Jake. They'd figured out that he wouldn't have his driver's license before graduation and were squabbling over who'd get to drive him to the ceremony.

Just as Jane intended, interacting with students from many different disciplines may be reaping benefits for my math- and physics-obsessed boy. A young literature student from the Honors College told him about Madeleine L'Engle's wonderful young adult novel *A Wrinkle in Time* and even showed him how to find it in the library and check it out. Whether she can get him to actually read it remains to be seen. Like many people with autism, Jake finds it difficult to read fiction. He says that for him, reading a made-up story is like converting a Microsoft Word document into an Excel spreadsheet.

Most important for me, at the Honors College we have seen Jake get in touch with his sense of humor. I have three boys and run a daycare, and if I didn't have a sense of humor, I wouldn't make it to lunchtime. I don't think Jimmy Fallon's writers have anything to worry about from these guys unless there's an urgent call for math jokes. But it warms my heart to see one of Jake's new friends swipe the baseball cap off his head and turn it the 'wrong' way – which for Jake means facing front – while the two of them laugh about why the chicken crossed the Möbius strip. (To get to the same side, of course.)

The biggest change is that Jake is finally capable of real conversation. Now, when I ask him how his day went, he doesn't just give me a blow-by-blow account of his schedule. Instead, he tells me about the practical joke his friend Nathaniel pulled on his friend Tracy, or what his buddy Owen did when he flunked the calculus pop quiz and what Owen thinks his parents will do when they find out. He asks me about the daycare and tells me dumb blonde jokes because he knows they'll make me roll my eyes. Because Jake is finally part of a back-and-forth discussion at school, he and I are finally having the conversation I always hoped we would.

His brothers benefit, too. One afternoon we turned on the TV to find that one station was broadcasting live from the Mecum car auction. For once, Wesley stood still, and I could almost hear the celestial music. Here were all the cars he'd ever dreamed of: Corvettes, Camaros, collectibles such as the car from *Knight Rider*, and of course a selection of his beloved Maseratis. As soon as we heard that the auction was taking place in Indianapolis, we were out the door. The boys tied their shoes in the backseat.

To get in, we had to register as 'bidders.' Pretty funny, given that we had only $5,200 in the bank. But the kids understood that we wouldn't be able to buy anything; we were there just to look. All three of them lit up with excitement once we got inside. Even I had to admit it was an amazing spectacle. The auction featured every car I'd ever heard of and a lot I hadn't. Wes took the lead, walking around each car and looking at every detail, down to the hubcaps. Many of the entrants even let him look under the hood. The whole time, Jake dug into his encyclopedic memory, unearthing fact after fact about the cars.

I never thought I'd find myself crying at a car auction, but I found it deeply moving to see my three boys walk off, heads together, talking excitedly about what they were seeing. In particular, it seemed as if Jake and Wes had finally found common ground.

We went back the next day, and the next. Finally, the auctioneer got down to the last cars on the lot. We watched an Oldsmobile sell for $3,000 and a Volkswagen go for $2,500. Next, a blue-gray Nissan Z, barely old enough to be a classic, sputtered across the red-carpeted floor. The bidding started at $500 and climbed in hundred-dollar increments up to $1,000. I snuck a glance at Wesley. He was head over heels in love. Catching Mike's eye, I knew he'd seen it, too.

At $1,500, the auctioneer got ready to call it: 'Once . . . twice . . .' Without a word, Mike hoisted Wesley up onto his shoulders and helped him hold up our bidding card. The gavel came down, and the Nissan was ours. Mike and I grinned at each other. In true 'muchness' fashion, we had just bought our middle son a car.

Were we out of our minds? Probably. All the dealers in the audience turned to smile at the little boy on his dad's shoulders. I'm sure every one of them remembered what it felt like to fall in love with a car for the first time, although I'd bet that very few of them knew what it felt like to get it! But all Wes cared about was what Jake thought, and Jake was beaming, ear to ear. He held Wes's hand the whole time we were doing the paperwork.

When we got home, Wesley ran upstairs and dumped out his coin collection. 'What're you doing?' I asked, stopping at the door of his room.

'Looking for my lucky penny,' he said, rooting through the change.

I smiled. My grandfather always had a shiny quarter for each of his thirteen grandchildren, and he always alerted us to lucky pennies lying on the ground. (I never suspected anything at the time, but now that I think about it, what *were* all those pennies doing out there in the Indiana countryside?) Whenever we passed a fountain, Grandpa John would give us a penny to toss in, reminding us to make a wish.

I'd always offered my own children pennies to toss. Jake had never been interested, and Ethan didn't seem to care much either. But right from the start, Wesley had taken this wishing business very seriously. There was a fountain in the hospital where he'd go for therapy as a very little boy, and he'd often stand in front of it, carefully formulating his wish before tossing in the coin. Even when he got older, whenever we passed a fountain I'd slip him a coin to toss in.

Digging through the coins on his bedroom floor, Wes found his lucky penny. He polished it, looked at it, and then polished it again. 'I can't believe it, Mom. Today is the day my wish came true!'

Thinking that he would have been wishing for a fast car, I couldn't stop myself from teasing him a little. 'Really?' I said. 'You wished for a Nissan Z?'

He looked confused for a moment, then shook his head.

'No, I never wished for a Nissan. I never wished for a car at all. The only thing I ever wished for was that Jake would play cars with me.'

# Thanksgiving

Michael put his arm around me, and the two of us looked out a small interior window on the second floor of Jacob's Place. Below us was the gym, where forty autistic kids and their families were playing and hanging out.

'Does it feel the way you thought it would?' I asked him.

'Better.'

'For me, too. I can't put the feeling into words. What's it feel like to you?'

'Thanksgiving,' he said. 'It feels exactly like Thanksgiving.'

In January 2011, I got a call from the head of the town council in Kirklin. He wanted to have a ribbon-cutting ceremony to celebrate the opening of Jacob's Place two days later.

The center wasn't done by any stretch of the imagination, and we didn't have a stick of furniture. I spent the next two days driving around picking up whatever furniture our friends could spare and purchasing a huge, lipstick-red circular couch with our credit card. We were so moved that the town wanted to make a fuss. Just a few years before, I hadn't been able to convince anyone to rent me a space because our sports program was for autistic kids. Now we had a place of our own.

The ribbon cutting took place in the morning. Lots of families from Little Light and Youth Sports for Autism made the drive out. The mayor gave a speech, and the religious leaders of the town got together and said a prayer. About twenty kids helped me cut the ribbon, and then Mike and I stood holding hands and watching as our ten-year-long dream became a reality.

That afternoon, we got our first glimpse of what the weekends would be like at Jacob's Place. The front room is a lounge, flooded with light from the big storefront windows. One wall is taken up by an old mahogany bar, donated to us and complete with an antique Coca-Cola mirror. Eventually, we'll sell candy there to fund some of the activities. There's an old-fashioned popcorn machine, which we fire up on game night. In keeping with the candy store theme, we commissioned an artist to make a mural out of different-colored jelly beans, just like I'd done with the children at the daycare. The opposite wall is taken up by that enormous red velvet couch.

There are interior windows everywhere, so that parents can keep an eye on their kids (and vice versa) without having to be right on top of one another. Off the lounge, there's a small room where the kids can watch videos and play games, and upstairs there's a raftered study space with big tables where they can read or be tutored. There's also a small, quiet room completely covered in soft cushions, with giant beanbags they can snuggle into. The lighting in there is on a dimmer. If kids find themselves overstimulated, they can duck in for a few minutes of sensory relief.

Once a month, we move the basketball stuff out of the way and use our video projector to throw a movie up against the big back wall. (It's expensive to buy the rights to films, so we don't do this as often as we'd like to, but we did buy the HBO movie about autism awareness activist Dr Temple Grandin, and all the moms in the audience cried.) We're still not fully funded, and there's a lot we still want to do. A wall in the stairwell has been half primer, half celery green for a while, and some of the furniture, all of which has been donated, is not in the best condition. But a couple of times a month, a group of moms gather around that red couch just to talk, while the popcorn machine hums along and the kids do martial arts in the back room. This is my lifelong goal, to be running a place where nobody ever tells a kid what he or she can't do or tries to 'fix' anyone. It's Jake's hope to have these safe spaces for autistic kids all over the country, because we all need other people and other families – a community – to help us through.

That first day, I could see it as it would be: Moms drinking tea and talking about doctor's appointments and food aversions, while their kids explored every nook and cranny of the building, eventually ending up in a game of tag in the gym. Dads playing catch with their sons, using the soft, squishy balls that we'd bought.

A reporter from a tiny local newspaper called the Frankfort *Times* was there, and she talked to Michael and me, as well as to Jake. Small local papers had done a number of stories about Little Light and the sports program, and we were always happy for the publicity. We wanted people in the area to know that the charity was there for them. The article, when it appeared, was a brief description of the building and the services we hoped to provide.

Then we got a call from *The Indianapolis Star*. I still don't know how the reporter heard about Jake, whether it was through the Frankfort *Times*, the Kirklin Town Council, or someone else, but the reporter asked if he could come out to talk to us. Of course, we said yes. Interest from the *Star* was very exciting, even if it turned out to be only a little piece in a way-back section of the paper. When the reporter showed up at our house, Michael and I were meeting with our accountant to talk about refinancing our home. After a few quick questions, I turned the interview over to Jake, confident that he'd represent the charity well. He knew everything, and I thought it might even be interesting for the reporter to hear firsthand what sorts of things the kids were doing there with their friends.

'Don't forget to tell him about family game night,' I reminded

Jake, then went back into our meeting. Ten or fifteen minutes later, I heard the front door close. When I asked him later, Jake said that their chat had gone well. It never occurred to me to ask what they'd talked about.

Later that week, just as daycare was starting, the *Star* reporter showed up again at our house. He asked me for a few pictures of Jake for an article that would appear in the Sunday paper. That night, Dr Darold Treffert called to ask our permission to talk to the *Star* reporter about Jake. Dr Treffert lives and works in Wisconsin, so I was impressed by the rigorous reporting for a little article about an autism charity in Kirklin, Indiana, population under eight hundred.

On Sunday morning, we woke up early to get the paper. I was really excited. Even if the article was buried behind the ads for yard sales and free kittens, it was still a big deal to us. We piled into the car and drove to Kroger, a grocery store about a mile up the road from our house. When we pulled into the parking lot and got out of the car, we heard people nearby saying, 'There he is! There he is!'

Mike and I looked around, confused. Our town doesn't get very many celebrities, but once in a while a NASCAR driver will come through, and people will make a big fuss. But there wasn't any NASCAR driver in the Kroger parking lot. All those people were pointing and looking at Jake! Jake, who was pulling up his shorts and giving Ethan a hard time about a Katy Perry song he liked. Before we knew it, there was a crowd gathering around our son, and they were asking him to recite pi.

When I saw Jake's face on the front page of *The Indianapolis Star*, I was shocked. 'Why?' I kept asking Michael, truly confused. 'Why does anybody care about Jake?'

It's not that I didn't think he was special, but I'm his mother; I'm *supposed* to think that. I understood that Jake was unusual, but he'd never seemed 'cover of *The Indianapolis Star*' unusual.

All our friends knew about what he was doing, and nobody had ever made a big deal out of it. Putting him on the front page of the paper seemed a little extreme.

By the time we got home, the phone was ringing off the hook. I talked to Jake's old elementary school teachers and the parents of kids he hardly knew, as well as our friends. Everyone was reaching out. We hadn't kept in touch with a lot of these people, so they had no idea what he'd been up to. One of his former teachers thought that we'd left her school because we'd moved. Talking to them, I started to understand how strange Jake's story must have seemed to an outsider. The most common reaction was incredulity: 'Is he really doing all this stuff?'

By the afternoon, I was exhausted. It seemed that we'd caught up with everyone we'd ever met, and all this on the heels of the charity's successful first day, which had been a huge event in itself. By early evening, the story had been picked up by the Associated Press, and consequently by almost every major media outlet in the world. By the time we woke up the next morning, it was everywhere.

Honestly, I've never experienced anything in my entire life like the next few days. Every morning show I'd ever heard of, and every newspaper and television station, called us. We'd pick up the phone, and a radio announcer would be on the other end saying, 'You're on the air!' Our neighborhood is normally completely quiet. Aside from birds or the occasional kid yelling to a friend as they wheel past on their bikes, you never hear *anything* on our block. So it was very unusual to wake up to the sound of a commotion.

'You have got to be kidding me,' I heard Mike say from downstairs. There were reporters camped out on our lawn.

People called from Hollywood. Jake got job and scholarship offers from all over the world. Research firms and think tanks called, along with Stephen Wolfram, the man who wrote the

Mathematica software and developed WolframAlpha, a computational knowledge engine. Later, a friend sent me a Chinese newspaper. The only thing I could read were the words 'Jacob Barnett, age 12,' floating in a sea of Chinese characters.

We could barely leave our house. There were girls outside holding up signs that read, 'We love Jacob!' Wherever we were – at Dunkin' Donuts, at our brunch restaurant, at the grocery store – people came up and asked Jake for his autograph or to take a picture with him. (To his credit, Wes made only one effort to cash in on his brother's newfound notoriety. 'Maybe we can get to see [skateboarder and actor] Tony Hawk now?' he said hopefully.)

A therapist who had been working with a kid in my daycare for a solid year screamed like a teenager when Jake opened the door. That was the most ridiculous thing I'd ever seen. 'You were here last week. Nothing has changed between last week and this week,' I said.

We were scheduled to go to a wedding the next weekend, but I canceled. At that point, Jake would have upstaged the bride and groom.

The glaring spotlight was overwhelming and, frankly, pretty unpleasant. Reporters can be very persistent when they're on the hunt for a story, and some of them were aggressive. A lot of the charity our family does is anonymous because I really do feel that it's more Christian that way, so this flood of attention was unwelcome, to say the least. And I was scared. People were acting crazy. I caught a pair of tabloid reporters from London trying to break into our basement. That night, I made Jake a bed on the chaise longue in our bedroom, and he slept there for a month.

It was also increasingly hard to protect him from what other people were saying about him, as when a tabloid in the UK said that he'd make the perfect supervillain. That comment hurt his feelings. 'Why would they say that without knowing me?' he kept asking us. 'You know I would never do anything to hurt anyone, right?'

The media eventually moved on, but the experience was a transformative one for Michael and me. For years, we'd thought of ourselves as living in the shadow of Jake's autism diagnosis. Now we have a different perspective. Jake is still autistic. His autism is not something he has overcome, but something he overcomes every day. He is still acutely sensitive to all sorts of things that go completely unnoticed by the rest of us: bright lights, the humming of an incandescent bulb, the change from concrete to tile underfoot. He takes pride in the ways in which he is different, and given the chance to drop the label, he has chosen to keep it. But the media helped Michael and me understand that autism is no longer the dominant theme of our journey with Jake.

Initially and for a long time afterward, I didn't understand why people responded to Jake the way they did. I think I have a better understanding of it now. Growing up with my sister, Stephanie, an art prodigy, and marrying Michael and mothering my children may have skewed my understanding of how unusual these gifts actually are. As soon as the piece in *The Indianapolis Star* came out, I talked to Dr Treffert, who explained that there's a scale of gifted children ranging from mildly to moderately to highly to exceptionally to profoundly gifted. Jake belongs in the profoundly gifted group. According to Miraca Gross in her book *Exceptionally Gifted Children*, there is less than one profoundly gifted person per one million. People like Jake are extremely rare.

Finally, all the feedback from people who learned about Jake helped shed light on why his story captured the imaginations of so many. Narnie said it best: 'Jake is good news.' People right away tapped into the fact that Jake is determined to do something good with his gifts. At a time when newspapers are filled with doom and gloom about America's children and their terrible reading scores and growing rates of obesity, about guns in schools and *Teen Mom* on TV, there's Jake. Indiana's public schools are struggling so much with their budgets that some of them have cut bus service. There's not a lot of good news about kids in this country, but Jake is indeed good news.

Jake's story is an American story, too. Whenever you read about those terrible test scores, the article always ends in the same way. China, or India, or wherever is going to take over because their kids can do math and our kids are hopeless. Of course, that's not true, but many of the people who contacted us said that's why they were so heartened to know that Jake was out there. And even though I'm glad that children all over the world who love math are surging forward, I confess that seeing the Wikipedia page about Jake that began 'Jacob Barnett, American mathematician,' made my heart soar.

It's important to Michael and me to explain that there's nothing supernatural or otherworldly about Jake. Some devotees of the mystical healer and psychic Edgar Cayce believe that Jake is Cayce's reincarnation, as predicted by Cayce himself. This is a normal Saturday for me: I pick up the phone and have a conversation with someone who believes that my son is the fulfillment of some mystical prediction.

But Jake is not supernatural. He doesn't even come from a private school in Manhattan. He lives in a cornfield in Indiana. He doesn't look different from other kids his age, and he doesn't act differently either, at least not most of the time. He's just a goofy, adorable kid in a backward baseball cap who can do incredible things. Wrapped up in a very ordinary-looking package is this extraordinary mind.

Michael and I agreed to do the CBS newsmagazine show *60 Minutes* partly to dispel any kind of supernatural myth. The first time the producer called, we honestly felt as if we'd entered the Twilight Zone. 'We're going to hear Rod Serling's voice-over any minute now,' Mike wrote on our phone pad, cracking me up. But after we talked to the producer, we believed the show was committed to doing a thoughtful piece. I felt that I could trust them not to make Jake seem like some freak of nature. And I knew that if we gave hope to even one mom who was being told by experts all the things her autistic kid couldn't do, it would be worth it.

Knowing 60 *Minutes* will be filming in your house is an excellent way to get your husband to deal with all those annoying little projects he's been putting off. If you'd told me ten years ago I'd be yelling, 'Jacob Barnett, you'd better be darn sure that Van de Graaff generator of yours doesn't electrocute Morley Safer' up the stairs – well, I just don't know what I would have said.

# A Roller-Coaster Ride

After the article appeared in *The Indianapolis Star*, we were inundated by requests for interviews. A lot of them came from academics interested in talking to Jake. One email in particular stood out, from a doctor at Ohio State University who studies child prodigies.

I'll be totally honest. I approached the email with a kind of horror. There was something a little unseemly about the idea of allowing my child to be used for scientific research, and I wasn't interested in it at all. Mike couldn't resist ribbing Jake about it: 'We're donating you to science!'

Jake responded dryly, 'They can study me when I'm dead.'

But as soon as I opened Dr Joanne Ruthsatz's message, I could see that I had judged her too quickly. First of all, the research she was doing was itself compelling. Dr Ruthsatz specializes in the genetic underpinnings that prodigies and autistic people have in common. Jake was already very interested in that topic, particularly because it has the potential to help a lot of people who are genuinely suffering.

In addition, Dr Ruthsatz sounded like a real person, and she also sounded like someone who would treat Jake like a real person, not a rat in a maze. Her playful energy and her passion for her research were contagious. She invited us to come to Ohio.

By that point, Michael and I were starting to think that it might not be a bad idea to get away for a while. The media storm had abated slightly, but we were still getting many calls a day and being approached whenever we went out. The clincher was that Dr Ruthsatz could get us passes to Cedar Point, a gigantic amusement park in Sandusky, Ohio, with more than seventy-five different rides, including *sixteen* roller coasters.

We drove to Ohio, and Dr Ruthsatz arrived at our hotel the next morning to administer a new IQ assessment of Jake. The way she set up the test confirmed the good feeling I'd had about her. While Mike took Ethan and Wes to the pool, Jake was comfortably ensconced in a quiet sunroom looking out onto a pretty little garden. Seated in a wing chair in front of a window, with a tray of muffins in front of him, he began the test.

The Stanford-Binet IQ test is designed in such a way that as long as you're answering questions correctly within each category, the tester keeps going. The questions get progressively harder as you proceed, until you eventually reach your ceiling in each cognitive area. Answering two consecutive questions incorrectly establishes that ceiling. The second wrong answer acts like a silent buzzer, directing the tester to move on to the next category. Very few people make it to the outer reaches of any one category, let alone more than one category.

Watching Jake, I could see that the harder the questions became, the more fun he seemed to be having. To give you one example, Dr Ruthsatz read a list of sixty animals to Jake in a completely random order. He repeated them back, in exactly the same order. Next, she showed him a list of the animals, again randomly organized, this time by arbitrarily assigned colors (zebra = green, tiger = purple, dog = blue). Again, he repeated them all back correctly. Then, some twenty minutes later and after several unrelated problems, Jake was again prompted to repeat the animals back to Dr Ruthsatz. This he did perfectly, still in the right order, in their correct color groupings, and with a huge grin on his face. That was when she turned to me and said, 'That's never been done before. Never, in history.'

Jake was clearly having a blast, but watching them became increasingly uncomfortable for me. The harder the questions got – and by the end, the level of difficulty was almost comical – the more overwhelmed I felt. How could *anyone*, let alone my own son, be answering these questions? It felt like flying too close to the sun, both breathtaking and terrifying. Of course, I knew that Jake's IQ was high, and I knew that most twelve-year-olds weren't studying quantum field theory. But maybe because I was on the other side of the table, a spectator to these amazing feats for the first time, what I saw that morning affected me in a new way. And at the end of the test, when Dr Ruthsatz quietly closed the booklet and turned to me with tears in her eyes, I actually felt queasy.

Jake had maxed out the test. To reach the end of just one category is extremely rare. Dr Ruthsatz had seen this happen only a very few times over the course of her career. And she had never seen anyone do what Jake had done, which was to max out the test in so many cognitive areas.

You don't often come across someone who can tell you something you don't know about your own child, but that weekend Dr Ruthsatz helped me understand more about Jake's incredible mind and how it works. She explained, for instance, that Jake had maxed out in 'working memory,' the part of the brain we use when we look up a phone number and commit it to memory long enough to dial it. Most of us have to say the number over and over in order to keep it in our heads, even for a brief time. It's different for Jake, and not just with a ten-digit phone number, but with twenty-page equations. And while you and I would probably forget that phone number seconds after we dialed it, for Jake it never disappears. He doesn't remember a fact so much as he relives learning it, which is why he doesn't need to rememorize it in order to retrieve it a week, a month, or even a year later. After he's seen it, read it, and learned it, the material is there for him whenever he needs it.

That's why he could learn pi to the two hundredth digit and

recite it forward and backward with equal ease. He sees that two-hundred-digit string of numbers in his mind's eye, and he can hold on to it as easily as we can hold on to two or three digits.

This turbocharged working memory is common in prodigies, part of what makes them able to do what they do. Dr Ruthsatz believes that prodigies actually use a different part of their brains for working memory than the rest of us do – the part, in fact, that we use for storing the things we never forget, such as riding a bike. That, she believes, is what makes a prodigy's ability to remember higher-order information so stable and fixed. For Jake, remembering that equation is like remembering how to swim for you and me.

Thinking about it another way, it would be impossible for most people to recite a two-hundred-digit number from memory, but if someone wrote it out for you on a piece of paper, you'd be able to recite it backward and forward with ease, because you'd be *reading* it. That's exactly what the experience is like for Jake when he's recalling a long string of numbers, a list of sixty animals, a complex graph, and so forth. As Dr Ruthsatz explained it to me, instead of a single sheet of paper containing that two-hundred-digit number, Jake's working memory is a piece of paper the size of a football field.

The truth is, we have no idea how powerful Jake's working memory is, since it exceeded the measure of the test. What is certain is that he remembers everything he's ever learned, and he has all that information immediately accessible to him whenever he wants it. Everyone, even physics professors, use formula sheets. You can find hundreds of them on the Internet, and laminated examples are sold in college bookstores. Students are encouraged to carry them everywhere, including into exams. Nobody on earth could be expected to memorize all the formulas they might need to solve higher-order math and science problems. But Jake has never used a formula sheet in his life.

Although Jake's working memory is extraordinary in certain areas, it's not very good in others. His memory for tastes, for instance, is precise, because he's actually reliving every meal. He can instantly recall physical characteristics of a scene, especially anything that has a pattern to it, which is how he could draw each and every one of the hubcap designs of the cars he saw in the Best Buy parking lot. At the same time, he has a hard time remembering smells, which are powerful memory joggers for most people, and like many autistic people, he has a lot of trouble remembering conversations and what other people have said.

Dr Ruthsatz was also struck by Jake's incredibly advanced visual-spatial system, which is extremely rare even in prodigies. If his working memory explains how he can play a piece of classical music after hearing it once, then his visual-spatial abilities are why four-year-old Jake could look at a map for a minute or two and then chart a flawless course through downtown Chicago for me. Or why, more recently, Wesley was so insistent that Jake play with him one afternoon when Jake had research to do. I'd gotten the boys a crate of Popsicle sticks, and they'd been building forts and towns for their toy soldiers.

'You don't need Jake to build,' I reminded Wes.

He rolled his eyes and said, 'Mom, *I* cannot build Washington, D. C.'

Apparently, after we'd returned from a trip to New York, Jake had built Wes a perfect replica of the city, complete with major landmarks, road systems, and the place we'd stayed. After our trip to Washington, he'd built a replica of that city, too, complete with a tiny, perfect Capitol dome made of overlapping Popsicle sticks. Jake also had built Wes a model of Oahu, because one of Mike's videogames contained a detailed map of the island. With Google Maps, Wesley explained, there wasn't any city Jake couldn't build. 'He can build me anywhere I want to go,' he said.

257

Beyond Popsicle-stick cities, this advanced visual-spatial system is a key element in Jake's ability to do high-level math and physics. Specifically, Dr Ruthsatz was able to clarify for me that it is the key to what Jake means when he says that he 'does math' in many, many dimensions.

Mathematicians knew the earth wasn't flat long before Ferdinand Magellan's fleet proved it. Similarly, many mathematicians hypothesize that there are more dimensions than the three we can perceive, even though they can't yet prove it. Most people find it relatively easy to think in three dimensions. It's not hard for you to conjure up the image of an apple or to imagine turning it upside down and around in space. You and I can do that in a way an ant crawling across the surface of that apple never could. To the ant, the 'world' of that apple is flat, but we can zoom out and see that it is round.

Jake agrees that there are likely many more dimensions than three, but unlike many scientists, even those who work in this field, Jake is able to conceptualize objects as they might appear in those other dimensions. He doesn't see them, per se, but he can do the tremendously complex math that would allow for other dimensions, and his visual-spatial gifts allow him to fully process what that math means. So just as you and I know the rules that apply to the apple we're holding in our mind's eye – we can visualize what it would be like to cut it in half, to turn it on its side, or to throw it and watch it smash into bits against a wall – Jake is equally agile with the properties and rules that apply to vastly more complex, multidimensional shapes.

This unique marriage of a turbocharged working memory, advanced powers of visual-spatial cognition, and an extraordinary attention to physical detail enables Jake to explore higher math and physics as very few people can. As Dr Ruthsatz said, 'He can see beyond what most of us can cognitively comprehend.'

Dr Ruthsatz was also able to answer a number of other questions that had been mysteries to us. She explained that when baby Jake was looking right past his therapists, he probably wasn't staring blankly into space, but concentrating the full force of his focus on the play of light on the wall. When he was rearranging the big box of crayons or putting himself to sleep by his shadow clock, Jake was already engaging the passions that still animate him today: light, the rules governing the movement of objects in space, the different dimensions of space, and the role time plays. In the same way that we can look at an artist's early work and see the beginnings of the themes and preoccupations that later come to define his or her masterpieces, Jake has been working since babyhood on the very same things he's interested in today.

Dr Ruthsatz helped me to see how wide-ranging Jake's interests are and how unusual that makes him. She was, for instance, amused to learn that Jake has eight whiteboards in his room, each one dedicated to original research in completely different areas of math and physics. Most scientists choose a particular facet of their fields and spend their careers doing research in that area. By contrast, any given day finds Jake switching with ease between subjects such as general relativity, dark matter, string theory, quantum field theory, biophysics, the spin Hall effect, and gamma-ray bursts.

How, you might be asking yourself, could his extraordinary gifts have been a surprise to me? After all, I cleaned up crayons arranged in the order of the color spectrum when he was three, watched him play perfectly a piece of music he'd heard only once at age seven, and called one of the world's foremost physicists to validate his original theory in astrophysics when he was nine.

I've struggled with this question myself. There are, of course, a number of explanations, but I think the real answer lies in my relationship to Jake. Yes, I was the person who drove him down to the university at ten years old and watched him answer questions that stumped his professors. But I was also the person reminding him to pick up the dirty socks scattered all over his bedroom floor when it was time to do laundry, and the person who ordered him fuzzy Crocs from Zappos when it was clear that for all the physics he knew, he'd never remember to tie his own shoelaces. If I had stopped and let myself bask in the awe of Jake's amazing abilities – if I had stopped to ponder how unusual he really is – I don't think I could have been a good mother to him.

The only compass I've ever followed is to let Jake do the things he loves and to make sure he gets to have a childhood. As shaky as that weekend with Dr Ruthsatz made me feel, I knew it was time to go back to being Jake's mom.

So the five of us went to Cedar Point, and I held the corn dogs and soda while my sons rode every single one of those sixteen roller coasters with their dad.

# A First Summer Job

Whether you're a camp counselor or scooping ice cream, early work experiences help a young person assume the kind of responsibilities that come with adulthood. So I always knew that my children would eventually have summer jobs. Jake's happened to be as a paid researcher in quantum physics at IUPUI.

A mention in *The Indianapolis Star* was the first I'd heard of Jake doing research. Then, a month later, Jake got a packet in the mail, formally inviting him to be part of an undergraduate research program in the physics department at IUPUI. I was startled to learn that he'd be getting paid, too.

It was an amazing opportunity, and yet I wasn't sure I wanted Jake to do it. Mostly, it felt like too big a step. Jake was just finishing up his freshman year. The university was adamant that he was ready for bigger challenges, and his professors said they would be derelict not to provide him with them. 'Enough of the book work. You are here to do some science,' his physics professor, Dr John Ross, told him. But I wondered whether they weren't also motivated by the fact that many elite academic institutions were now actively courting Jake.

I couldn't help worrying that we were going too fast and putting too much pressure on a twelve-year-old. I also didn't want Jake to spend his entire summer chained to a computer screen. I wanted him to ride his bike and play paintball with his friends and to swim at the pool until his nose was a blur of freckles running together. I was haunted by the vision of all those gifted kids we'd seen over the years studying for math competitions while other kids their age took part in fun summertime activities.

Jake, of course, shared none of my worries about the workload. 'It's all I've ever wanted, Mom!' That's what he kept saying, and I could see it was true. He'd be working with Dr Yogesh Joglekar, researching condensed matter physics as it relates to fiber optics, which involves Jake's guiding passion, how light travels through space. I knew Dr Joglekar and trusted him, and Jake was so excited about the chance that at the end of the day, we couldn't say no. As Mike pointed out, Jake has always been a researcher at heart. He is relentlessly curious about how the world works. While you and I take it for granted that there are things we'll never understand, Jake has never been able to complacently accept that, and when an explanation eludes him, it drives him nuts.

At the beginning of the summer, all the students who had been chosen for the research program were invited to a meeting held at the law school. It's a beautiful building, with heavily varnished wood paneling, marble, and Greek statues everywhere. The first thing I noticed was how professional everyone seemed. Jake's classmates, even though they often have eight inches and a hundred pounds on him, are college students. They wear jeans and baseball caps and have baby faces and problem skin and dubious hygiene. They look, in short, like kids. The undergraduate researchers, by contrast, were carrying leather briefcases and wearing somber, professional-looking dresses and suits. I'd pulled him away from playing Frisbee with his brothers to come, so Jake was in what we call his 'uniform' – backward baseball cap, T-shirt, shorts, and flip-flops – while I was wearing a hot-pink sundress with a bow in front at the waist. Given how we were dressed, I was a little alarmed to see the head of the program making her way over to us.

'You're Jake's mom,' she said, shaking my hand. 'We're so

pleased he's going to participate in the program. We expect great things from him.' I assume she knew, as I did not, that his appointment to this program was breaking a world record. That day, Jake would become the youngest astrophysics researcher in the world.

As we sat and waited for the speakers to begin, I couldn't help thinking about my own first summer job on a farm. Along with a group of Mexican migrant workers, I walked up and down row after row of corn, thinning, de-tasseling, and finally pollinating it. It was backbreaking work in overpowering heat. Sweat would pool at the bottom of the huge waders we wore. At lunch, we'd sit on overturned buckets and eat our sandwiches in the back of a semitrailer so hot that the air rose up in waves. As a joke, the farmers would put dead mice in our lockers. I learned not to scream because it only made them laugh harder.

I was terrified of the farm dogs patrolling the cornstalks, so my mom sent me an electronic device designed to repel them. She'd found the device advertised in the back of a magazine, but I guess she hadn't read the ad carefully enough, because it did just the opposite and attracted the dogs in wild, snarling masses. That's how I found myself 'treed' in the bed of a pickup, shaking with fear, until one of the farmers took the device away from me and crushed it under his boot heel.

The next summer, I worked at Wendy's, where the smell of pickles, mustard, ketchup, and grease-soaked meat lodged so deeply in my clothes and hair that I felt as though it was seeping out of my pores. I smelled like that for months. No shower could make me feel clean. When I left that job for one at a pizza parlor, I was honest with my boss about my reasons for leaving: 'I just need to smell like something else for a change.'

Those were my first summer jobs, and this was Jake's. It's every parent's hope that his or her child will do better and go further than he or she has, and here we were. All I could do was laugh and shake my head.

The woman who runs the program welcomed us by telling the moving story of her own beginnings in academic research. When the letter arrived inviting her to be a fellow at her college, it mentioned a stipend. Her working-class father couldn't imagine that someone would pay her to study, or to think, or to write. He was convinced that the number on that paper represented the amount of money they'd have to pay in order for her to participate, and he almost didn't let her go. Until the day she cashed the first check, he remained convinced that it was some kind of scam. She told the story with compassion, and I felt my face grow hot. Sitting there in my sundress, I could relate to her dad.

Then she began to talk about the mentoring program. Every undergraduate researcher in the room would be paired up with an older scholar, someone with more experience, who could give the undergraduate the tools he or she would need to succeed in their chosen field. Both parties were expected to take that relationship very seriously. Jake's mentor would be Dr Jokelgar. Not only would the researchers meet one-on-one with their mentors every week, but they would also attend a weekly luncheon, dressed in formal clothes, for a lecture on a larger topic related to professional development or scientific ethics.

I had fully expected to be bored during this ceremony, but I found myself weeping. By assigning Jake a mentor, it was as if the university was making a commitment to him: 'We are going to support you and give you the direction and leadership you need.' It was time for me to share him and to allow him to get the help he deserved.

Jake was less emotional. 'Seriously? I'm gonna have to wear a *suit*?'

He didn't have one either. On the rare occasions when we

had to dress up, Jake had always been able to get away with a clean pair of dark pants and a nice sweater. So off we went to the Macy's at the mall. While the tailor knelt at his ankles, pins in his mouth, to alter the length of the pants, Jake shuffled out of his flip-flops and showed the world his dusty summer feet.

'He was playing Frisbee at the playground,' I found myself explaining to the poor guy. (He earned his commission that day. He had to show me how to tie a tie, too.) When he wanted to know why we were buying the suit, Jake and I just looked at each other. 'We have a wedding to go to later in the summer,' I said, which was true, and considerably less complicated to explain.

When the tie was on and the suit was all pinned up, I stood back and looked at my little boy. He looked great – almost.

'Jake, you have to take off the baseball cap.'

He wasn't happy, but he did. His hair was long and wild-looking, pointing up every which way. 'I guess you're going to need a haircut, too.'

'No, Mom! I can't get a haircut! This is my *science* hair!'

I laughed out loud. Mentor or no mentor, this was still my baby.

When you teach your child to ride a bike, you walk up and down the street by his side. He needs you to hold him up until he learns to balance on his own. Sometimes he falls, but very quickly the skills come together, and even though your hand is still right there, something amazing happens: He finds his balance and takes off.

That day, I saw a boy riding his bike solo for the very first time. I had been scared I'd be stuck there, watching him ride off over the horizon. But the amazing thing about Jake is that he didn't leave us in the dust. And he never will. He never minds waiting at the corner for us, or swinging around in a loop to pick us up. He circles back for me after each class at the university, sharing funny comments people made and errors he found in the textbook and new ideas he supports or refutes. He circles back for the kids he helps and tutors. Right now, he's writing a book to help math-phobic kids. That's how driven he is to help other people, especially other children, to see the beauty of math and science. He wants to bring all of us with him. That's what's beautiful about Jake.

I'd have to learn to trust other people with him. Mostly, I'd have to learn to share. For me, that's really what this book is, the chance to share Jake and his gifts with the world.

# A Celebration

Aside from whatever misgivings he had about dressing up, Jake loved doing research that summer. And strangely, he also had a great deal of free time. It seemed as if he was always biking down the block with his buddies from the neighborhood or heading off with his brothers to shoot hoops. He didn't appear to be doing much work, and I began to feel a little concerned.

When I asked him about it, he explained that Dr Joglekar had been giving him assignments every week and that he had been completing them. I hadn't seen him hitting the books because he had, so far, been able to do the problems in his head during our forty-five-minute car ride home from the university. This week, he said, would be the exception. He didn't think he'd be able to solve the latest problem he'd been given in time for his meeting on Tuesday.

I launched into a stern lecture about the importance of a strong work ethic. 'You have a *job* now, Jake. You're being paid, and people are counting on you to do whatever is asked of you. These problems are not optional. I expect you to stay in and do what you have to do this weekend in order to have your work completed by Tuesday.'

'I'm not sure I can,' he said. That shook me a little, since I'd never seen Jake even remotely concerned about anything math related. 'In that case, you give it your best effort,' I told him. 'Take a crack at it. And remember, there's no shame in asking for help.'

'I don't think there's anyone to ask, Mom.'

A couple of hours later, I heard him laughing with Wes as they left the house and headed over to the park. I opened the upstairs window and called down, 'Jake, did you get your work done?'

'Yes, Mom, I think I've got something I can use.'

'Good. I'm glad you got through that, honey. I'm proud of you.'

Of course, at the time, I didn't have the slightest inkling of how proud I should have been.

Jake called me the following Tuesday, as he always did, to let me know when he was leaving his appointment with Dr Joglekar. He was as excited as I'd ever heard him.

'I did it, Mom, I did it!'

'Slow down, honey. What did you do?'

'I solved it! I solved the problem!'

'That's great! I'm so glad you stuck with it.'

'No, Mom, you don't understand. It was an open problem, a problem in math nobody has been able to solve. And I solved it!'

I had misunderstood. This hadn't been any ordinary homework assignment, but the kind of problem that career mathematicians take months, years, even decades to unravel. Yet in two hours, between working on his jump shot and playing on the Xbox, Jake had solved it. In hindsight, I'm thankful that during my lecture on the importance of a strong work ethic, I'd had no idea what I'd been asking him to do.

With the completion of that assignment, Jake's summer research was officially done. Solving that open problem was a huge breakthrough, with major implications not only for his adviser's research but also for math and fiber-optics technology. He put together a presentation on the breakthrough for a symposium at the university, and he and Dr Joglekar began preparing a paper for submission to major journals.

This was a new experience for Jake, and it excited him. He was very driven to understand what the correct format was for a research paper like this one and to get it right. I didn't fully understand why he was so charged up until I realized that the paper was a way for him to communicate with other scientists and maybe even foster a conversation with them. Once more, Jake was learning a new language, one that would finally allow him to talk about all the things he loved so much.

The paper, 'Origin of Maximal Symmetry Breaking in Even PT-Symmetric Lattices,' was accepted for publication in the physics journal *Physical Review A*. (And no, I can't tell you what that title means.) Jake's name would be on the paper with Dr Joglekar's, an uncommon honor for any student, much less an undergraduate, much less one as young as Jake.

The afternoon before Jake was to present his research, he came in from playing in the yard. My day wasn't going so well, and he knew it. With a smile, he handed me a bouquet of *thirty-eight* four-leaf clovers. I took the daycare kids out to search for more, thinking he might have stumbled on a patch of them. But we were out there for the better part of an hour, and we found only three.

It made me laugh. Sometimes being with Jake is like watching someone walk on water without knowing they're doing anything the least bit amazing. It may sound corny, but it's an honor to be his mother, to have an inside track on what he sees and thinks about and on how his extraordinary mind works. The true wonder for me is that my autistic son knows how to cheer me up with a bouquet of clovers only he can find.

People often ask about Jake's future. So far, we're making it up as we go along. I do believe that he will make a significant scientific contribution to the world, mostly because that's what he says he wants to do, and I've never seen Jake abandon a goal. He's spent most of his life trying to understand the governing equations behind the universe.

I was relieved to learn from Dr Ruthsatz that child prodigies do not burn out quickly, as the myth would have it. She's been working with prodigies for fourteen years, and every one of them has gone on to succeed in his or her field. Although he has the makings of a good businessman, Jake seems to have inherited the family-wide lack of interest in money as a motivation. He's completely uninterested, for example, when people from Silicon Valley come calling. He's more compelled to explain to others how the world works. Ultimately, Jake wants to help people by finding solutions to practical, real-world problems. In that way, he reminds me of Grandpa John.

At the end of the summer, Jake presented his research. People thronged around him, asking questions. Business leaders from the community came over to shake his hand. As we stood and watched our son, Mike grabbed my hand in his own. I looked down at our intertwined fingers and couldn't help remembering how tightly I'd held on to him during that first, devastating evaluation with Stephanie Westcott, the day Jake was diagnosed with autism. We'd come a long, long way from that day.

Jake posed for group photographs with the other researchers and their professors. 60 *Minutes* was there filming. To cap the whole thing off, there was a ceremony in a soaring marble and glass room in the IUPUI Campus Center. But I had a surprise up my sleeve for Jake. We were going to counter all this sophistication with some good old Indiana fun.

One night earlier in the summer, Narnie had come over while we were watching the movie *Talladega Nights*, a favorite in our house. In the movie, race car driver Ricky Bobby (played by Will Ferrell, so you can only imagine) gets physically thrown out of an Applebee's. Watching the scene reminded me how Heather, my daycare assistant, had told Jake that he was going to win a big award someday and when he did, I was going to cheer so loud I'd get us all kicked out of a restaurant. As I was telling this story to Narnie, the two of us looked at each other, and a lightbulb went off.

It was perfect. A regular kid doesn't toast a success – I don't care how illustrious it is – with champagne at a fancy restaurant with white tablecloths. A regular kid high-fives his friends and eats as many hot wings as he can. So we were going to go out with our friends to have a good time, and if people wanted to toast Jake, they could raise their root beer floats.

I drove by the Applebee's near us and spoke with the manager. I told him the whole story, and we came up with a plan I felt sure would crack Jake up.

While Mike and I were watching Jake present his research, Narnie subbed in for me at the daycare. On the side, she got Ethan and Wesley totally NASCARed up, Talladega-style. She covered them in temporary tattoos, and they made ripped-up T-shirts that read 'Jake – you rock!' She even put do-rags on them.

When we walked into Applebee's with Jake, everyone was there, ready to celebrate Barnett-style. There were friends from Little Light, friends who'd been in the daycare when he was little, and all of his friends from elementary school. I wanted Jake to know that no matter how many conjectures he solved, there would always be a group of people who remembered what he looked like the day I dressed him and all the other daycare kids up like Santa's reindeer.

It was an amazing night. We set up the poster Jake had made to present his research, and he told us (in the most general terms) what he'd learned. He ate a gigantic hamburger and had a sundae for dessert. We stayed late, because everyone had a story to tell about Jake.

At the end of the night, all of us hooted and clapped and screamed our heads off in celebration of him, Ricky Bobby–style. And when it was time to get 'kicked out,' the waitresses picked Jake up, put him on their shoulders, and carried him right out of that Applebee's with a huge grin on his face.

# Postscript

'He can do anything he wants.'

That's what Jake's physics professor Dr Ross said when the *Indianapolis Star* reporter asked him what he thought Jacob would do with his talents. When I read those words, a chill went down my spine. This is how far we've come, from the special ed teachers who didn't believe Jacob could ever learn to read, to a university physics professor who sees his unlimited potential. *That's* the kind of ceiling I want my son's teachers to be setting for him. More important, it's the ceiling I want teachers and parents to set for every child, and for all of us to set for ourselves.

I wrote this book because I believe Jake's story is emblematic for all children. Though his gifts are unique, his story highlights the possibility we all have of realizing what is extraordinary in ourselves, and maybe even opens the door to the possibility that 'genius' might not be all that rare. I'm not suggesting every autistic child is a prodigy, or every typical child, for that matter. But if you fuel a child's innate spark, it will *always* point the way to far greater heights than you could ever have imagined.

It's hard to trust your child to find his or her own path, especially when we're told every day by professionals that children must fit into rigid boxes. We all want to give our kids the best opportunities we can, which is why it feels like such a disservice if we don't push them in the 'right' direction. Celebrating your children's passions rather than redirecting them, especially when those passions don't line up neatly with a checklist for future success, can feel like jumping off a cliff. It certainly did for me. But that leap of faith is necessary if your kids are going to fly.

If a child who was never supposed to talk or read can rise to such improbable heights, imagine what children without such challenges might achieve, and how far they might soar if we encouraged them to unfurl their wings – past any horizon, past even our wildest expectations. By sharing our story, I hope that will happen.

# He just wanted a decent book to read ...

Not too much to ask, is it? It was in 1935 when Allen Lane, Managing Director of Bodley Head Publishers, stood on a platform at Exeter railway station looking for something good to read on his journey back to London. His choice was limited to popular magazines and poor-quality paperbacks – the same choice faced every day by the vast majority of readers, few of whom could afford hardbacks. Lane's disappointment and subsequent anger at the range of books generally available led him to found a company – and change the world.

*'We believed in the existence in this country of a vast reading public for intelligent books at a low price, and staked everything on it'*
**Sir Allen Lane, 1902–1970, founder of Penguin Books**

The quality paperback had arrived – and not just in bookshops. Lane was adamant that his Penguins should appear in chain stores and tobacconists, and should cost no more than a packet of cigarettes.

Reading habits (and cigarette prices) have changed since 1935, but Penguin still believes in publishing the best books for everybody to enjoy. We still believe that good design costs no more than bad design, and we still believe that quality books published passionately and responsibly make the world a better place.

So wherever you see the little bird – whether it's on a piece of prize-winning literary fiction or a celebrity autobiography, political tour de force or historical masterpiece, a serial-killer thriller, reference book, world classic or a piece of pure escapism – you can bet that it represents the very best that the genre has to offer.

**Whatever you like to read – trust Penguin.**